ONE SIGNAL
PUBLISHERS

ATRIA

SEEING OTHERS

How Recognition Works—and How It Can Heal a Divided World

MICHÈLE LAMONT

ONE SIGNAL PUBLISHERS
ATRIA

NEW YORK LONDON TORONTO SYDNEY NEW DELHI

ONE SIGNAL PUBLISHERS

ATRIA

An Imprint of Simon & Schuster, Inc.
1230 Avenue of the Americas
New York, NY 10020

First One Signal Publishers/Atria Books hardcover edition September 2023

ONE SIGNAL PUBLISHERS / ATRIA BOOKS and colophon are trademarks of Simon & Schuster, Inc.

For information about special discounts for bulk purchases, please contact Simon & Schuster Special Sales at 1-866-506-1949 or business@simonandschuster.com.

The Simon & Schuster Speakers Bureau can bring authors to your live event. For more information or to book an event, contact the Simon & Schuster Speakers Bureau at 1-866-248-3049 or visit our website at www.simonspeakers.com.

Interior design by Timothy Shaner, NightandDayDesign.biz

Manufactured in the United States of America

1 3 5 7 9 10 8 6 4 2

Library of Congress Cataloging-in-Publication Data has been applied for.

ISBN 978-1-9821-5378-6
ISBN 978-1-9821-5380-9 (ebook)

To Pierre and Chloe

CONTENTS

SEEING OTHERS

INTRODUCTION

THE POWER OF RECOGNITION

In June 2020, I talked with the Pulitzer Prize–winning journalist and historian Nikole Hannah-Jones, just as massive Black Lives Matter protests were spreading across the United States following the murder of George Floyd. During our interview, she described how her endeavor, the 1619 Project, took shape and grew. Originally a special issue of the *New York Times Magazine* published in August 2019, this series of essays marked the four hundredth anniversary of the first enslaved Africans arriving in Jamestown, Virginia. Hannah-Jones's opening essay pointedly challenged white readers, starting with its title, "America Wasn't a Democracy, Until Black Americans Made It One." The project provided an alternative vision of American history, covering the era of slavery, the promise of equality, and the formation of the American dream. It also exposed the harms caused by a national narrative that sidelines Black history and suggested that a better society is possible if we can replace that narrative with a more inclusive one—a narrative that recognizes the value and dignity of Black people's experiences.

In her work as a journalist, Hannah-Jones strives to show what she calls "the intentional architecture of inequality of American society." Though she has often found herself searching for hope, she recognizes that the 1619 Project gave hope to others. As she puts it, seeing how America's system of racial domination was created helps us see "that it can be uncreated." This optimism explains in part why the 2019 special magazine issue immediately ran out of print and why the book that eventually arose from the project became an instant hit, staying at the top of the *New York Times* bestsellers list for months on end.

With support from the Pulitzer Foundation, the project was also developed into a set of history curricula that came to be taught in over 3,500 US classrooms in 2020 alone. As the project became more prominent, it ignited passionate debates around the country. That same year, then-president Donald Trump hastily assembled a "1776 Commission" to write a different version of history that he felt would better fit within a "patriotic education"—an account that downplayed the significance of slavery and racism in America's past and included no input from professional historians. In several states, conservative lawmakers attempted to bar teachers from any 1619 Project–based teaching and worked to ban many other books addressing racism from school libraries and curricula.

At the heart of all this were deep questions about *who matters*—not only in the United States, but also far beyond. And the fight over the 1619 Project is just one of many intensely polarizing debates that have played out across the US and around the world in recent years, on topics ranging from Black Lives Matter, MeToo, and abortion to the minimum wage and the fight for workers' dignity. Marginalized groups have always struggled to find acceptance and justice, but in recent years a new wave of energy and activism has forced an important shift. It may be that this search for recognition calls for an entirely new frame of understanding our social world, and for entirely new ways of envisioning a more equitable society.

INTRODUCTION

For almost forty years, I have studied the impact of culture on inequality with the goal of deepening our understanding of how the world works. In particular, I am interested in how groups gain recognition from one another, how they come to be seen as valuable, and what that recognition does for their quality of life. To answer these questions, we need to understand how people conceive of their own worth and how they assess that of others—whether in moral, economic, professional, or cultural terms. Part of this task, for example, has involved learning about how people of color experience racism differently in different countries. Another part has involved understanding some of the factors driving the growing influence of the far right and white nationalism. Ultimately, these insights can help us combat narrow and hateful conceptions of who matters, and find ways of encouraging a more expansive means of understanding people's worth.

As we approach this task, we need to understand not only the material circumstances that drive people's decisions, but also how they make sense of their own lives. This is why I feel it is important to share my perspective as a sociologist. When it comes to understanding how we determine who matters, other prominent disciplines can have troublesome blind spots. To simplify, psychologists tend to focus on what is happening inside the minds of individuals, while economists focus on material circumstances and the distribution of resources. But there is a more intangible, collective, cultural dimension of worth that both frequently overlook. This will be our focus in the chapters ahead. Instead of adding to the growing library of books that tell us why we're divided and how we fail, I decided to write a book about people who make hope possible and accessible, a book that seeks to understand how we can broaden the circle of people who matter.

In order to take on this task, my research team and I have, since 2019, spoken with a long list of change agents, ranging from Hollywood creatives to activists and thinkers, as well as a substantial number of young people from the American Midwest and the East Coast. Both groups we interviewed have helped us see how new ideas about worth are taking shape. These interviews, together with my decades of experience as a sociologist, have led me to an inescapable conclusion: dignity affects quality of life just as much as material resources do. When we think about how to improve society, then, we cannot ignore worth any more than we can poverty or inequality. We need to focus on the extent to which different groups are "seen" by others, whether they have a seat at the table, and whether they feel welcomed, valued, and listened to. We know it is possible to do all this because worth is socially determined. That is to say, it is not handed down from above based on neutral criteria. Rather, *we* decide who matters—all of us, every day, by creating, supporting, and spreading new narratives about the worth of all groups. This is why worth should be factored in explicitly—in every social interaction on the street, as well as every legal and policy decision that our elected officials make.

This is not to say that money and power do not matter. But whether groups are recognized and afforded dignity is *just as* important to their flourishing as human beings, just as vital to their drive to be all they can be. This is a radical idea, far from accepted in our materialist, individualist, and achievement-oriented societies. Bolstering this claim, economists recently found that 60 percent of what makes work meaningful to people comes from factors other than money, such as having autonomy, feeling a sense of competence or mastery, and forming connections with others.

Key to understanding the power of recognition, dignity, and worth are the narratives we tell ourselves about why and how our world works. Consider, for instance, the narrative of meritocracy, which explains success as the inevitable result of hard work and little else. Such a narrative not only encourages people to blame themselves for their failures and financial hardships, it also conceals the deeper structural obstacles that have long held back entire groups because of their race, gender, or sexual orientation. Developing *grit* (or personal resilience) is often offered as the path to success by psychologists, governments, and policy makers without regard for the different types of support to which people have access. But grit is not determined by individual will; it is facilitated by material resources and social networks, and by narratives and institutions (such as schools) that empower people and recognize the value of their identity and experiences. To counter such misleading and harmful narratives, we need new ones—narratives that empower people and recognize the value of their experiences. By allowing people to live their lives with dignity, such narratives can also help mobilize them to engage in civic life.

Changing the story in this way can have a dramatic effect on all manner of social problems. Much attention in public life today is devoted to division and tribalism—that is, to our tendency to identify with people who share our characteristics and affiliations. But the lines that divide us are not immutable. By transforming the narratives we tell ourselves about different groups, and extending recognition and dignity to others, we can erode the lines of division and create more opportunities for understanding between class and racial groups. We know this is possible because it has happened frequently throughout history. In 1973, for instance, 90 percent of Americans disapproved of homosexual relations, but by 2019 that number had fallen to 21 percent. Another study showed that, from 2002 to 2019, the percentage of Americans who believed homosexuality should be accepted by society rose by 21 points, from 51 percent to 72 percent. Many people contributed to this rising level of acceptance, especially participants in social movements, as well as journalists, social scientists, and medical and legal experts. Together, they pushed us as a society to tell a new story about who matters, and to acknowledge the dignity and worth of gay people.

Why does this matter? What we stand to gain is a more meaningful, just, and fair society, for the largest number, and hopefully for our children and our children's children. After all, justice and fairness are not only about who gets what, but also about dignity, respect, and the ability to be valued for who we are, free from discrimination. This holds not only for the United States but also for other advanced societies. Adopting diversity, equity, and inclusion (DEI) initiatives has become enormously popular in many countries—and has become almost a requirement for some organizations. But they are clearly not enough.

I propose that we shift perspectives to make sense of the role that recognition plays in our lives. When I say "recognition," I am not talking about mere identification, as when you recognize someone you know on the street; rather, I mean "seeing others" and acknowledging people's existence and positive worth, actively making them visible and valued, reducing their marginalization, and openly integrating them into a group. In the aftermath of the 2008 US presidential election, for instance, many observers noted a building sense of hope about race relations in America. With the historic election of Barack Obama, the country's first Black president, pictures of his family started circulating in the media. Many white Americans lived in isolated, largely segregated communities, and understood Black people largely through crude depictions in the media and racist stereotypes. Seeing images of this Black middle-class family challenged many preconceptions about African Americans. At the same time, many Black families reported feeling "seen" for who they really are, at long last. Of course, there was also racist backlash to this phenomenon, which psychologists came to call the "Obama effect."

The term "worth," too, can be misunderstood. When I use it, I mean something other than "social status," or the place of individuals in hierarchies based on competence, authority, or money. Rather, I am referring to a vast range of criteria that people use to determine personal and collective value, from altruism and creativity to professional success. However, worth and social status can be intimately linked, but the way they are linked often differs based on class. My past work has shown that professionals and managers (the roughly top 20 percent of the college-educated population whom I will call the upper-middle class) believe their worth comes mostly from their education and expertise, their occupational and economic success, and their expensive lifestyles. For them, worth stems from social status. But this is not necessarily so for the working class, whose low social status is often in tension with their conception of worth, which is shaped more by their contributions to their family, friends, and community, and generally their sense of morality and dignity, or what they believe they deserve in terms of respect. This, they share with many other groups that face discrimination, including people of color, queer people, and different religious groups. Recognizing the common struggles of these groups is one of the most essential steps for fixing our divided world. Having one's sense of worth affirmed is not a luxury but a universal need that is central to our identity as human beings and our quality of life.

Without the validation of social status that elites enjoy, workers and other marginalized groups must look for other means of bolstering their sense of worth. Right-wing populists have often successfully addressed the working class's need for such validation in campaign speeches and other public fora. In the last decade, the Republican Party has been more successful than the Democratic Party at attracting the non–college educated, in particular. Instead of depicting "everyday Americans" as "deplorables" as Hillary Clinton was perceived to do in the 2016 presidential campaign, her opponent Donald Trump affirmed their worth in his various electoral speeches, explaining their loss of social status as a result of globalization and immigration. Liberals and progressive professionals must fully understand the ways in which they alienate many workers and prioritize affirming their worth, recognizing what we can gain from increasing recognition for all.

Again, I am motivated by hope, because we urgently need new ways to dissuade people from the appeal of right-wing extremism that is fed by cynicism and a desire to "buck the system." However, important as these marginal ideologies and groups are, they will not be a central focus of this book, given the plethora of recent studies on them. We will touch briefly, however, upon the non–college educated and the downwardly mobile middle and working classes, exploring why they may find populist ideologies attractive. I also ask how we can change our collective thinking so that we can influence their perceptions and expectations.

If we aim to truly *recognize* all groups, we have to question negative portrayals or stigmas. We also have to change how we evaluate people and stress what is common, as well as what is different. We have to reconsider how we rank the sufferings of various groups. This is essential to our collective future, and particularly urgent after decades of growing inequality, which has worsened during the pandemic. Better understanding how recognition—"seeing others"—works will help us capture where it happens, how it could happen more, and how we can all contribute to it through the choices we make in our daily lives.

Some have argued that social change should not focus on racial, ethnic, or gender discrimination, because these identity issues, they say, divert us from more pressing matters like economic inequality and poverty. This is wrong. If certain neighborhoods, schools, professions, and social circles are inaccessible for marginalized groups due to racism, for example, poverty cannot be addressed without addressing racism as well. For such groups, economic stability can be nearly impossible to achieve while living under extreme social stigmas. The latter affect their access to jobs and countless other valued resources. In other words, when it comes to economics and identity, it is impossible to say which is more important. Forty years of research and having written several books that touch on both class and race lead me to firmly believe that we have to consider both!

Before going any further, it is worth saying a bit more about the many inspiring people who were kind enough to be interviewed for this book and whose words and perspectives helped guide my analysis. This book will include learnings from over 180 people on how we can reshape our societies to make them more equitable by promoting recognition. I call these interviewees *change agents*, just as many of them call themselves. They play an important role in shaping how we see one another. Just like Nikole Hannah-Jones, these change agents give us the fresh perspective that allows us to see our environment in a new light. The change agents we interviewed included labor and community organizers, philanthropists, public policy experts, corporate types who promote a more equitable economy, LGBTQ+ advocates, Black Lives Matter activists, socialists, and feminists, as well as artists, thinkers, and seventy-five popular stand-up comics and Hollywood creatives (see Appendix A for a full list). All are in the business of producing intentional cultural change, and their works include cultural touchstones as commonplace as a hit song on the radio, a *New York Times* bestseller, or a blockbuster film.

Of course, being a change agent does not imply any specific ideological leaning. Change agents can shift our perspective in both positive and harmful ways, and many are nativists, racists, or far-right extremists. Think of popular commentators such as Tucker Carlson, Joe Rogan, and Ben Shapiro, who so often use their platforms to deny certain groups recognition and to restrict who is considered worthy. Although I do not focus on these harmful change agents here, they do play an important role in our political landscape, and they will come up from time to time.

I listen to another group of cultural innovators, as well—young people. To better understand their perspectives, my research team spoke with eighty middle-class and working-class American college students in the Midwest and on the East Coast. Although not representative of everyone in their age group (about 50 percent of Americans their age attend college), these young people do offer important insight into the obstacles standing in their generation's way, their goals, and what motivates them. Like the professional change agents, they, too, are cultural producers, actively shaping the road ahead even as they begin to drive upon it themselves. They differ from the change agents in that they are younger, have yet to fully enter their work lives, and are not involved professionally in the creation of new narratives. They are often influenced by change agents when they reflect about the kind of society they would like to live in.

When discussing young people, the media often use the label "Gen Z," referring to those born between 1997 and 2012. I focus specifically on a subset of that group who were at the start of their adult lives when we conducted our interviews, college students, or those born between 1997 and 2003. A large part of my interest in this narrower group is related to the unique circumstances of their early adulthood. Just as they were setting out to find a partner, a vocation, or a purpose that would flip the light switch and lend meaning to it all, navigating adulthood became much more of a challenge, as profound, society-wide problems emerged, including growing inequality, social polarization, new threats to American democracy, and a global pandemic. All of this pulled the rug from under their feet just as they were preparing to start off on their own. Some among them wonder: What is the point of living with purpose anyway?

We are in the midst of a conflict over where we are heading as a society. And the stakes are high for today's young Americans, who belong to one of the first generations less likely to do better than their grandparents. So many are frustrated to find that the narrow but well-worn paths to success used by previous generations now lead to dead ends. They are asking boomers (born between 1946 and 1964) and Gen Xers (born between 1965 and 1980) to move aside. They are forging ahead, and some are leading the change "from the bottom up." This is why we all have to pay heed. Many are inventing their own narratives, which often differ from those of their parents. How can we use these narratives to see the way forward?

Many change agents and young people we talked to have important new ideas about who matters and what our society should be about. They want the coming years to be guided by new principles—we should not allow ourselves, they say, to be silent in the face of inequity, the denigration of marginalized groups, police violence, and many other glaring societal problems. They develop, adopt, and diffuse what sociologists call "scripts of self," or narratives about what kind of people we should be. While some embrace the traditional narrative that wealth on its own creates personal worth, many place great importance on authenticity, sustainability, inclusion, meaning, and connection. And many feel that our society's unrelenting focus on success does not move them.

Throughout our history, many groups have been stigmatized and assigned various negative traits: women (especially older women), people of color, queer people, undocumented immigrants, Muslims, the Roma, Indigenous people, incarcerated populations, people with disabilities, those who did not go to college, and others. Time and again, more privileged and influential groups have defined these people as inconsequential, unintelligent, invisible, "less than"—in other words, as deserving of indifference or scorn. And too many of us sit complacently on the sidelines, buying into the narrative that marginalized groups "deserve" their stigma. Recognition cuts against this tendency by celebrating the plurality of our paths, by broadening how we think about worth, and by valuing people *for* their identities and differences—not in spite of them.

There are three main avenues for building recognition: through political activism and the law, through culture and media, and through our own interpersonal experiences and networks. Of course, these tools are not new, and they have frequently been deployed simultaneously. Since the 1960s, a new wave of political activism succeeded in expanding rights for some marginalized groups, primarily women and Black people. Those shifts were accomplished not only through political and legal means, but also through changes in the culture and in ordinary people's lives; they were about challenging stereotypes, being heard and seen, and expanding constricting roles.

To understand the power of political and legal activism, consider the efforts to legalize same-sex marriage over the past few decades, which have been correlated with a rapid decline in the number of attempted suicides among LGBTQ+ high school students. Even though marriage is often far from high schoolers' minds, these laws and court rulings sent a message to LGBTQ+ youth that they matter and are deserving of the same dignity afforded to everyone else. Of course, the legalization of same sex marriage did not end homophobia, solve discrimination, or even stop bigoted politicians from continuing to push antigay legislation. But these legalization efforts did serve an important function, broadening the definition of the mainstream and saying, even to young people uninterested in marriage: "We see you; we value you, and we invite you to take a seat at the table alongside us." Importantly, this monumental accomplishment was made possible not only through political and legal advocacy, but with the support of massive social movements and the diffusion of new narratives, which frequently took the form of slogans like "love is love" and "we're just like you."

One difficulty with efforts to fight for recognition in political and legal spheres is that they often come up against a reactionary backlash. We all know that progress is not linear. This has been perhaps most clearly exemplified in recent times by the American Supreme Court's June 2022 decision reversing its nearly fifty-year-old ruling in *Roe v. Wade*, which had declared reproductive rights to be constitutionally protected and which still has the support of a significant majority of the US population. At the same time, many LGBTQ rights, and particularly trans rights, have been threatened by conservative lawmakers. Backlashes like these may slow down social progress, but they have not stopped the forward march of human rights over the last decades.

Political and legal advocacy are some of the most powerful ways of extending recognition to a marginalized group and allowing them to gain formal social acceptance at the national level. But cultural industries and the narratives they popularize can be just as powerful. Screenwriter Joe Robert Cole described to me how he saw the film he cowrote, *Black Panther*, the first Marvel movie with a predominantly Black cast, and how he understood the blockbuster's cultural impact. His film touched so many, he said, because "the audience could feel what it feels like *to be seen, to be viewed as great*"—a powerful experience "for people who are not used to [being] viewed as important." Many viewers—not only in the US, but around the globe—celebrated seeing Black superheroes represented on such a massive scale and in such a mainstream context.

Examples of popular culture's ability to expand recognition abound. Popular TV shows such as *Glee*, *Will & Grace*, and *Modern Family* have all contributed to normalizing gay people. *Transparent* played a similar role for trans people. Hollywood creative Joey Soloway explained their intent in the making of this award-winning show that features a trans woman who transitions later in life. The story opens as she comes to embrace her new identity and works to redefine her relationships with her adult children. Soloway explained how the show used storytelling to make the reality of trans people "more understandable, and less aberrant" for mainstream audiences.

While recognition plays out collectively in politics and culture, it also operates on a more intimate, interpersonal level. This happens through face-to-face relationships, as when those close to us acknowledge and support who we are, validate our priorities, and support our struggles—regardless of whether our identities and choices conform to mainstream expectations. This interpersonal form of recognition also happens when we make decisions about whom to befriend, what matters to us, and how to lead our lives.

As I will show toward the end of the book, we can all contribute to including more people around the table. This kind of everyday recognition has an impact not only on our well-being, but also on social solidarity and inclusion.

As we work to achieve a more equitable society, we need to interrogate how we evaluate worth in ourselves and in others. Many people are already pushing in this direction, and the quest for recognition is becoming a powerful movement of its own. Broadening recognition could very well be an alternative source of collective hope. By the end of this book, we will understand more deeply how recognition can redefine the status quo. Once we reduce stigma, celebrate difference, and embrace the diversity of what humans are and can do, we can perhaps experience the promises of dignity for all.

Before we dive in, it is worth saying a bit more about how my personal experiences have shaped my views on worth, recognition, and dignity. These topics first became important to me when I encountered sexism growing up. It manifested even in matters as ordinary as the division of chores in my otherwise-loving family: my older brother mowed the lawn, and I did the dishes. But mowing the lawn happened only once every three weeks—doing the dishes happened almost every day. As a feminist—even back then—I would not have it. Whenever I was silenced, which happened again and again, it only strengthened my determination to claim my space.

These and other early experiences put me on a path of working to understand recognition and inequality. I was born and grew up in Canada, which has a long colonial history of marginalizing the French-speaking, culturally and ethnically distinct *Québécois*—my people. I came of age in the seventies, at the apex of the fight to affirm our cultural distinctiveness and gain our political independence from English-speaking Canada. Like the American Civil Rights Movement, this movement involved public displays of cultural pride in the form of songs, plays, and other creative expressions. These celebrations worked hand in hand with protests and denunciations of economic exploitation, political subjugation, linguistic subordination, and social injustice. This cultural revolution, my first experience of collective mobilization, convinced me that recognition is central to our societies—and just as necessary as economic equality in our struggle to build a more just world. It also showed me that those who condemn so-called identity politics as a narcissistic dead end are missing something essential about what motivates people.

My geographic location played an important role in this education, as well. I grew up as a monolingual francophone near the Outaouais (or Ottawa) River, which separates the provinces of Ontario and Québec and serves as an important symbolic divide between French-speaking and English-speaking worlds. As I developed my first friendships with English-Canadian students in college while discovering Monty Python, I began thinking about how boundaries between groups take shape, when and how they can be crossed and weakened, and at what cost. As I grew as a researcher, this concern extended beyond boundaries between ethnic groups to groups with different cultural and moral orientations, different social classes, and different intellectual fields.

As a twenty-year-old graduate student in late-seventies Paris, I experienced the aftermath of the insurgent and often anarchistic student protest movement of May 1968, which partly succeeded in upturning the traditional social order, with slogans such as "it is forbidden to forbid" and "all power to the imagination." This taught me that profound change is possible. I also found myself drawn to a growing postcolonial and anti-imperialist sentiment that I shared with friends who hailed from all corners of the earth—including

Brazilian and Greek militants who had fought the US-backed military dictatorships in their countries, as well as Hungarian and Cambodian neighbors who had escaped repressive regimes.

When I was a postdoctoral researcher at Stanford University in the early eighties, I witnessed the earliest iteration of Silicon Valley's privileged elite, just as yuppie culture and personal computers were taking off. Here was a totally foreign—and profoundly harmful—new way of determining who matters, which was a conduit for the growing inequality to come. After four years of bohemian student life in Paris, I could barely make sense of the Californian orgy of consumption, especially the taste for insanely expensive ultralight bikes and fancy cars. At the same time, I became friends with well-supported young researchers who were professionalized by attentive Stanford faculty—in strong contrast to the near-total absence of mentoring that prevailed in Parisian universities.

Even with the advantage of coming from an educated, middle-class family, I felt and continue to feel like an "outsider" within academia, as a woman in a male-dominated profession, as an immigrant with an accent, and as someone who hails from the academic "periphery," with foreign graduate degrees—although I recognize many may not think of me that way, given my decades of teaching in uber-elite universities such as Princeton and Harvard. These experiences left me curious about how exclusion and inequality are connected to one another differently across national contexts.

In the late eighties, as my career continued to progress, my interests came to focus on how and why people make status distinctions between groups of people differently in different places. This had started from my earliest observations of divisions based on—to simplify greatly—language in Canada, culture and religion in France, and race and money in the US. I became interested in how cultural differences can create social isolation between groups. Long before the Trump era, when journalists and academics began to pay real attention to how populist politicians drew on these divisions, I wrote a book about working people's efforts to seek respect and affirmation of their dignity. Soon, these topics came to define my intellectual mission. I became convinced that they matter deeply, not only for each of us individually, but for our collective future and that of the next generation, as well.

I am also writing as a woman and the mother of three young adults who are themselves searching for a future they can embrace. My experience with them as they became adults motivates this book—not entirely, but in large part. I think of my kids, and their friends, having observed so many hours of their living room hangouts spent sketching out their futures, their ideals, and the impacts they hope to make in the world. I have also witnessed their periods of hesitation when facing the future. The experience of attending college during a global pandemic was unfulfilling and exacerbated the inherent difficulty of finding direction at that age. Like many of their peers, they have had to navigate uncertainty and a certain amount of anxiety as they have made sense of abrupt social change.

Beyond my kids and their circles of friends are some eighty graduate students in their twenties or thirties I have mentored over the last decades. They took on the academic path for the creativity and (perhaps) security and fulfillment it can offer. Many are puzzled about the future as well, and study sociology and society to make sense of it all. Like me, in recent years they have had their share of mental health challenges and have dealt with painful personal and institutional crises. And each cohort has grown more and more critical of universities.

Of course, some readers may wonder why they should listen to the message of a white, middle-aged, female Harvard professor who works in a literal ivory tower—William James Hall, where my office is located, is, in fact, a tall, white, tower-like building. They may wonder: Is this going to be another experience in "boomer-splaining"? To the skeptics, I would say that we all have a partial vision of the world, as well as our own unique blind spots. But we also know that "non-fish" can sometimes perceive the water better than the fish who live their lives immersed in it. I bring to the table a great deal of evidence and decades of research that help me make sense of the strange and the familiar alike—not perfectly, but with a passionate and unrelenting commitment.

In 1993, the moral philosopher and social critic Cornel West published his book *Race Matters,* which went on to sell half a million copies. This series of eight essays was a powerful call to address racial inequality and the various obstacles facing African Americans in the contemporary United States. As we celebrate the thirtieth anniversary of this landmark book, we must continue to remember the essence of his message—and broaden it to other marginalized groups. Much progress has already been made. Many negative stereotypes have been sapped of the destructive power they once had—about women, queer people, and more. Slowly but surely, the lenses through which stigmatized groups are perceived have changed. Just maybe, they can change further. And as you will read next, this change may not be optional, even as we contemplate backlash in a number of crucial areas. Our work is not done.

CHAPTER 1

THE VIEW FROM ABOVE

THE UPPER-MIDDLE CLASS AND THE FAILURES OF THE AMERICAN DREAM

In the United States, our hopes have long been shaped by what we call the "American dream." More than any other group, those who became adults in the period immediately after World War II embraced this dream and benefited from a period of unparalleled economic growth and technological innovation, fed by faith in the exceptional destiny of the country as a land of riches where hard work is always rewarded. All this had the effect of solidifying the American ideal of a prosperous, suburban life with a nuclear family and white picket fence.

However, the decades since the postwar boom have revealed fractures in this dream. For some, it was clear from the start that certain groups would be excluded from it. For others, the hollowness of its promises has become evident only in recent years. Still, the dominant national narrative of equal opportunity and upward mobility persisted, even in the face of increasing skepticism.

Today, we find ourselves in a new gilded age of extreme wealth concentration and inequality. Indeed, according to a recent report by the Pew Foundation, "From 1983 to 2016, the share of aggregate wealth going to upper-income families increased from 60% to 79%. Meanwhile, the share held by middle-income families was cut nearly in half, falling from 32% to 17%. Lower-income families had only 4% of aggregate wealth in 2016, down from 7% in 1983."

To many, the growing economic inequality has made it clear that their hard work and personal sacrifices will never be rewarded. The end of upward mobility in America (and many other Western democracies) has left the middle and lower classes, the "99 percent," abandoned with little else on which to pin its hopes. One result has been a major mental health crisis up and down the social ladder over the last decade—evident in grim statistics like the US suicide rate, which increased by 35 percent between 1999 and 2018.

The 2008 Great Recession left many, even those at the top, ever more depressed and anxious about their finances, and more protective of the levers available to preserve their standing. The upper-middle class, whose lives were already fixated on work and competition, became even more fearful of losing their privileged position. They opened the gates to a winner-take-all economy that leaves workers and lower-income people feeling exploited, ignored, silenced, and worthless. At the same time, emerging digital media platforms were increasingly pushing images of photo-filtered perfection to a fractured world, creating idealized and unrealistic expectations of economic success, achievement, and consumption.

Despite the American dream's inability to deliver for most, its persistence acts as a balm to political and social unrest. It provided hope for a better future, even if largely unattainable. But if we are going to build a world where everyone feels truly valued and included, we have to rethink our dominant *measuring sticks*, or the models of ideal self that we use to think about our identities and likely future, which are offered to us through shared narratives about the perfect life and who matters in society. Think, for example, of the archetypal corporate white male worker who is always available for more work. These models shape who we are, who we think we should be, what we think is possible, what our objectives are, and how we approach them. These are unrealistic for most people, and particularly for women, who still often have the prime responsibility for raising children. But with our traditional models of upward mobility generally out of reach for most people, what will feed our hopes and dreams? Where are the new ideals that will inspire us?

These questions matter not only for the United States but for other countries as well. While many societies have come to define their own values and identity at least partly in contrast to the United States, especially since the Trump presidency, many also continue to take inspiration from the US, despite many indications that the image and quality of life in this country is in steady decline.

Because of these dire economic realities, social movements for equality in the United States have multiplied in recent years. These movement have also influenced social progress around the world. For instance, the 2020 Black Lives Matter (BLM) movements inspired a wave of protests worldwide in support of racial justice. And advances for gay rights in the US have also fueled the rapid spread of support for the LGBTQ+ community in many other parts of the world—though certainly not all. But country-specific recognition movements also developed independently in a range of countries, such as the Catalan independence demonstrations in Spain, the Hong Kong Umbrella and subsequent movements in favor of greater autonomy from China, and the Indigeneous protest movements across the Americas, as well as in Aotearoa New Zealand and Australia.

To understand what future is possible for our societies, we first need to look at why change is needed. Again, there is a great need for greater economic equality, but thinking only in terms of economics won't do: it does not capture fully what motivates the cynicism toward the American dream.

During the last decades of the nineteenth century, the first Gilded Age was a period of unequaled opulence and inequality. This era was ruled by the plutocracy of the Carnegies, Vanderbilts, and Rockefellers, who capitalized on technical progress to amass fortunes and grow the American economy to new heights. But it was also a time when millions of workers and new immigrants lived in squalor in crowded cities, in abject poverty with no social protections.

Today, the "Second Gilded Age" reproduces a familiar pattern of widening inequality: we now have an exceptional concentration of wealth in the hands of the top 1 percent of American households. As of 2021, this tiny group holds 32 percent of the national wealth, a higher portion than at any point since at least 1962. This transformation has been massively covered by the media, studied by social scientists, and discussed by politicians—especially Democrats.

At the same time, it has become far more difficult for Americans of various classes to move up the social ladder: in 1970, 92 percent of young people born in 1940 were out-earning their parents by age thirty, but by 2014, for those born in 1984, that number had fallen to 50 percent. This occured in the context of rapidly growing income inequality: In 1965, the ratio of CEO-to-worker compensation was 21-to-1. By 2020, the ratio had ballooned to 351-to-1. Moreover, as of 2017, the US had greater income inequality than any of the other G7 countries (Canada, France, Germany, Italy, Japan, and the United Kingdom) based on the Gini coefficient, a standard measure of country-level inequality. These divergent fates of Americans have made it increasingly difficult to believe that a rising tide of economic prosperity will eventually lift all boats.

This rise of inequality has roots in recent history, arriving after decades of neoliberal policies that first came to prominence under President Ronald Reagan in the US and Prime Minister Margaret Thatcher in the UK. As these policies gained momentum globally, they soon came to be seen by many as the only path to national prosperity. Neoliberal policy makers deregulated markets and progressively removed barriers to profit-making. Their "market fundamentalism" implemented austerity policies, rolled back progressive taxes, erected wealth protections for a chosen elite, and abandoned to the private sector many functions traditionally performed by the public sector, from garbage collection to the management of prisons. They encouraged the maximization of competition, stressing the need to systemically quantify and measure performance. This accelerated the concentration of wealth, as the working class's compensation declined by roughly 43 percent between 1979 and 2017 (adjusted for inflation and the relative increase in productivity).

The effects of inequality show up in every aspect of daily life. For example, epidemiologists have found that growing inequality is correlated with worsening health and subjective well-being for all members of a society, including those at the top.

But if the American dream has proven empty in many ways, why has its influence endured? For most of the twentieth century, this myth worked as a powerful cultural engine. The term was first coined by J. T. Adams in his 1931 bestseller *The Epic of America*, where he described it as a panacea for the problems of the world, the key to a harmonious and more equal society. It promised a life "which should be better and richer and fuller for every man, with opportunity for each according to his ability or achievement." But more than material goods, it also promised to remove barriers to personal achievement, creating what Adams imagined as "a dream of social order in which each man and each woman shall be able to attain to the fullest stature of which they are innately capable, and be recognized by others for what they are, regardless of the fortuitous circumstances of birth or position."

As a remarkably efficient "hope machine," the American dream proved capable of appealing to hearts and mind, and to stimulate business and shape policy. Indeed, it provided a vocabulary with which to make sense of life for a great many people and for a great many years. Still today, it continues to feed the aspirations of many, particularly for immigrants coming to the United States. A close cousin of the notions of "American exceptionalism" and "manifest destiny" that animate our national myths, the American dream also has a darker side. Frequently, the dream has obfuscated the fact that the country's riches were gained at the expense of Native Americans, enslaved people, underpaid women, Asian Americans, and other exploited groups—topics now at the center of new efforts to reconsider American history.

The dream was a work of folklore anchoring a collective identity. It provided American citizens with a purpose to guide their actions (the goal of building prosperity), standards to determine who belongs (one's degree of material wealth and college education), notions of who deserves our trust (those who are industrious)—and of which groups deserve to be forsaken (those who are lazy and not self-reliant). The boundary organized around the American dream is also the moral boundary that structures the class system.

Many people continue to put their confidence in this version of the American dream, even as its promised rewards fail to consistently materialize. As many surveys have shown, at least 60 percent of Americans believe the US is still a country of opportunity where material success is within reach for all. The vast majority believe that inequality can be explained by the fact that some don't work as hard as others, while one survey revealed that the majority of those interviewed believe hard work is "the most important reason that people have gotten ahead."

For many workers, the dream has often been equated with making a decent living and passing on money to your kids. It was related to the promise of consumption and growing earnings which seemed attainable for many—especially for white men. Still today, many equate realizing the dream with joining the middle class, which now requires a college degree, which is still out of reach for the majority. For others, it also means becoming an executive, professional, or entrepreneur, and reaching the "comfort level" traditionally available to the top 20 percent of the population. Interviews with working-class people conducted in 2016 revealed that "most insist that the American dream exists or that hard work pays off," even as their own hard work and that of their friends and families fail to provide them financial security. Tellingly, in 2022, the final episode of *The Simpsons* depicted Homer as unable to achieve the American dream given the decline in income for American workers.

In practice, considerable disagreement exists around the specific meaning of the dream. Is it to raise a family? To contribute to the community? To attain a certain level of wealth? This fluidity contributes to the popularity of the myth since it can take on different meanings for different people.

For example, many African Americans—a group often hindered from enjoying the full fruits of American progress and prosperity—attest to having *their own* "American dream" and define it in any number of ways. In fact, working-class Black people are more likely to believe in the American dream than the middle-class, perhaps because in many cases, they live in more segregated neighborhoods and have fewer interactions with white people, and thus perceive racism less frequently and acutely. Understanding distinctions like these was one impetus of a 2016 book I wrote with several colleagues called *Getting Respect*. We spent years studying how African Americans experience discrimination differently from groups facing stigmatization and exclusion in other countries. We found that in 2007–2008, an overwhelming majority of these interviewees embraced self-reliance and individualism, which are central to neoliberal models of self. More than a decade later, in 2020, we followed up with fifteen of them to hear how their views had evolved. A majority—middle class and working class alike—continued to embrace these values. They said they believed the American dream was attainable and they emphasized the importance of hard work as the key to success.

For instance, Geoffrey, an insurance salesman, said the American dream is "attainable for everybody, but the thing is that you have to work for it, right? You have to work for these things and unless you work for these things, you're not going to get it. And then you can't complain." He was not alone in his views. But a number of them also believed that pursuing the American dream means placing too much emphasis on materialism. In this, they resemble younger cohorts who favor less materialistic and more experiential definitions of the American dream.

Rather than dispose of the dream entirely, many Americans continue to believe in its value but suggest that more people should have access to it. The persistence of this American dream may seem puzzling to non-Americans. At times, it seems as though believing in it acts as proof of citizenship, proof of belonging. Thus it is perhaps not surprising that the group with the firmest belief in their access to upward mobility is immigrants. Often, the dream has inspired them to leave their country, community, and family for a better future.

For many, belief in the American dream goes hand in hand with a tendency to accept the present order of things. The late author and journalist Barbara Ehrenreich, for example, in her classic 2001 book *Nickel and Dimed*, wrote about her experience working poorly paid service jobs in order to learn about the difficulties facing the working class. While working as a maid, she asks her fellow workers if they resent the rich people whose mansions they clean. Many say that they don't—given that they, too, hope to become rich someday. She doesn't have the heart to tell them that given the realities of class in America, they'll likely never attain that goal. It comes down to simple math: 100 percent of the population cannot be squeezed into the top 20 percent of the income distribution. This fundamental disconnect is what makes the American dream an impossible dream for most—an unfulfillable promise.

While many continue to believe in the dream, others are becoming increasingly disillusioned. Between 1998 and 2019, the percentage of Americans who believe the system is fair shrank by more than half, falling from 68 to 29. As of 2017, a majority of adults believed that life for the next generation will be worse, while 78 percent of Americans believed "it will take the next generation more efforts to advance." Tellingly, more people have come to perceive the dream as attainable for themselves, but not for society as a whole.

These surveys suggest that the American dream is increasingly viewed less as a promise than as a mass deception. Those who feel tricked by a flimsy social contract may give up on the concept of shared citizenship and just "do their own thing"—living at the margins of, or in opposition to, mainstream society. This tendency helps explain why so many people, mostly working class, choose not to participate in the political process—only 46 percent of low-income, eligible voters voted in the 2016 presidential election, while 68 percent of higher-income people did. It can also help explain the appeal of antistate ideologies like the alt-right and libertarian doctrines. A functional society can't be maintained when one of its core principles strains under the weight of suspicion. If we are to achieve a better future—or even just a manageable one—we will have to offset this failure with other narratives of hope. Given the political polarization of so many advanced industrial societies and growing political abstention among those at the bottom of the labor market, this is now a most urgent task.

Many more privileged Americans aren't so aware that upward mobility is becoming unachievable for some groups, in part because they are insulated within neighborhoods and social circles. However, wealthy people also tend to underestimate their place in the economic hierarchy, believing that they are farther from the top than is really the case—and this is true not only in the US, but in France, Germany, Russia, and Spain as well. Since the 2008 recession, middle-class American adults also underestimate their economic situation despite their middle-class household income: 12 percent fewer self-identify as middle class and 13 percent more wrongly identify as working class. In 2022, a total of 53 percent of the middle-income population self-identified correctly as middle class, down from 65 percent in 2008.

Poor people are also frequently isolated in their neighborhoods and thus less likely to have access to news, which gives them a poorer understanding of upward mobility and how unlikely they are to actually achieve it. Paradoxically, they overestimate their chances of upward mobility to an even greater degree than more privileged people. But this belief in the American dream may simply be the expression of a desire to be seen as "belonging," as having "the right values." Above all, it is enormously challenging to keep faith when everyone around you faces mounting difficulties—including unemployment, precarity, economic drift, cost of education, family disruption, and health challenges, to name just a few. Some may feel that their struggles are individual, but it's clear from recent studies that many of them are widely shared.

Economists, along with the politicians who rely on them, are often concerned with finding ways to either "grow the pie" of the economy, or to shift its pieces around to benefit more people. But this approach can overlook how other conditions can affect that distribution. While expanding the pool of resources available to the working class and the poor is important, it is clearly not sufficient. We also have to reconsider the models of self that come with the American dream, and how they are obscuring the bigger picture and hindering progress on redistributing the pie.

The hegemony of the American dream manifests in the emphasis Americans put on the neoliberal virtues of material success, self-reliance, individualism, entrepreneurialism, and competitiveness. These criteria of worth have gained more and more influence as "models of ideal selves," and encourage many to internalize blame for the increasing precarity of their lives. This model can also lead people to seek out a scapegoat group to blame. Of course, neither option is helpful from the perspective of progressive mobilization.

These neoliberal virtues have also nourished patriotism and support for America's dominant position on the world stage. One reason they are especially effective in doing so is that they extend to downwardly mobile people one of the few high-status identities available to them: their "winning" status as Americans, as citizens of the most powerful country in the world. The disparity between this identity and the punishing, untenable economic position of the downwardly mobile can drive those of them who are white toward embracing that part of their identity, too. This nationalism, in turn, can lead some to become attracted to the white supremacist movement, and to denounce immigrants and Black Americans as less worthy.

From Ronald Reagan to Donald Trump, neoliberalism has come to be understood as a precondition for a successful society. Entrepreneurialism, competitiveness, economic success, and self-reliance are increasingly equated with deservingness and merit. Generations have felt the need to measure their self-worth, and the need to judge others, by these limiting ideals. And as they gain influence, these values have served as indicators of cultural citizenship and belonging. In the end, they have fed considerable social instability, a mental health crisis, a decline in trust, and much more.

The group that best demonstrates the neoliberal virtues of material success, competitiveness, efficacy, entrepreneurialism, and self-reliance is the upper-middle class: college-educated managers and professionals. This group benefited enormously as the winners in a "winner-take-all" economy and continued to solidify its position during the economic changes of recent decades. Compared to the middle- and lower-income classes, the upper-middle class's income has grown significantly for several decades. By 2016, the average income of upper-middle-class people was 2.4 times higher than that of middle-income people and 7.3 times that of lower-income people.

It's not hard to understand how inequality generates chronic stress, including mental and physical wear and tear for those on the lower half of the social ladder. Typically, working-class families must contend with poverty, powerlessness at work, bigotry, and other factors. But in recent years, inequality has been stressful for the upper-middle and middle class as well, especially since 2008: an intensified "fear of falling" is spreading within these groups, with wide-ranging ramifications. Mental health problems are increasingly affecting adults in the middle- and upper-income bracket (defined here as greater than $50,000). While anxiety among this income group had been lesser than for the lower income group, it grew at similar rates for all groups from 2008 to 2018. Maintaining their position requires enduring intense competition, working nonstop, forgoing personal time, and dealing with status anxiety. The rates of suicide for those in higher income groups is close to that of those who make less than $30,000. Concerns about money, job stability, and overwork are cited as the most common reasons for this change; long work hours are particularly associated with risk of depression.

This top group has also been challenged in one of the most intimate sectors of life: family planning. In recent years, fertility has plummeted for the top quartile of wage earners. The numbers are even more shocking in comparison to those in the lower rungs. A considerable percentage of people earning between $50,000 and $100,000 expect to have fewer children than they had hoped because of their "inability to afford" more children. That sentiment is held by 21 percent of that income group, compared to only 14 percent of those who earn less than $50,000. Higher-income parents feel pressured to affirm and pass on the privileges of wealth, and to achieve this the financial costs of parenthood have increased, through private school tuition, tutors, and expensive sports. And they feel psychological pressures as well. They cannot resist "helicopter parenting," going to great—and, at times, inappropriate—lengths to ensure their kids' success. For instance, a growing number are hiring independent educational consultants to guide their children through college applications.

And yet, many high-income families are blind to the many ways they pass on class privileges, and to how, in doing so, they block others from climbing as high as they have. In a 2002 survey that asked students at a competitive high school to rank factors determining a person's future, 71.5 percent of respondents ranked individual effort at the top, ahead of factors like their parents' background, social support, and quality of education. A study of privileged students at an elite boarding school also found a strong belief in hard work as the key to success.

The subjects of intense parental investment, mostly middle and upper-middle-class youth, face significant pressure to succeed. Lives of hyper-competition lead to significant struggles with burnout, anxiety, and feelings of being overwhelmed. Studies show that these pressures have increased over the decades; whereas just 18 percent of freshmen, most of whom are middle class, said they were overwhelmed in 1985, 43 percent were overwhelmed in 2019. In the words of Katherine, a white student from Massachusetts, "our generation faces a lot of pressure and competition . . . a feeling of competition constantly is just exhausting. You're competing with everyone over internships, over this, over that, and you're worried." These responses and behaviors are more prevalent among college students than in the general population, with college students being 2.5 times more likely to abuse substances than the general population. But it may be that they are more often diagnosed. Some researchers argue that those high-income kids are at most risk.

The "wellness" culture has spread considerably among the middle class over the last decades. Between 2002 and 2019, there has been a 48 percent increase in the number of adults who received mental health treatment or counseling in the US, at roughly the same time that psychologists found that "socially prescribed perfectionism" increased by 32 percent (between 1989 and 2016). Treatment for mental health has become more available over time, making the rise in the use of mental health services a period trend, rather than attributable only to an increase in psychological distress itself.

While Twitter and Instagram humorists may downplay (or even ridicule) the mental health struggles of the upper-middle class as a "first-world problem," such issues can nevertheless be significant. Increasingly, expensive neighborhoods have been stratifying into multiple enclaves, with the most exclusive areas reserved for the wealthiest of the wealthy. This, in turn, has pushed the affluent to anxiously compare their station to that of even higher-income people. Inside this affluent bubble, people can easily lose perspective and forget the magnitude of the advantages they enjoy.

Still, many upper-middle-class people find comfort in spending time with and comparing themselves to those who are most like them (what sociologists call "class homophily"). Many have a poor understanding of the world beyond their familiar and homogeneous neighborhood, which also leads them to underestimate the problems facing the poor. Compounding this trend is the growing spatial segregation between classes. As economic inequality grew over the last several decades, so too did physical separation between classes in neighborhoods, workplaces, and schools (see Figure 1). As a result, fewer Americans today are in contact with people from other income groups than in 1970. The magnitude of the change is staggering!

Figure 1: Income inequality and segregation

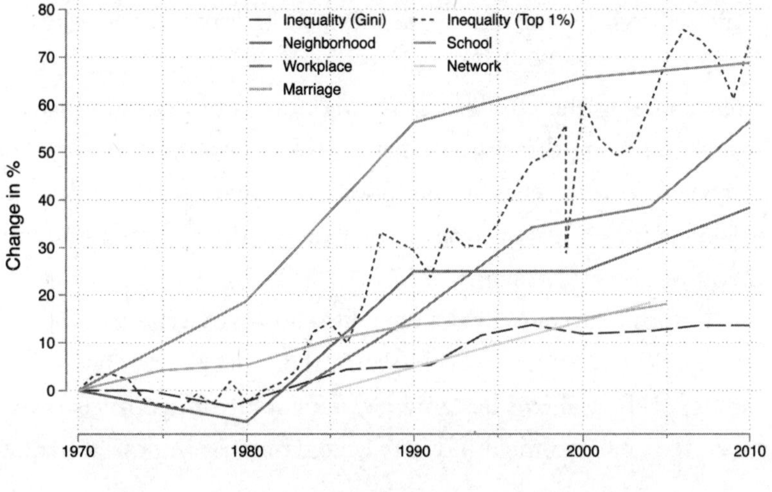

The upper-middle class's values and lifestyle are often given outsized representation in the media, in advertising, and at colleges and workplaces. And their patterns of consumption are often presented as a model to be emulated by everyone, even though the resources needed to do so are available only to a tiny, shrinking minority. As a result, the upper-middle class has become more influential and culturally dominant, while also growing ever more physically distant from other class groups.

One example will resonate with many of us: in 2016, a study of over four hundred primetime American sitcoms, totaling sixty-eight years of television, found that 80 percent of the shows' characters were upper-middle class, while just 10 percent were working class. In the vast majority of cases, the working-class men were represented as buffoons or as incompetent, immature, ignorant, and irresponsible.

In a recent study, the political scientist Eunji Kim compared the effect of watching rags-to-riches reality TV shows (like *Shark Tank*, *American Idol*, and *American Ninja Warrior*) with the effect of watching other reality TV shows. She found that watching stories of upward mobility had a significant effect on the viewer's own belief in the American dream, particularly among Republicans and the "politically optimistic." Kim's study established that watching these shows was just as likely to lead viewers to embrace the *American dream* as being the children of immigrants. These shows inspire hope, but it is one-dimensional, based on socioeconomic success and individual achievement—a conception that downplays the collective as well as inequality of means. Such shows also fail to foster any alternative criteria of worth.

If exposure to rags-to-riches reality shows strengthens belief in the American dream, we may be seeing the social effects now, as the number of these shows has grown exponentially in recent years. In effect, the entertainment industry is now functioning as a gigantic publicity machine for upper-middle-class values like consumerism and neoliberalism. The reality of the working class is largely absent in entertainment. This can encourage workers to progressively identify themselves with and normalize the upper-middle-class world they observe. They also may come to consider their own conditions as lacking—as a shameful aberration from the acceptable norm.

Beyond just reality shows, contemporary television inundates us with rags-to-riches stories of people transcending a distant, dark, and shameful past—as well as stories of people who just happen to already be rich. What we don't do is normalize the experiences of working-class people. For instance, the 1980s and '90s working-class sitcom *Roseanne*—and its 2018 reboot—portray characters whom few would identify with. The same is true of Homer in *The Simpsons*, a caricature of the bumbling idiot.

In contrast, several recent shows feature wealthy people visiting fancy resorts or "self-improvement retreats" (*White Lotus*, *Nine Perfect Strangers*), or people living in exclusive neighborhoods—*The Real Housewives* series being only one example. But these shows depict a lifestyle unattainable for most viewers. While these shows explore the ugliness of the wealthy and hardly glorify them, they also offer "eye candy" for envious consumers.

The effect of these portrayals on Americans' understanding of themselves and their support for the American dream can be seen clearly in opinion surveys. Earlier in this chapter, we noted the strength of Americans' belief in meritocracy and hard work—but as rags-to-riches narratives have pervaded the airwaves, that belief is only growing stronger and stronger. A majority of Americans still believe that the rich owe their position to hard work. This belief is much stronger among Republicans (75 percent) than Democrats (38 percent), according to one 2019 national survey. But the embrace of meritocracy has increased from 90 percent to 96 percent between

1980 and 2010, and is thus strong across the political spectrum. This is considerably higher than in many other places. In France, for example, belief in meritocracy remained stable, at 55 percent, over the same period. This belief in meritocracy goes hand in hand with the reluctance of some Americans to tax the rich, since some stubbornly still believe in trickle-down economics, thinking that if the rich get richer, everyone else will rise with them. (Or that one day they may be rich themselves and benefit from low taxes.)

This normative world also supports a narrow definition of what the middle-class ideal should be. The nuclear family with the white picket fence is envisioned by many as a suburban white family, living a life away from "crime-ridden" Black and Brown urban neighborhoods where homelessness abounds. Because this ideal is drawn so narrowly, worth, purity, and goodness are defined as belonging to fairly comfortable white people, and everyone else is often presumed undeserving, even as the American dream is increasingly unreachable for the majority. This world of comfort and security is likely to be threatened by radical ideas such as "defund the police," reparation, abolishing prisons, and even desegregating schools.

As the lifestyle and values of the upper-middle class gained more legitimacy and influence, a large segment of the population came to perceive itself more negatively and feel their dignity tumbling, at the same time as some embraced meritocracy. The transformation of the boundaries in American society has had a negative effect not only on the top of the social ladder, but also on the less privileged two-thirds of the population and those who experience growing exclusion. This is an even bigger part of the problem at hand.

CHAPTER 2

THE VIEW FROM BELOW

THE WORKING CLASS AND THE MARGINALIZED

Now that we have considered the plight of people at the top, it's time to turn our attention to "the bottom half"—and to groups that have found themselves increasingly excluded.

As we've already seen, an array of structural changes in recent decades has steadily deteriorated workers' economic standing. Many have seen their income decline year after year since the 1970s, as the minimum wage has failed to keep up with inflation. At the same time, workers have also seen their rate of union membership tumble. From 1954 to 2022, union membership in the US fell from 34.8 percent to just 11.6 percent. Along with these economic losses, many workers have also lost social status. This is especially true of male workers, who once largely defined themselves through their identity as steadfast providers for their families. When stagnant wages and disappearing jobs began to erode that identity, some of these men felt shamefully emasculated. At the same time, fewer got married, had children, or maintained strong networks of friends, and joined civic and religious organizations. And because of the dominant neoliberal narrative that attributed economic difficulties to individual failings, a growing number came to believe that their failures were personal rather than systemic. This fed their growing isolation, as well as political cynicism and apathy, but also, in some cases, their radicalization and support for populism in the United States and beyond.

The situation is even more dire for those living under the poverty line given the erosion of government programs like public housing, unemployment benefits, and disability income. Until the US government provided relief for COVID-19, a growing proportion faced extreme poverty as essential safety net programs such as food stamps have been cut again and again. In 2020–21, government relief has improved their situation in the short term and showed what the US is capable of when political consensus is possible. But for many the situation remains hopeless.

All these trends stand in sharp contrast to the positive meritocratic message of "work hard and you'll rise up." This dissonance sends a message to those at the bottom that their difficulties stem from their presumed lack of drive, that they deserve to be cast aside. In this way, the working class and the poor are vilified and made to feel "less than"—less competitive, hardworking, intelligent, disciplined, entrepreneurial, and motivated than professionals and managers. Essentially, the American dream and its myth of meritocracy draw boundaries between those who matter and those who don't. This becomes the basis of the social hierarchy, protected by an ironclad moralistic justification that has only gained influence under neoliberalism.

The vicious cycle of our current economic model centered on growth at all costs has led to a widespread toll on mental health for the population at large, including increased reports of anxiety, depression, and suicidal ideation. These effects were of course accentuated by the 2020 COVID pandemic. According to one national study published in February 2021, 41 percent of surveyed adult Americans said they had experienced anxiety and depression symptoms since the start of the pandemic, and 13 percent reported new or increased substance abuse.

The opioid crisis provides evidence of the dire situation facing the lower half of society in particular: The numerous fatalities from the crisis fit into what the economists Anne Case and Angus Deaton have famously called "deaths of despair"—or deaths caused by suicide, overdose, or alcohol abuse, largely concentrated among white, non–college educated people. Case and Deaton documented a rise in these deaths, which they associated with rising inequality, the dysfunctional US health care system, and the inadequacy of the social safety net. After all, growing inequality feeds mistrust and anxiety about social status. If workers can no longer aspire to middle-class status, what does that mean for stabilizing middle-class social institutions like work, church, family, and social clubs? If the majority of people feel a divide between who they think they should be and what society makes possible, how can they be moved by a shared social vision of communal life?

In the early 1990s, I interviewed blue-collar and low-status white-collar workers living near Paris and New York for a book I was writing called *The Dignity of Working Men*. At the time, the differences between the two groups of workers were stark. One was that American workers were far more attracted to promises of upward mobility than their French counterparts and sought to emulate the upper-middle class. Unfortunately, they were also more likely to think of themselves as "losers," whereas French workers demonstrated more class solidarity and expressed cynicism about upper-middle-class values, including its "bourgeois lifestyles."

To be certain, some American workers were also fairly critical of the "people above"—or "the Ken and Barbie people," as one worker put it. These more critical workers called their upper-middle-class peers "workaholics," viewed them as obsessed with material success and professional status, and as domineering and self-centered, lacking in concern for others. Even so, many admired them.

In contrast to American workers, the French put more weight on being there for their pals through thick or thin—and less on displays of consumerism. The French, of course, were drawing on a long history of vilifying the rich and took inspiration from their country's long and rich socialist, republican, and Catholic traditions, which celebrate solidarity, including toward the poor, and condemn capitalism as exploitative and inhumane. These communal and prosocial values were, of course, far less present in the US, where individualism dominates.

These interviews took place roughly three decades ago, but given all that's taken place since then—the growth in inequality, the declining standards of living among the non–college educated, and the increasing differentiation between urban and rural populations—it seems likely that using material success as a measure of personal worth was even more harmful after 2000 than in the early nineties, with all but a few left empty-handed. Both in the US and beyond, these workers are hanging on to the notion of self-reliance while also trying to cope with growing uncertainty and precarity. They have seen their relative status deteriorate at great speed. Many analysts suggest that this economic anxiety and status drop explain their racial resentment toward minority workers, support for the populist right, xenophobia, and other ills.

The Dignity of Working Men also showed how the American interviewees drew strong moral boundaries between themselves and those they saw as poor, contrasting their own discipline with the alleged laziness and helplessness of low-income people. One remarkable but unsurprising finding was that white workers had a particularly low opinion of the African American poor. They were particularly contemptuous of welfare recipients, who take shameful government-sponsored “handouts.” Rather than see the systemic economic failures for what they were, many believed that the poor brought about their condition through moral and ethical failings. At the same time, the 2008 financial crisis made even more workers resentful of the financial elite, as they felt their status destabilized even further as they lost homes and experienced mass unemployment, while the federal government saved the banks.

Welfare recipients still face intense stigmatization in America, although more Americans now express support for progressive taxation. Many Americans—particularly Republicans—continue to embrace individual and moral explanations over structural explanations for poverty, blaming the poor for their plight. In other Western democracies, too, empathy for welfare recipients has declined in recent years. As a result, here and elsewhere, low-income populations recede from the national conversation, to the point that their interests become nearly invisible.

Given the grinding conditions in which they live, impoverished people have rarely mobilized politically to defend their rights and assert their humanity. But on occasion they have managed to come together. These rare instances include the 1968 Poor People’s March on Washington, an effort to gain economic justice for poor people in the United States led by Martin Luther King. More recently, the Occupy Movement of 2011 denounced the selfishness of the “one percent,” but this effort rapidly lost steam. In similar ways, other social problems fed by inequality and poverty can too easily fall out of sight, including mass incarceration and student debt.

One of the main contributions of the book is to argue that stigmatization extends across a number of groups that are often pitted against one another. This chapter is about all the groups that are experiencing exclusion, not only the working class.

For religious, ethno-racial, and sexual minority groups, the situation can be very difficult. Many of these groups experienced an expansion of rights and recognition in the more than half-century since World War II. Groups who benefited included religious minorities, people of color, the LGBTQ+ community, and women. Yet during Donald Trump's presidency, many observers, both in academia and in the media, documented a stark rise in hate crimes, particularly against immigrants, Latinx, Muslims, and African Americans. At the same time, Republican politicians attempted to roll back LGBTQ+ rights, abortion rights, and protections against discrimination in the workplace. In all cases, common neoliberal measures of self have been leveraged in identity politics, pitting those judged self-reliant against other groups. This often resulted in a hardening of boundaries toward groups typically aligned with progressive policy gains (with parallel changes occurring in Europe).

The growing stigmatization of poverty is doubly harmful for groups already facing discrimination—groups like African Americans, Hispanics, and immigrants, who are often presumed to take advantage of welfare. This was a persistent theme in the interviews I conducted in the early 1990s for *The Dignity of Working Men*, as the workers I talked with denounced "leeches" and "sponges," targeting in particular those they perceived as "outsiders" from immigrant backgrounds.

Whereas for much of the twentieth century we saw more and more inclusion and tolerance, we are now witnessing a reversal of that trend at some levels. Stigmatized groups, and especially immigrants, are facing tougher conditions, as anti-immigrant, right-wing, populist political movements gain momentum in both the United States and Europe—although different countries have different stories. The United States saw a growth in warmth toward several immigrant groups in recent years, but Hispanics continue to be presumed "illegal" and to take advantage of public resources, such as welfare.

Blatant racism directed at African Americans has also been rekindled, challenging common narratives of racial progress, while institutional and spatial segregation has also increased dramatically—especially within schools. Between 1983 and 2004, opinion polling from the American National Election Survey showed a steady increase in positive feelings toward African Americans among all groups, but starting in 2005, those numbers started to slightly decline, especially among Republicans. This can be explained in part by white people's insecurity about their own position in society. In 2017, 55 percent of white Americans believed there "is discrimination against white people today," while only 43 percent disagreed with that statement. By 2021, 65 percent of white Americans thought their group experience some or a lot of discrimination.

For its part, the LGBTQ+ community has seen steadier improvement. This is not surprising given that the LGBTQ+ community is not clearly associated with the poor (while poverty is high among the young, those living in "double income, no kids" middle-class households are not atypical). Thus, some segments of this population (e.g., professional middle-age gay men) have encountered less pushback than others (e.g., younger trans people) and are more regularly featured in the media.

However, the LGBTQ+ community also faces an accelerated cultural war and risks losing ground as the homophobic agenda of the Christian right and Republican politicians has rapidly gained political and legal traction, especially in the South, where gender-affirming health care for trans children has been the focus of intense battles, and denounced as "child abuse" in Texas and Florida. Conservative Supreme Court justices, meanwhile, have suggested that they are open to overturning *Obergefell v. Hodges*, the decision that legalized same-sex marriage in all fifty states.

Working-class and low-income women also face great difficulties. The wage gap between men and women persists, while abortion rights are under attack across the United States, in Latin America, and elsewhere. The reversal of *Roe v. Wade* by the Supreme Court in 2022 affects negatively not only the health and well-being of women across all classes, but also their sense that they matter and are perceived as fully independent and competent citizens by their government.

Overall, the boundaries between different groups are hardening, even in the aftermath of massive demonstrations in support of racial justice across 140 American cities in summer 2020. By 2021, support for the movement had declined significantly among white people—although the shift was much more significant among white Republicans than among white Democrats. In all cases, common neoliberal models of self have strengthened group boundaries and intensified intergroup competition (with parallel changes in Europe over recent decades).

CHAPTER 3

MEETING THE MOMENT

HOW WE FIGHT FOR A MORE INCLUSIVE WORLD

This has so far been a bleak assessment of modern American society. What I hope to have shown is that every class and many identity groups are harmed by the current economic and social changes, except perhaps for a tiny sliver at the top of the class structure—the wealthiest of the wealthy. Every other group, to one degree or another, finds itself reeling from an onslaught of difficulties, disappointments, and anxieties, grasping for dignity and stability.

What are the solutions to this state of affairs? We have already considered how neoliberal scripts self-promote individual salvation in the form of individual mobility. For their part, psychologists and public policy experts often embrace grit (a character trait or individual resource similar to IQ), while the consumerist media and the therapeutic culture favor narrow, palliative solutions focused on individual gratification and self-care. But wellness and lifestyle products, and health and fitness activities like mindfulness, meditation, and yoga, can get us only so far. They can certainly make a difference on an individual level, but they fail to address the root problem. In fact, individualist approaches may harm more than they help, since they pull people's attention away from potentially more meaningful efforts. They are part of the problem, not solutions. Ultimately, if we truly want to address current challenges, we need to focus on addressing exclusion in our daily lives. We need to ask ourselves hard questions about how we decide who matters and what we can do to create a more inclusive society.

Many people who think deeply about these problems favor economic solutions. The Democratic Party in the US, for example, often raises the possibility of redistributing resources by enacting more progressive taxation policies and closing tax loopholes, allowing the poor to get tax relief and obliging the rich to pay their fair share. There are many other economic policies that reformers hope will lead to a more egalitarian society, such as mandating gender wage equality, creating a system of universal basic income, and extending health care to all. These changes are crucial and do show real promise.

However, political or institutional reforms will never be sufficient to produce the change we need unless we are also able to change our narratives. The ways that different groups are made to feel excluded often is not driven primarily or solely by economic factors. Consider, for example, NIMBY movements: they are often both about preserving the value of real estate and about keeping distance from low-income people and people of color, as we see in conflicts about the construction of affordable housing. Middle-class or rich people are more likely to evoke "preserving historic architecture" and "quality of life" than their desire to have few children from non–college educated families in their local schools. This also holds when it comes to white resentment about affirmative action and diversity in the workplace—claims about unqualified, undeserving people of color "taking the place" of more deserving "hardworking" white people. These common arguments belie a desire to maintain a homogeneous environment and status, and to hoard resources for the only group that is nationally valued—the top of the social pyramid, where whites are overrepresented.

Social scientists have documented in detail how Gifted and Talented programs in public schools, which were in many cases created to appeal to white middle-class parents, end up exacerbating segregation. Although American public schools today are largely segregated by class and race, that segregation is not an official policy, but rather an effect of broader racial and class segregation between neighborhoods. Some of this stems from exclusionary governmental and institutional policies like redlining—but clearly, individual white families' choices about where they live and where they send their kids to school also play an important role, as shown in the popular NPR podcast *Nice White Parents*. For change to last, we need to transform how we think about who matters. Americans often judge a person's worth based not only on meritocratic factors like their dedication to their work, but also on their proximity to whiteness, their distance from poverty, or how "American" they are perceived to be (in self-presentation, accent, or familiarity with American sports and culture). Only once we are able to shift our national conversation and adopt a much broader conception of who "belongs" will we be able to make any progress.

Fostering change is a multidimensional puzzle. Economic and policy changes and cultural changes are all needed—and each plays a vital role in shaping the other. Fortunately, we can focus on more than one thing at once: we can push simultaneously for greater recognition *and* greater material equality. In my past work I have argued that moral boundaries feed social boundaries—which is to say, the moral judgments that each of us make about our peers inform how we understand the lines between groups based on the resources, networks, and spaces they access. It's easier to distance yourself from people who are different if you believe that their differences are signs of being undeserving because they are uneducated, vulgar, or phony or because they are lazy, have low moral standards, or take advantage of others (in my previous books, I found that the first traits are more often mentioned by the upper-middle class, whereas the latter are mentioned more by the working class).

We have already seen that different classes and identity groups are growing more and more physically separated from one another as people increasingly seek out neighborhoods, workplaces, schools, and social circles composed of people with similar backgrounds to their own. As shown in Figure 1, there has also been a decline in marriages and friendships between these groups. If we want to address inequality, we must confront the stereotypes used to justify this spatial segregation, the narratives that lead some to (consciously or not) perceive other groups as less worthy. Without this crucial step, even if we are able to enact policy changes to encourage integration, those efforts are likely to backfire and stoke resentment. This is exactly the sort of backlash we see against affirmative action in college admission decisions and practices designed to encourage more diversity in workplace hiring. I do not mean to say that we should defer all meaningful policy action until there is universal agreement that all groups are equally worthy—but without changing hearts and minds, we will always face an uphill battle to enact meaningful change through policy.

Most of all, we must resist the temptation of superficial measures. Diversity and inclusion cannot be treated as mere buzzwords, but must be accompanied by substantive changes—in our collective values, our social scripts, and our measures of worth. The dangers of making such shallow commitments without truly rethinking our lived values are clearly described by the historian Lily Geismer in her book *Don't Blame Us: Suburban Liberals and the Transformation of the Democratic Party*. Focusing on the Boston metropolitan area, the book shows how upper-middle-class neighborhoods have remained racially homogeneous for decades despite the professed progressivism of those who live there.

This is the world I have lived in for twenty years, in my own town of Brookline, Massachusetts, and our family experienced these shifts as my three kids grew up in Brookline's public schools, attending a "Title 1" elementary school with a high proportion of low-income students. There, my children saw the demographic composition of their peer group become more and more homogeneous as they got older. In the earlier years, several of their buddies were Cape Verdeans and Dominicans who lived in the public housing project nearby. But as they entered high school, they found themselves in more homogeneous circles, as academic tracking "magically" came to parallel class and ethnic or racial lines. In such a context, conventional solutions don't go far enough. Changing our attitudes and narratives is a prerequisite to meaningful change. And fortunately, once again, important changes are already happening.

Before going any farther, it is worth pausing to make clear what we're talking about when we use the term *narrative*. Narratives are more than just stories—they are perspectives about society and social relations that allow people to make sense of the world. Generally, they are known or shared by group members and shape their lives, including how they decide who is worthy or unworthy.

Former president Trump, for instance, advanced a narrative in which immigrants (and especially those from Central America) pose an existential threat to the United States. When launching his presidential campaign in 2015, he implied that all Mexican immigrants coming to the US were rapists and drug dealers, ignoring the reality that US immigrants are far more law-abiding than average. Narratives can be loud and obvious, as in this case, but they can also be subtle—they can be ways of seeing that make some visible, while moving others to the background. In other words, narratives are how we describe reality to ourselves and to others—and they encompass everything from our identities and experiences to our social environments and groups.

Of course, we are more likely to buy into narratives when they are already embraced by our peers. They become more powerful the more popular they are. And they can shape our views in both positive and negative ways. They can, for example, help a group imagine a different future, as happened when second-wave feminists spread new narratives that helped women "see" patriarchy and claim a greater autonomy. Narratives can also feed our sense of agency, that is, our capacity to shape the world we live in, as well as our *social resilience*, our collective capacity to respond to the challenges we face. This capacity is grounded in the environment we inhabit, including the narratives we are exposed to, and the institutions that structure our lives (governments, schools, church, community associations, etc.).

Of course, narratives change over time. In France, a strong Catholic and socialist tradition has helped foster national narratives that stress civic responsibility and solidarity toward the poor. These narratives help explain one of the conclusions I drew in my book *The Dignity of Working Men*, which is that French workers do not feel they are losers as much as their American counterparts do, despite similar material conditions. American workers have not always been made to feel this way. In the post–World War II era, when unions were particularly strong in the United States, US workers could draw on a much more egalitarian narrative, informed by the same values of solidarity that are stronger among the French. By the 1990s, when I conducted my research with workers from New Jersey and New York, unions had lost much of their power, having suffered major setbacks during the Reagan administration and before. At that point, while American and French workers were both contending with difficult economic conditions, American responses were shaped by a more individualist national narrative, and were thus more likely to feel stigmatized and devalued, and to have less compassion for people below them and less solidarity with other workers. They were more likely to seek individualist solutions in upward mobility, whereas although increasingly individualists, to this day the French remain more likely to mobilize collectively and take to the streets to have their demands addressed. Massive demonstrations throughout Paris's major avenues have been a regular feature of daily life for decades.

While narratives can shift over time, they can also become another thing for people to fight over. For example, narratives about the history of marginalized groups are frequently contested, as seen during the uproar caused in the early 2020s by right-wing activists fighting against what they call Critical Race Theory—which they use as a catchall term for any lesson or teaching that acknowledges the experiences of marginalized racial groups. But ignoring this history creates another narrative entirely. Consider the many injustices and atrocities that Black people in the United States have endured over the centuries. Discounting this long history of slavery and segregation changes how everyone thinks about both American and African American identity, and ultimately denies Black people dignity and recognition. Progress toward racial equality will continue to be slow and sporadic until our narratives can fully incorporate this painful American history of injustice. This is precisely the objective of Nikole Hannah-Jones's 1619 Project.

Her story illustrates how change agents can produce new narratives that ensure everyone matters.

Hopefully by now, the power of narratives to shape how we perceive the world is becoming clear. They stand to determine whether certain groups are admired or scorned, listened to or ignored, respected or shamed. This brings us to a crucial point: all of these—narratives, stigmas, stereotypes, and social hierarchies—are produced by human beings and thus changeable. This means that conflicts between groups cannot be explained primarily by moral tribalism (or biology, human nature, and cultural evolutionism). In fact, eugenics was based entirely on reinforcing existing social and racial hierarchies and had no relationship to science or reality.

The ability of narratives to produce social change has been documented time and again by social analysts. This is doubly true of narratives produced and disseminated through popular culture—which can have a direct effect on behavior by getting people to relate to members of another group and thus to narrow recognition gaps. For instance, an important psychological experiment published in 2012 showed that Latinos who watched a Telemundo soap opera in which a character helps with the 2010 census were less mistrustful of the US government and more likely to support participation in the census. In 2014, another important study found that the TV show *16 and Pregnant* ultimately led to a reduction in teen births in the eighteen months after its premiere. The authors suggested that the show "accounted for about one-third of the overall decline in teen births in the United States during that period."

Acknowledging the importance of narratives and recognition, the Rockefeller Foundation in 2015 paid for some twenty thousand public school students in New York City to attend the Broadway musical *Hamilton*. The blockbuster musical cast actors of color to play the Founding Fathers and used hip-hop, a musical genre created by people of color, to retell the story of the nation's founding. These choices centered people of color in a space where they have been traditionally excluded—histories of the nation's founding. The musical challenged the idea of who built the country, who belongs in America, and who can be included in a national identity. During performances, crowds often cheered loudly to the line "Immigrants, we get the job done," an important reminder that the US is a nation of immigrants whose contributions are frequently overlooked.

Similarly, the film *Black Panther*, featuring primarily African American actors, was released during Black History Month in 2018. In addition to expanding many white moviegoers' conception of what superheroes look like, the film inspired community activist Frederick Joseph to launch an important crowdfunding effort "to ensure the Boys & Girls Club of Harlem could all secure seats to what will likely be a lasting role model in the superhero genre." The GoFundMe page for this effort emphasized how the film could contribute to closing the recognition gap for low-income African American kids: "This representation is truly fundamental for young people, especially those who are often underserved, unprivileged, and marginalized both nationally and globally."

Of course, many different factions have tried to leverage the power of narratives. In the 1990s, Republicans increased their influence by transforming the way Americans think of politics. For example, a political action committee associated with Newt Gingrich, who was then the Republican House minority whip, circulated a document to the party's candidates titled "Language: A Key Mechanism of Control." It invited them to label Democrats with words like "decay," "failure," "crisis," "pathetic," "liberal," "radical," "corrupt," and "taxes," while defining Republicans with words like "opportunity," "moral," "courage," "flag," "children," "common sense," "hard work," and "freedom." Gingrich later told the *New York*

Times his goal was "reshaping the entire nation through the news media." Which is exactly what the party did, with the support of talk radio shows and, later, Fox News and other outlets.

If narratives are so important to explaining our world, why are they underdiscussed in conversations about inequality? One reason is that economists play such a dominant role in these discussions and bring to them a specific type of expertise and knowledge, which is deeply rooted in quantification and cost-benefit analysis with direct policy implications.

In her 2010 book *Economists and Societies*, the sociologist Marion Fourcade showed that for much of the twentieth century, economists held an enormous amount of influence over how governments understood social change. This was especially true in the United States, where economists shaped policy in profound ways and played an outsized role in evaluating the effectiveness of the very policies they prescribed. In her book *Thinking like an Economist*, Elizabeth Popp Berman took this analysis further, exploring how economics provides a partial understanding of the world, drawing attention only to certain kinds of problems while obscuring others, and pushing us only toward a narrow set of solutions. As Berman shows, quantitative methods took priority over qualitative methods, which are typically used to study narratives. In this way, economists came to dominate research on social change, putting much greater emphasis on resource distribution. For example, when faced with rising inequality, some economists might argue for lowering tax rates for the rich to incentivize people to make more money. Others may promote more distributional measures. Yet, a few prominent economists have become interested in identity and narratives, decrying how their disciplines have committed "sins of omission." Others have attempted to engage more systematically with insights from sociology.

As economists gained influence, we also saw the rise of cognitive psychology in microeconomics, or the study of economic decision-making. Beginning in the 1980s and '90s, cognitive psychologists began turning their focus to economics, and ultimately revolutionized our understanding of decision-making. Prominent articles and books on the topic appeared, including Steven Pinker's *How the Mind Works*, Richard H. Thaler and Cass Sunstein's *Nudge*, and Daniel Kahneman's *Thinking Fast and Slow*. They gave rise to a new and influential knowledge industry: the science of nudging, or shaping behavior with subtle cues and other noncoercive means. For example, displaying healthy foods like fruits and vegetables at eye level in grocery stores would be a nudge to buy healthy food. In 2015, this area of study assumed a new level of influence, as the Obama administration established a "social and behavioral science team" tasked with deploying this approach in governmental policy.

Nevertheless, despite its popularity, this cognitive approach shares some of the shortcomings that typically constrain the broader field of economics. Both minimize or ignore the cultural context in which decisions are made, so their solutions are necessarily limited. In my view, our focus should be less on nudging the individual, or what happens inside our brains, than on how we can create and disseminate new narratives that will be readily available and help foster social change. When economists and behavioral scientists overlook narratives, they miss crucial aspects of our reality. We do not live our lives in the controlled environment of a laboratory. Therefore, we need broader and more dynamic frameworks to make sense of the world that surrounds us.

In recent years, many psychologists have also focused their attention on what they call *moral tribalism*, an allegedly innate instinct to segregate different groups and favor one's own group over others. The concept has been used, for example, to explain the growing political polarization and sectarianism in the United States and elsewhere. Its proponents often ground it in utilitarianism, human nature, and anthropological evolutionism.

But this theory often errs in assuming that the lines between different groups are set in stone. Not all groups are tribes, since the degree to which groups are cohesive, or have "groupness," depends on a range of factors, including the availability of jobs and the competition for these jobs, the frequency of their contact with other groups, and the history of their relationship with those groups. The boundaries (the various types of lines that we draw as we evaluate people, such as moral or socioeconomic boundaries) are changeable—as we've seen in a widened acceptance for gay people, which may have seemed unimaginable just a few decades ago. We know boundaries are changeable because *we make them*—they are created through a process that we all participate in. Moreover, perceptions of the social distance and competition between groups are highly variable across contexts.

Although tribalism is often explained by a generally ill-defined "human nature," cultural evolutionism, and vague references to how we are "wired to do X," there is nothing natural about "seeing race," even in babies and toddlers—like everything else, racial categories have to be taught. These perceptions are changeable and can be acted upon. We have the ability to reimagine the future and what kind of society we want to live in. How we go about changing these boundaries and ensuring that all groups feel valued is at the center of *Seeing Others*.

CHAPTER 4

BEING THE CHANGE WE WISH TO SEE

CHANGE AGENTS AND THE QUEST FOR DIGNITY AND RECOGNITION

When we connected in 2020, Catherine Opie was coming back from a monthlong RV trip through the American South. A famous artist and a professor of photography at UCLA, she had been taking pictures of African American communities to witness the disproportionate impact the COVID-related economic downturn had on them. Opie also acts as one of the most influential tastemakers in the world of contemporary art, serving on the board of the Andy Warhol Foundation, where she has a leading role in shaping her field. Her work creating representations of queer communities in Los Angeles, San Francisco, and beyond draws worldwide acclaim.

Through her art, Opie works to make stigmatized groups visible—and to help them be seen by others as they see themselves. While she portrays LGBTQ+ people in affirmative, humanizing ways, she also aims to persuade potentially prejudiced audiences to reframe how they view these groups. Opie's mission was inspired by her own personal experience. She has a strong memory of coming out to her father, a realtor, as he discovered her artwork.

Influenced by the German-Swiss sixteenth-century portraitist Hans Holbein the Younger, in her early work, Opie took portraits of her extended circles of friends from the leather S&M scene in Los Angeles and San Francisco, whom she calls her "Noble Family." These subjects are represented with "obsessive exactitude" against colorful backgrounds, wearing "aristocratic clothing." In an interview published at the time, she spelled out her objectives for the project: "They think we [in the leather community] are child molesters and everything that's attached to that. We have had a bad rap. I decided to do a body of work that was about being really out, and about being out about my sexuality. Instead of just showing the tattoos and the piercings and the markings on the body, I wanted to do a series of portraits of this community that were incredibly noble." In another series, she represents domestic scenes of lesbian couples at home, holding their children and dogs.

Opie wished to save others from the internal struggles she experienced when she was coming out. Her art recognizes and destigmatizes differences by drawing attention to the dignity and normalcy of traditionally ostracized groups. Early on, Opie was inspired by the influential queer philosopher Judith Butler in her desire to document the performative dimension of queer identity.

Opie embraces the political dimension of her art and underscores how it is contributing to redefining who "belongs" in American society. She aims to redraw the boundaries of acceptability, and even of dignity and worthiness, and to demonstrate the variety of American communities, the range of people who create bonds between each other. She says she is moved by our shared humanity, "whatever and whoever [we] are," and "the fact that we have to coexist on this finite planet."

To do this, Opie leverages the power of documentary photography, making private worlds public. And she is far from the only photographer to embrace such a mission. Indeed, many artists have been attracted to photography as a medium for raising the visibility of marginalized communities, including communities of color. This power of "representation" is at the center of strategies for broadening recognition to more people.

Deborah Willis is the photography curator at the famed Smithsonian National Museum for African American History & Culture in Washington, DC, and she is another prolific contributor to this artistic space. A dynamic woman in her late sixties, she is also a MacArthur "Genius Grant" award recipient, and the curator of photographs and prints at the Schomburg Center for Research in Black Culture in Harlem. Her exhibit, *Posing Beauty: African American Images from the 1890s to the Present* (2009), has toured worldwide. Her work has played a pivotal role in legitimizing and canonizing photography that serves and represents the Black community.

Her son, Hank Willis Thomas, is a celebrated Black photographer in his own right, with his own artistic vision. He is famous for his artwork that comments on icons of American sports and popular culture. For instance, one of his most famous pieces depicts a Nike swish branded on the skull of a Black man, as a critique of the brand's commodification of Black culture. The piece also powerfully refers to the history of branding as part of American slavery.

Thomas's For Freedom project, inspired by Norman Rockwell's iconic 1943 paintings *Four Freedoms* (from want, of speech, of worship, and from fear), contrasts the originals with a new version representing the racial diversity of contemporary America. I also spoke to Thomas about another project of his, *Question Bridge: Black Males*, a video (available on YouTube) in which 150 Black men from twelve American cities and different walks of life answered the same question: "What does it mean to be a Black man today?" From their response, Thomas learned that "Most of what we [Black men] have in common are the prejudgments that people place upon us."

When we spoke, Thomas said his goal with this work was to "deconstruct the whole notion of Black male identity." He said that today's stereotype of Black male identity is a product of European imagination, a cultural cudgel in deep need of reconsideration. As a cultural engineer of sorts, Thomas aims to illuminate both our differences and our often-overlooked shared humanity. Together with Opie and Deborah Willis, he is committed to the notion of universality as much as to the recognition of African Americans. These artists aim to denounce injustice and reduce stigma as they reveal the many facets of groups traditionally devalued in mainstream representations.

Throughout American history, and even today, the media often centered our attention on the individual as hero (most often a white male), through classics such as *The Great Gatsby* (1925), *Citizen Kane* (1941), and more recent examples, such as *American Psycho* (2000), *The Wolf of Wall Street* (2013), and *Nomadland* (2021). To counter these narrow norms, a plethora of contemporary artists are producing counternarratives, hoping to shape a different society in which our diversity is in full view. These artists value subjects based on various dimensions of their identity, including their common humanity, offering a counterpoint to neoliberal priorities, which isolate people, and push them to pursue individual success.

When I talked with these artists about their work, they expressed in various ways a goal of broadening our definitions of "who matters." Ultimately, each of them is working to make visible what brings us together as human beings, despite our outward differences. These creators are what I call "change agents," or cultural entrepreneurs who intentionally aim to transform how we perceive differences in others. Artists can act as important mediators to help us overcome those divisions. Think, for example, of James Baldwin, the Black writer and activist who helped Americans understand racism through books such as *The Fire Next Time* (1963), or the author Ta-Nehisi Coates, whose 2015 bestseller *Between the World and Me* was a kind of response to Baldwin. Such books are crucial entry points for understanding racism for Blacks and non-Blacks alike.

Change agents are not only preoccupied with recognition. They are also concerned with stigmatization, the mirror opposite of recognition, which, instead of calling attention to the value of differences, casts them as a mark of inferiority. Ultimately, stigmatization serves as a justification for discrimination, which is to say, denying people resources like education or housing based on their identity or characteristics. But recognition is so effective in challenging stigmatization because it works by reframing those very same differences as positive contributions.

Recognition is conferred in different ways. At the broadest level, it is a matter of which groups are granted political rights by societal consensus—the right to vote, to representation, to access public resources (like public education or medical care), to economic autonomy, and more. It is also a matter of which groups are granted cultural membership. As society becomes more inclusive and egalitarian, there will be a growing number of people who are considered worthy members of the community.

But recognition happens on another, less formal level, as well. And this form of recognition must take place before recognition becomes a matter of political rights. The Italian-Scottish political scientist Lorenza Fontana showed as much in her recent study of Indigenous people in Latin America organizing to gain access to land and various cultural rights, such as the protection of their language.

As marginalized groups are mobilizing and loudly denouncing the exploitation, mistreatment, and discrimination they experience, their demands gain visibility and, in many cases, traction. These contribute to recognition and form a virtual cycle in which groups can achieve more recognition and rights. But in so many cases, before any of this can happen, change agents have already been at work, creating new representations of these groups, of their history, their experiences, and their collective identity. Because this is such a critical part of the path we must walk to reach a more just and equitable world, it is worth dwelling a bit on the process by which ordinary people, participants in social movements, knowledge workers, and change agents come together to reframe how groups are perceived.

Today's cries for recognition are not new. In fact, there is a long history of this important step on the path toward social equality. This was, in a way, what the renowned sociologist W. E. B. Du Bois was writing about in an 1897 article for *The Atlantic* on what he called "double-consciousness." In it, he reflected on the experience of Black Americans who were compelled to assess their own worth through the dominant matrix of a profoundly racist society.

In this canonical text, Du Bois described the strange "sense of always looking at one's self through the eyes of others, of measuring one's soul by the tape of a world that looks on in amused contempt and pity. One feels his two-ness—an American, a Negro; two souls, two thoughts, two unreconciled strivings; two warring ideals in one dark body, whose dogged strength alone keeps it from being torn asunder."

Here, Du Bois acknowledges that while "I know my own worth, I also have to contend with how others see me, even if the two perspectives are at odds with one another." Together, these two aspects define a person's social identity. When Du Bois speaks of double-consciousness, he speaks of this gap, and more specifically, the gap between the humanity a Black person knows she has and the low status that white people routinely cast upon her. If we are to create a just society, this gap needs to be closed: white people need to recognize the equal humanity of Black people. Men need to acknowledge the full humanity of women and their right to self-determination. Zionist Israelis need to recognize the plight of Palestinians. This is what recognition is about, and what is captured so powerfully and simply in the phrase "Black Lives Matter."

The tension around recognition became especially clear to me in 2008, as some colleagues and I were starting to listen to over four hundred people of color about their experiences with racism for what was to become our 2016 book, *Getting Respect*. What was most striking to me was that the kinds of experiences they spoke about most frequently were experiences of being overlooked, underestimated, ignored, or insulted—rather than experiences of systemic discrimination in areas like housing or employment. We categorized these experiences collectively as "assaults on their worth," in contrast to more stereotypical kinds of discrimination in access to resources. Many researchers have understandably focused on the ways that people of color are deprived of resources, but for the people we interviewed, who lived in different countries around the world, the most salient experiences of racism were those that came not only in the form of discrimination and blatant racism or microaggression, but also in being underestimated, ignored, or "unseen."

The way we can prevent these experiences is by changing the dominant narratives about marginal groups. But one thing we need to acknowledge as we set about this is that different stigmatized groups deal with harmful narratives differently. For instance, while working on *Getting Respect*, my colleagues and I learned about the experiences of Oriental Jews in Israel, called Mizrahim, who have lower status in the labor market than Jews of European descent. But the Mizrahim (who originate from North Africa or the Middle East) frequently downplay experiences of discrimination, even as they struggle to be seen as full members of Israeli society. This contrasts with the African Americans we interviewed, who tended to feel that confronting racists is essential, even if it comes at a personal cost. For their part, some Black Brazilians we talked to were hesitant to "name racism," given the prevalence of a state ideology that presents their society as a heterogenous and tolerant "racial democracy."

One can't ignore recognition given how salient it has become in today's social mobilizations. Prior social movements, like the fight for women's suffrage or the Civil Rights Movement, sought recognition through winning voting rights and other legal changes. Today's social movements, however, are more focused on fighting for recognition itself, rejecting the impulse to assimilate, and pushing not for tolerance, but to be present and participate with "one's full self," demanding autonomy in self-definition and inclusion. Activists today are still seeking legal rights and protections (take the continued struggles over abortion access, for example) and pushing for policy solutions to redress systemic injustices, but many movements are combining these efforts with a mission of asserting the basic dignity of marginalized groups, as in the Movement for Black Lives, the MeToo phenomenon, and transnational mobilizations for women's and LGBTQ+ rights.

This is true of social and political movements across the ideological spectrum, and throughout the world. Antiabortion activists, for instance, argue that they are fighting for the basic dignity of fetuses, which they understand as unborn people. And in all manner of social movements—from low-caste farmers in India, to girls seeking educational access in Afghanistan, Iran, and Iraq, to Jews and queer people seeking protection from persecution in Hungary—people are also fighting for basic recognition of their whole selves.

Social movement scholar Erica Chenoweth argued in 2020 that the previous year had seen the "largest wave of mass, nonviolent antigovernment movements in recorded history." To back up this assertion, she examined movements from 1900 to 2019, including those in democratic countries like Brazil, Poland, and the US, as well as those in authoritarian states like Hong Kong, Iran, Bolivia, Lebanon, Egypt, and Turkey. Toward the end of this period, between 2010 and 2019, she noticed a dramatic rise in the number of social movements, with a particularly notable spike in the aftermath of the Women's March in 2017. In the United States, not only were the demonstrations larger than ever, but they were mobilizing a wider range of participants, with white people and people of color walking together in solidarity.

Many words have been used to describe different facets of the general trend toward increasing recognition. The term *social justice*, of course, has long been used but has seen a notable uptick in usage in recent years. The *New York Times* mentioned it on average roughly a hundred times a year from 1980 to 2000, but in 2020 it used the term more than seven hundred times. Another term that has become much more common in recent years is *woke*, which is used to describe someone who is attentive to subtle forms of discrimination and injustice. Although African American communities were likely using the term much earlier, one of its first popular appearances was in the R&B singer Erykah Badu's 2008 song "Master Teacher," which included the refrain "I stay woke." As Badu explained to NPR, the term referred to "being in touch with the struggle that

[Black] people have gone through . . . and understanding we've been fighting since the very day we touched down here." The term first became a subject of widespread attention from the media in 2014, as the Black Lives Matter movement began using it more frequently in protests and messaging following the murder of Michael Brown in Ferguson, Missouri. Although it originally was used to mean keeping one's eyes open, specifically to racial injustices, the term is now used more broadly to include awareness of injustices faced by other marginalized groups, as well—but this is largely because it has, at the same time, been mockingly appropriated by conservatives who were unaware of or insensitive to its original meaning, eager to lump together what they felt were exaggerated claims of discrimination from many different groups.

Across the political spectrum, some moderates have turned against the term, including those who stand in opposition to its cultural goals. Dubbed "cancel culture" by conservatives, wokeness also came to be massively criticized by Republicans for its alleged intolerance and elitism, and for threatening free speech rights within the First Amendment. In 2021, 80 percent of Republicans saw "cancel culture" as a "threat to freedom." In spring 2021, news outlets such as the *Financial Times*, the *Washington Post*, the *New York Times*, and the *New Yorker* reported a large number of highly politicized attacks on woke culture and defenses of freedom of speech. Thus, gradually, the term became almost completely unmoored from its original meaning and has been used (both derisively and not) to mean support for everything from defunding the police to gender affirmation surgeries.

But despite the push and pull over its exact meaning, "woke culture" has become a tool for dealing with the harms caused by our dominant culture, by affirming the distinctiveness of marginalized groups. Many groups are asserting their right to be recognized—to live authentically, instead of aiming to assimilate and camouflage who they are. In popular culture, the singer Lizzo used her cover art and music videos to affirm her pride in her curvy body, in defiance of dominant beauty standards insisting that women should be thin. In sports, football player Colin Kaepernick protested police brutality against Black people by taking a knee during the national anthem, against the official prohibition of the National Football League.

Finally, the term *identity politics* has also been used to talk about growing efforts to extend recognition and dignity to marginalized groups. This, too, has come to mean many things to many people, but in a most basic sense it refers to political action of different identity groups, which is to say, groups that are defined by characteristics like race, ethnicity, or sexual orientation, rather than by class. In the past, and still today, thinkers across the political spectrum have dismissed identity politics as irrelevant and a distraction from the other more serious issues pertaining to class. But class has both a cultural dimension (e.g., identity, status, and tastes and the meaning attached to consumption goods) as well as an economic dimension (e.g., how much people make, their position in the labor market). Racial groups, too, have both a cultural and an economic dimension.

Identity and material resources are both important factors, therefore, and both are needed to properly understand inequality. For one thing, economic inequality is often deeply rooted in identity-based discrimination and injustice. A major reason that Black people in the United States have accumulated less wealth than their white peers, for example, is that they were systemically excluded from homeownership through redlining, discrimination on the part of banks, and other explicitly racist practices. But these hurtful actions were always motivated by cultural beliefs about this group; identity is and has always been a basis for hateful attacks. If we hope to change people's minds and reduce stigma, we need to think deeply about the role that identity plays. The wind is changing, and many now acknowledge that dignity and respect should not be considered secondary or a luxury. And no amount of backlash, fatigue, or scolding from various quarters will change that fact.

Understanding the quest for dignity is essential for making sense of discontent on both sides of the ideological aisle. In her influential 2016 book *Strangers in Their Own Land*, the sociologist Arlie Hochschild argued that the increasing turn toward populism on the American right was motivated in part by a loss of dignity. In a separate study, my collaborators and I found that Donald Trump's speeches during the 2016 presidential campaign appealed directly to "America's forgotten workers" by recognizing their plight and by blaming globalization and immigration for it. He also gave words to their anger, tied to their feelings of emasculation, as the masculine role of the provider seemed ever more out of reach. His supporters were attracted to his slogan "Make American Great Again" as the proper response to this loss. In this context of economic decline, many felt "left behind," "overlooked," and "underestimated" by coastal elites and politicians such as Hillary Clinton, and were coaxed into action by a desire to reclaim American pride.

Then and now, Trump's supporters tend to see the world as a zero-sum game and therefore worry a great deal about keeping their place in the traditional pecking order. For them, extending recognition and dignity to another group necessarily means losing some of their own. In many cases, they seek to reaffirm the social dominance of the groups to which they predominantly belong: straight, white, older, and often Christian men.

As the demographic composition of the United States continues to shift and the share of the non-white population continues to grow, Trump supporters are responding with increasing anxiety. This phenomenon has inspired a conspiracy theory known as "the great replacement," which holds that liberal politicians are encouraging illicit immigration in order to "replace" groups that do not support them. A 2022 poll conducted by the Southern Poverty Law Center revealed that 67 percent of Republicans believe this. A different survey conducted the previous year found that fewer than half of Republicans believed the increasing diversity of American society to be a strength. In any case, whether they are ready for it or not, the change is already under way. In the coming decades, although immigration has been declining, the United States will be a majority-minority society, and many states and cities have already passed this benchmark. One of our nation's current challenges is to determine how to make white constituencies understand and respect the views of people of color.

Whether we are talking about the non–college educated or the many different marginalized groups held back by intolerance and discrimination, one lesson we can draw is that being denied basic dignity can have a profound effect on people's lives. Health researchers have found that recognition, stigmatization, and discrimination all affect our well-being. When people are devalued by the larger society, this assault on worth can batter their health. One manifestation of this trend, as we've already discussed, is the opioid epidemic, which has been driven in part by the declining economic prospects of non–college-educated white Americans, their perceived loss of social status, and the resulting sense of despair that they experience. This stigmatization translates into "wear and tear" on the body (called "allostatic load"), as well as an increase in depression and other mental health problems. For groups that must contend with racism and other forms of discrimination, these effects can be even more pernicious. For some people of color, the experience of constant racism can have a "weathering" effect, leading to higher overall levels of stress and ultimately, in many cases, to severe chronic health problems (stress, high blood pressure). All this has led to a large decline in life expectancy for different stigmatized groups. While the general trend since 1990 was for life expectancy to increase across the board, for all groups, since 2010, it has begun to decline for those without a bachelor's degree. And, as of 2019, Black and American Indian or Alaska Native (AIAN) groups experience the lowest life expectancy of all racial-ethnic groups, at seventy-one and seventy-three years, respectively, in comparison to their white counterparts at seventy-nine years. Notably, over the past two decades, the AIAN group has not experienced an increase in life expectancy. Growing inequality and the bifurcation in outcomes between college educated and the non–college educated feed into this perfect storm.

There are other reasons why stigmatization matters for our well-being: Many factors that drive stigmatization and rob different groups of their dignity are not about material resources—or rather, they shape how material resources are distributed, not the other way around. For instance, homophobia has led to precarious outcomes for many queer youth, as many are rejected by their families at an early age. In this case, stigmatization leads to homelessness. Also, while low-income people often feel isolated and depressed, their plight is not only due to poverty, but also to the feeling of worthlessness that comes with stigmatization. This may lead to the "why try" syndrome, as individuals lose faith in their ability to change their lives. If stigmatization creates inequality and affects us negatively, these are more reasons to closely understand it, and work to reduce it.

Having demonstrated the centrality of recognition to well-being, we can turn to the various pathways through which recognition diffuses.

CHAPTER 5

CHANGING HEARTS AND MINDS

HOW RECOGNITION CHAINS AMPLIFY THE CULTURAL AGENDA

The video "Quest Bridge," by photographer Hank Willis Thomas, whom we met in the previous chapter, features 150 Black men from across the US who all answer a seemingly simple question: "What does it mean to you to be a Black man?" The piece cut through stereotypes about Black male identity by showing the incredible diversity of responses—by showing, in Thomas's words, "[our] different shapes, colors, strengths, and weaknesses—our shared tragedy as fallible human beings." Recognizing the power of Thomas's work, a number of different organizations paid to help distribute "Quest Bridge" throughout the US. The Campaign for Black Male Achievement (CBMA) screened the video in museums and high schools across the country, in thirty-five different states, and distributed teaching materials to facilitate conversations about the complexity and multiplicity of Black masculinity.

One of the video's most important accomplishments, of course, was to extend recognition and dignity to Black men everywhere. CBMA's efforts amplified and extended the effects of that accomplishment many times, thanks in large part to its vast network that brings together 4,800 community leaders and 3,000 other organizations nationwide. CBMA supports many other programs, as well, including My Brother's Keeper Alliance, a widely publicized initiative of the Obama Foundation launched "to address persistent opportunity gaps faced by boys and young men of color and ensure that all young people can reach their full potential."

In the spring of 2020, I met with CBMA's president, a serious, middle-aged African American man named Shawn Dove. When I asked him why his organization supported Thomas's work, Dove said, "There's no cavalry coming to save the day in our communities as Black folks. We are the iconic leaders that we have been waiting for and the curators of the change we are seeking to see." Hope, he said, is fundamental to that work, adding that after four hundred years of racial oppression, "My challenge as a leader is managing the paradox of promise and peril [we] see every day. Focusing on the peril will drain your hope that change is possible."

CBMA's work is largely behind the scenes, yet it makes an enormous difference in terms of building and expanding new narratives. Dove said he is seeking "to provide a platform for leaders to tell the stories of their work, and the stories of the young men that they are engaging with." He also fosters strategic partnerships between the private sector, government, philanthropy, the academic community, and "most of the folks that are at the front lines." But the overall goal is to "create a framework of respect—not identifying people first by their problems and what is wrong with them, with Black people being the face of poverty and the face of crime." Concretely, this means that Dove often finds himself encouraging other nonprofits to see their mission not in terms of a problem that needs to be addressed, but rather as a matter of seeking out opportunities to make a difference. CBMA's work may happen in the background, but over time it slowly adds up and amplifies the new cultural agenda.

CBMA is part of what I call a "recognition chain," which is to say, a network of change agents and organizations that scales up and disseminates messages of recognition. In these chains, change agents join forces with foundations and other organizations to benefit from their infrastructure, and ultimately to see their recognition work reverberate far beyond their own individual or institutional reach.

Other kinds of change agents participate in these networks, too, including art critics, like my Harvard colleague Sarah Lewis, who has written about the power of art to expand who matters to fully include African Americans. In 2016, she edited a special issue of the leading photography journal *Aperture*, whose theme was "Vision and Justice." In this celebrated issue, she showed how "The century-long efforts to craft an image to pay honor to the full humanity of Black life is a corrective task for which photography and cinema have been central, even indispensable." Scholars like her play an important role in bringing attention to the work of Black photographers, and in making clear how that work is situated within a deeper tradition of aesthetics, politics, and recognition.

Another important group that takes part in recognition chains is middle- and upper-middle-class consumers of art. To better understand their motivations and the contributions they make in expanding recognition, Holyoke College professor Patricia Banks interviewed upper-middle-class Black people, asking them about how they decide what art to buy and/or put on their walls. Many said they felt it was important to see visual representations of people who look like them. Some remarked on the ways they were affected by the absence of such representations when they were growing up. Years later, for a different project, Banks interviewed some of the people and organizations who fund museums specifically intended to showcase African American art, asking about their rationale for doing so. Time and again, they emphasized the importance for African Americans of "being seen" and represented in their full humanity—of bridging the recognition gap they experience.

Art galleries also play an important part in recognition chains. The Jack Shainman Gallery in New York City, which represents Hank Willis Thomas and many other artists of color, is one prominent example. The space has been "celebrated for its multicultural roster of emerging and established artists and estates who engage in the social and cultural issues of their time."

But galleries are just one part of the equation. On a larger scale, recognition chains function like networks, connecting creators from marginalized communities to all sorts of helpful parties: the funders whose resources allow their narratives to flourish at a larger scale; the galleries, museums, and other institutions that publicize their works; and the audiences or "participants" who buy, consume, or appreciate them. Together, all these groups help disseminate new narratives about inclusion and gradually narrow recognition gaps, ultimately transforming how we understand the world. These chains or networks became especially important in the aftermath of the 2020 Black Lives Matter protests, as many institutions began investing more deliberately in works and artists focused on social justice and social change. While they operate in mainstream media, they often operate in their own circuits of circulation and diffusion, oriented specifically toward spreading recognition.

What Shawn Dove described above is a relatively recent and daring reorientation of how the nonprofit sector approaches its work. Take, for example, the Ford Foundation, which, with a $16 billion endowment as of 2022, is one of the world's largest private philanthropies. Under the leadership of Darren Walker, the foundation's president, who is Black and gay, the organization has focused on fighting inequality by changing narratives, or, by "changing hearts and minds." In 2013, when Walker first took the reins, this was a pathbreaking move, given that many other philanthropies were prioritizing only material needs and overlooking the place of culture in addressing inequality. Today, other foundations are following in Ford's footsteps, focusing on narrative change, building alliances, and contributing to recognition chains. This has been a sea change in the field of philanthropy, which was previously more focused on economic concerns.

Here is an example of how these organizations shape narratives. In collaboration with the National Domestic Workers Alliance, Ford's program Just Films assisted in the production of Alfonso Cuarón's 2018 film *Roma*, which tells the story of two domestic workers employed by an upper-middle-class family in Mexico City. In popular culture, domestic workers are invisible, often playing background roles. Their needs are typically subordinated to those of their employers. *Roma* helped reframe this group by showing them struggling with universal moral dilemmas (e.g., whether to get an abortion) and by bringing their intimate lives to the center of a film. As such, it also enables a closer identification between the audience and the characters. With the help of the Ford Foundation, the film reached audiences all over the world and won three Academy Awards.

Another important way that foundations, philanthropies, and cultural organizations narrow recognition gaps is by changing their leadership to become more reflective of the communities they serve. For instance, after the Black Lives Matter movement of summer

2020, many organizations put people of color in leadership roles. These included organizations in cultural sectors ranging from publishing to art museums and art leaders, higher education, and beyond. In June 2020, the Poetry Foundation, which with its $300 million endowment is the leading philanthropic organization for poetry, dismissed its former leader Henry Bienen (a past president of Northwestern University, a white man with strong Ivy League ties) and replaced him with Michelle T. Boone, a former commissioner of cultural affairs in the City of Chicago, a grassroots activist, and a woman of color. This leadership change came in response to a letter signed by 1,800 poets arguing that the foundation's leadership had been elitist, racist, and disconnected from the community.

Even if not broadly publicized and still in the process of consolidating, this new cohort of leaders is having a significant impact at the national level, bringing their experience and networks to bear on their organizations' important work of recognition building. At the same time, other leading foundations have recently decided to (or been pressured to) take the even more drastic step of significantly redirecting their funding strategies by supporting more projects that speak to racial and social justice. These include the Mellon, Luce, Spencer, and MacArthur foundations. The Gates Foundation has aimed to "change the conversation" on social mobility by moving the narrative focus from the individual to the structural factors that contribute to poverty. At the same time, progressive foundations such as the William and Flora Hewlett Foundation and the Omidyar Network also have committed themselves to fighting inequality. Moreover, the booming sector of "social justice philanthropy" provides flexible funding to a plethora of progressive social movements. To learn more about this, I spoke to Leah Hunt-Hendrix, an heir to her Texas family's oil fortune, who has cofounded three successful social justice organizations, bringing together a network of mostly millennial progressive donors. The success of movements such as Black Lives Matter is significantly magnified by the support of organizations like these, which play a central role in amplifying recognition.

As the philanthropic sector grows, its critics are multiplying. Some have argued that philanthropic organizations do more harm than good by improving conditions just enough to undermine calls for radical, systemic change, but not enough to make a lasting, meaningful difference in people's lives. For some of these critics, philanthropic organizations ultimately exist to discipline, control, and limit the impact of social movements and progressive advocacy—and they do so by insisting on quantitative evidence of their impact. Others view leading philanthropists as self-serving elitists who exercise disproportionate influence due to their social position, education, or social networks. For instance, the Chan-Zuckerberg Foundation and the Gates Foundation have been accused of attempting to conceal the misdeeds of their funders through philanthropy, just as did the Mellons, Carnegies, Rockefellers, and Fords of yesteryear. While these critiques may have some merit, and it is certainly not true that all philanthropies and nonprofits are guided by pure intentions, their work is nevertheless having an important effect: the narrative turn is happening in this organizational field, complementing in much-needed ways the traditional policy work done by economists.

Still, it remains to be seen whether these changes will result in a lasting transformation in funding priorities and agenda setting. For this to happen, significant changes in board and staff composition will be needed, together with a fundamental transformation in the relations of power between foundations and the recipients of their largesse.

Another crucial sector in which recognition chains operate is that of digital technology platforms. Take, for instance, Jack Conte, one of the founders of the highly successful digital platform Patreon, which connects content creators like podcasters, musicians, and stand-up comics to paying audiences. Patreon is one of the platforms that revolutionized the media industry over the last decade by making available new and different voices to highly differentiated publics. In our interview, Conte described at length the cultural impact of Patreon, which unleashed a flood of bottled-up creative energies across a range of cultural domains. Its mere existence fosters numerous taste communities independent from the control of traditional tastemakers who acted as gatekeepers in leading record companies or movie studios. This represents a significant shift in how creative work is supported and sustained, and has helped create the conditions for a more pluralistic cultural ecosystem. Like YouTube, Patreon has helped many creators of color, queer creators, and others from a variety of different marginalized groups to find and build their audience even when traditional media were unreceptive to their work. This includes celebrities such as Issa Rae, Lilly Singh, Awkwafina, Lil Nas X, and many more.

Another technology platform that has played an even more crucial and more visible prominent role in this field supporting recognition chains has been Netflix. To better understand its strategies and motivations, I talked with Channing Dungey, who at the time was the platform's executive vice president for international programming. Together with *Selma* director Ava DuVernay, these African American Hollywood powerhouse women are responsible for producing a massive amount of diverse content for the global market.

Dungey explained to me that the company directly aims to promote representation and recognition by producing diverse content and supporting creators of color. For example, Netflix produced Ava DuVernay's acclaimed 2016 documentary *The 13th*, which describes contemporary mass incarceration as an extension of slavery and a direct outcome of the Thirteenth Amendment adopted in 1865, which allowed involuntary servitude to continue as a punishment for a crime.

The platform also developed a multi-project deal to pull Shonda Rhimes away from ABC, where she had been in charge of numerous groundbreaking shows that did extraordinary work to expand representation, including *Grey's Anatomy*, *Scandal*, and *How to Get Away with Murder*. Since joining Netflix, Rhimes has produced one of the streaming company's biggest hits, *Bridgerton*, a period drama based on a series of books by Julia Quinn. Rhimes cast the show without regard to race, tapping Black and brown actors to play eighteenth-century English nobility. This celebrated show promotes recognition by making race incidental and challenging the association of whiteness with upper classness. Yet the show has also been criticized for ignoring power imbalances in interracial romantic relationships and overlooking crucial aspects of women's domination.

Women such as Rhimes and DuVernay, and many other power brokers at Netflix and elsewhere, deserve great credit for expanding the number and type of roles available to actors of color—and for, in doing so, contributing to the work of expanding recognition.

Now that we have explored the role that the nonprofit sector and technology platforms play in recognition chains, we must consider another important, yet largely invisible player: the so-called narrative industry. This sector consists of social change organizations such as Purpose, Swayable, and More in Common, which operate mostly in the fields of strategic communication, binding politics, social movements, and advocacy to produce social change, including by scaling up messages of recognition. Drawing on fields such as psychology, marketing, and brain science, and on experiments, surveys, social media analysis, and AI, these organizations work to fine-tune messages from groups advocating change to specific audiences and make them more resonant. This work can have an enormous effect, because without resonance, narratives never have the opportunity to take off in the public sphere and close recognition gaps.

To get a deeper sense of how the narrative industry works, I met with leaders of some of these narrative industry organizations. One of them, Nick Allardice, is a top executive at Change.org, an organization that promotes the use of community petitions worldwide as a tool for social change. Nick describes his work as "empowering people everywhere" to help create a world where "no one is powerless." He aims to provide "a technology solution: free, easy-to-use tools that allow people to collectively organize." As of 2019, the organization had 171 staff members, about 329 million users globally, and approximately 41,000 new campaigns each week.

Allardice is a believer in the power of personal narratives to reframe issues and motivate action. One of his favorite examples is medical marijuana, which was legalized in Australia thanks to the efforts of a former nurse named Lucy Haslam and her husband. As Allardice explained, "Her son had terminal cancer and cannabis oil happened to be one of the few things that alleviated his symptoms." His dad, a former cop, "basically became [a] drug dealer" to help his son. Their petition campaign on Change.org generated attention for their personal story as it attracted supporters and eventually went viral. Ultimately, their story helped shift people's perspectives and make legalization a reality.

Today, when a petition is launched on the platform, staff

automatically run experiments to determine which message would be the most convincing—what is "the unique set of variables that are right for it." In addition to serving as a platform for petitions, Change.org also allows users to make monetary contributions toward causes that are important to them, and in turn, to ask others for contributions. By and large, users tend to give small amounts—the average contribution is only $10—but collectively, these donations can make a big difference, and Allardice hopes in the future to direct even more funds into social impact initiatives. People might use the platform, for example, to lobby the local government for more green space, to raise funds for installing solar panels on the roof of a school, or to change an unsafe intersection. One of the first crowdfunding platforms, it is used for causes that range from the hyperlocal to the national or international, and anyone can launch a petition.

Allardice's previous work to destigmatize poverty has played a large part in shaping his vision for Change.org. He started in Australia, where, as a student, he volunteered to live on two Australian dollars a day in order to raise funds to fight poverty. While collecting pledges, he aimed to raise awareness about the daily realities of living in poverty. This commitment, as well as a concern with climate change, was shared by a group of millennial men who were involved in the Australian student movements with Allardice. Now jokingly calling themselves the "Australian Mafia," they were among the first in their country to engage in digital campaigning and organizing, and are now living in the US, where they have massively contributed to expanding this field. This and similar networks that work toward recognition of marginalized groups draw on skills that differ from those found in traditional cultural fields.

Another member of this Australian mafia is Jeremy Heimans, the cofounder and CEO of Purpose, a for-profit public-benefit corporation that leverages social media to support social movements. With the slogan "Purpose Moves People to Remake the World," this organization collaborates with all kinds of progressive organizations, helping them tailor their messaging for targeted audiences, including those concerned with shifting identities, racial justice, and LGBTQ+ rights. For instance, with their research, the team was able to determine that campaigns for "quality of air" were more effective in India than messaging about "climate change."

But Purpose is just one player in a much larger field of similar organizations building momentum for progressive causes. While algorithm-assisted research can leave some with an impression of manipulation and propaganda, these organizations are quite effective at setting the cultural agenda and slowly reframing how groups are perceived, one problem at the time, using technology to disseminate new narratives of recognition. They are creating an underground revolution by expanding the role that narratives play through the systematic and technologically assisted production of social change.

Recognition chains work through the media, which shapes how certain narratives gain traction and influence our views. There are a variety of approaches to studying and understanding the media. Some focus on the content that passes through the media—for instance, whether messages about a group present them as likable or undeserving. Others focus on how messages are received, such as, for instance, the way that audiences decide which television characters they find most relatable. Yet others focus on the effect of the media on behavior.

In all cases, networks serve an important function, shaping how people represent themselves and exchange ideas. In his classic study

Imagined Communities, the historian Benedict Anderson described how representations of different groups (whether religious, regional, occupational, or otherwise) in books and periodicals helped give shape to national collective identities in Europe. In Anderson's account, literacy was essential to the distribution of shared identities, since it was mostly through print media that shared group identities were able to coalesce. Sociologist Heather Haveman also wrote about the importance of magazines and newspapers in bringing nineteenth-century Americans together around their specific leisure activities, occupations, ethnic groups, religious affiliations, or geographic locations.

The same logic applies to many other types of identities. For group identities to spread and social movements to be popularized, resources are needed. This has been true across history, from the Protestant Reformation to the Enlightenment to the spread of socialism.

But while the media have exercised enormous influence over group dynamics and recognition, new digital media are coming to play perhaps an even bigger role, as newspapers and other print publications face increasingly dire economic challenges and new distribution platforms such as Netflix and Patreon expand. Understanding these structural changes and their impact on how ideas travel and are adopted is essential to making sense of recognition chains.

Whereas in the past, traditionally dominant groups exercised enormous influence over the media, today's new media are more inclusive. This is happening at the same time that traditional gatekeepers in cultural industries such as film, music, and radio have lost their monopoly on decision-making and are now serving more differentiated publics. As such, the growth and diversification of the media are helping strengthen recognition chains, as we have seen with Ava DuVernay and Shonda Rhimes. The online space in particular is democratized to such an extent that it stands to overwhelm us with its noisy and chaotic swirl of views, a space for broadening horizons but also for echo chambers and filter bubbles.

But as new digital platforms gain power and popularity, ordinary people are increasingly turning to these new sources of information, and particularly to social media and podcasts, which play an important role in recognition chains. Thus far, however, the most active users of these platforms remain concentrated among a relatively small group. In 2018, for instance, 22 percent of the American population used Twitter, which seems significant, but in fact, 80 percent of all US activity on the platform was attributable to a narrow subset, the most active 10 percent of users. And of course, as many different commentators and analysts have noted, where people get their information varies considerably across age groups and level of education. Younger generations get more of their information on social media; 48 percent of Americans under thirty consume their political news primarily through social media, and an additional 21 percent consume their news through other forms of online media, such as online publications (like *Politico* or *Slate*). The more highly educated are 13 percentage points more likely to use social media in general than those who did not pursue postsecondary education. They are especially attracted to platforms that facilitate discussion like Twitter and Reddit, as well as professional platforms like LinkedIn.

Thus it is not surprising that at least for now, television remains the primary medium for the vast majority in the US. According to *The Atlantic*, Americans in 2018 were still watching nearly eight hours of television per household per day. Nightly local TV news remains an important source of information for the bulk of the population.

At the same time, other forms of media are in trouble. Print journalism, for instance, has been in an accelerating crisis for several decades, and its downfall has dramatically affected our ability to understand and learn more about the world around us. Of course, many newspapers have shut down in the internet era as advertising revenue collapsed, but even the strongest of those that have survived lack anything close to the power and reach of the new online media platforms. The *New York Times*, for example, one of the most powerful remaining print outlets, had 7.6 million subscribers globally at the end of 2021 (including both print and online), with revenue of more than $2 billion for the full year of 2021. Compare that to Facebook's annual revenue of $39.3 billion and its 2.9 billion monthly active users globally; and to Twitter's $5.07 billion and 217 million monthly active users. All this means that newspapers are less able to do their important work of relaying information about current events. In 2020, only 3 percent of Americans cited print newspapers as their favorite source of information, and only 10 percent of those surveyed said that they access print publications online often. In February 2022, only 11 percent of American millennials said that newspapers are their most frequent news source, while 44 percent reported that daily news consumption came through social media. As revenues and readership have fallen, newspapers have had to make painful cuts, sacrificing costly investigative reporting and other important projects. The crisis has reached the point that nonprofits like ProPublica and the Center for Investigative Reporting have had to step in to fill the gap. The crisis is even more acute in local newspaper coverage—the medium that is the closest to representing local communities and their interests. Coverage of state legislatures has declined by 35 percent since 2003.

To appeal to more people, there has been a rush toward Fox

News–style "infotainment," which harkens back to the yellow journalism of Hearst, Pulitzer, and others in the late nineteenth century. This has had enormous consequences for how people experience political life and has helped drive intolerance and ideological polarization. While opinions about the specific policies that distinguish Democrats from Republicans have changed little, members of both parties are more and more inclined to say that they strongly dislike the other group. Consequently, politics has increasingly become an arena dominated by identities and emotions, in which reasoned differences of opinion about policies matter less and less.

Beyond the media, other institutions help shape public life and our views of the world around us, many of which have seen their influence decline in recent years. Unions and the labor movement, for example, once played an important part in cultivating solidarity among workers, but over the last half-century their power has greatly diminished. As we discussed in an earlier chapter, the United States has seen its share of unionized workers decline from a high of nearly 35 percent in the mid-1950s to less than 12 percent today. But labor has recently been reenergized by the "Fight for $15" movement, unionization drives at major companies like Starbucks and Amazon, and a massive mobilization around the working conditions for domestic and restaurant workers during the pandemic. When I talked with leaders of these two movements, Ai-jen Poo of the National Domestic Workers Alliance and Saru Jayaraman of the One Fair Wage Campaign for restaurant workers, they emphasized the potential of this renewal. Steven Greenhouse, who covered labor for the *New York Times* for thirty years, also remarked on this revitalization of the labor movement in our interview. All three noted that messages about the importance of solidarity and workers' rights had gained resonance within the broader culture, at the same time that the ideal of the American dream had become less influential than ever. Jayaraman in particular attributed the popularity of the campaign to increase the minimum wage for restaurant workers to the fact that "not just a sliver but the majority of people [are] unable to buy a house or pay their college loan . . . are unable to take care of themselves, still living at home with their parents." In her view, "among millennials, I don't think anybody even uses this American dream anymore. It's so clichéd and has so little resonance."

Religion is another institution that has been losing steam in recent years, with the number of Americans who consider religion to be central in their lives rapidly declining. But there is a notable difference in the sharpness of decline between political parties. The Public Religion Research Institute found that the share of religiously affiliated Democrats declined by more than 20 percent between 2016 and 2006, from 96 percent to 73 percent. The decline was much less significant among Republicans, dropping from 96 percent to 88 percent over the same period.

Despite these changes, religious institutions continue to shape narratives about recognition, dignity, and how we determine worth as a society. To learn more about this, my research team talked with Reverend Alvin Herring, the executive director of Faith in Action, an international network that aims to create "a society free of economic oppression, racism, and discrimination, in which every person lives in a safe and healthy environment." His religious leadership is focused on addressing inequality and reducing the stigmas that deprive people of the care and safety they deserve. Religious leaders from other faith traditions share this sense of altruism and concern for universal dignity, such as Imam Omar Suleiman of Faith Forward Dallas at Thanks-Giving Square. He explained that the more deeply he becomes committed to his faith as an Orthodox Muslim, the more committed he becomes to humanity. For him, lifting up our shared humanity is essential to reducing stigmatization.

Education is another public institution that has increasingly come to shape our perceptions about society. Curricula in K–12 schools in the US, for example, have become a major political battleground, particularly when it comes to the subject of history, which is often pitted against creationism or nationalist narratives about our past (as we saw with the 1619 Project); many conservative politicians (e.g., Florida governor Ron DeSantis) are passing legislation prohibiting teachers from talking about the history of discrimination in America, the object of critical race theory. But teaching this history is a vital task, even if it clashes with some of the country's most important ideals, such as the myth of American exceptionalism or America's Manifest Destiny.

For its part, higher education has also gained in cultural importance after several decades of growing enrollment. Fifty percent of US eighteen-year-olds today are heading to college, where they learn about the ideals of the enlightenment, moral tolerance, and democratic inclusion. However, as of 2021, 24 percent of freshmen drop out of college. In general, 40 percent of undergraduates drop out. At the same time, higher education is making valuable contributions to the fight against discrimination by bringing people of different backgrounds together and exposing students to unfamiliar views.

Higher education also provides the space and freedom scholars needed to write on important topics that contribute to closing recognition gaps. My Harvard colleague Henry Louis Gates plays a leading role in redefining the American cultural canon around race, as did English professor Catharine Stimpson, who contributed to defining the canon of gender studies through her editorship of the pioneer women studies journal *Signs*, and as an editor of a widely used textbook that helped institutionalize the field. For her part, Kimberlé Crenshaw, a Columbia University law professor who brought intersectionality into contemporary thinking, equipped us to think about gender and racial identity together (to become aware of the relative invisibility of the murder of young Black women by the police, for instance).

Many other types of organizations and advocacy are central to the public sphere, where our collective narratives take shape. We are in an era of heightened activism, with many social movements concerned with climate change, immigration, women's rights, LGBTQ+ rights, feminism, and antiracism, to mention only a few. For example, the organization Marshall Plan for Moms aims to pay women for the care work they provide and proposed a plan for "the world we want our children to inherit" (albeit with mitigated success). They contribute to shifting the focus toward collective action, at a time when mothers are facing significant challenges following the pandemic.

Change agents and recognition chains operate on the right as much as they do on the left. Throughout history, some change agents have aligned themselves with immoral causes. There is nothing inherently moral or progressive in their role.

On the right and the far right, many promote recognition for a white "manosphere" whose members often feel displaced by demographic and economic changes. This includes Joe Rogan, an antivax comedian and Spotify podcaster who criticizes cancel culture and defends gun rights. Internet influencers such as far-right and white nationalist Nick Fuentes also have a considerable impact (he hosts the show *America First*, which was suspended from YouTube for violating its hate speech policy). Others, such as Tucker Carlson (star anchor at Fox News), are less niche and have been able to build a major following and play a central role in amplifying narratives from the right and far right. These change agents magnify political backlash through their own recognition chains. They use narratives for feeding different kinds of hope. Progress is far from linear, and we see plenty of backlash amid competing versions of what progress means. While I do not make these tensions visible, conservative change agents also feed the public sphere with notions that slowly but surely spread and change views.

Such leaders animate various alt-right organizations such as Young Americans for Freedom, a conservative and libertarian youth organization active on campuses; and the Groyper Movement, a splinter group from the America First Political Action Conference, which assembles white nationalist and far-right activists. These movements tend to promote nihilism and a lack of trust in governments, and are associated with violence, mixed martial arts, and military and gaming culture. These are beyond the scope of my study, even if some supply recognition narratives to downwardly mobile working-class men and others.

It is difficult to predict the fate of the different institutions that shape recognition chains, and which of them will gain the most resonance. But as their narratives multiply and reinforce one another, slowly but surely they will allow people to imagine different realities for themselves and others. Indeed, such chains connect producers of new narratives with philanthropists and foundations, experts in strategic communication, new platforms, and other cultural institutions to magnify their combined impact. As we will see, they also involve a public or movement participants. Thus, recognition is far more than the work of a self-serving progressive elite: it requires collaboration between many people who work toward some form of social change. Together, they can have real impact on how marginalized groups are perceived, and perceive themselves, and open the way to new paths of action. To more fully understand how this happens, we need to take an even closer look at the strategies change agents say they mobilize for recognition work.

CHAPTER 6

STRATEGIES FOR TRANSFORMATION

THE WORK OF CHANGE AGENTS IN HOLLYWOOD AND BEYOND

Native American poet Natalie Diaz won a Pulitzer Prize in 2021 for her collection *Postcolonial Love Poem*, in which she wrote, "I am doing my best to not become a museum / of myself. I am doing my best to breathe in and out. / I am begging: *Let me be lonely but not invisible.*" When I met with Diaz to discuss her work, she described the book as a "hymn against erasure." Similarly but differently, Desmond Meade, of the Florida Rights Restoration Coalition, ran a campaign to allow convicted felons to win back their voting rights by amending the state's constitution. In his words, these former felons "ran their campaign on love," by mobilizing their family and friends to knock on doors and put rights restoration on the ballot. For her part, Cristina Jiménez, who co-founded United We Dream, the largest immigrant youth–led organization in the United States, celebrates the role of narratives in humanizing undocumented immigrants—as she said, "it is not about immigrants being criminals, but about families and children, and family separation and detention." In each of these cases, we can see individuals waging a fight for recognition on behalf of the groups they are part of—to be seen, heard, and valued—but we can also see that each has adopted their own unique strategies for achieving that recognition.

As we continue our exploration of how we decide who matters, it is worth reflecting on the remarkable diversity of different strategies for shifting the narrative—and different kinds of change agents who are engaged in that work. The change agents whom my research team and I spoke with come from all walks of life and represent a vast number of different professions and skill sets.

Let's start with comedians and creatives working in Hollywood, many of whom use their characters, jokes, or narratives to challenge stereotypes about stigmatized groups. To gain a broader understanding of what happens in this field, my research team and I talked with seventy-five comedians and Hollywood creatives whose work has achieved a certain level of prominence and cultural significance—focusing specifically on those who have garnered awards or demonstrated an unusual ability to reach younger generations. The Hollywood creatives include actors, but we focused also on those who work behind the scenes, including showrunners, producers, directors, and screenwriters—and in fact most of them have worked in more than one of these roles over the course of their careers. They include such prominent figures as Joe Robert Cole (*Black Panther*), Lee Daniels (*The Butler*, *Empire*), Bill Hader (*Barry*), Dan Fogelman (*This Is Us*), Julie Plec (*The Vampire Diaries*), Michelle and Robert King (*The Good Wife*), Michael Schur (*Parks and Recreation*, *The Good Place*, *The Office*), and John Wells (*Shameless*, *The West Wing*). We also spoke with major comedians including Cristela Alonzo, Neal Brennan, Jim Norton, Iliza Shlesinger, and Reggie Watts.

Take, for instance, W. Kamau Bell, a popular stand-up comic and host of CNN's *The United Shades of America*. When I spoke to him, Bell, a middle-aged and middle-class Black father who is married to a white woman, told me that in his work, he seeks to bridge racial divides by confronting social problems with humor and honesty. One of his objectives, he said, is to help white viewers reframe how they perceive African Americans. But this is just one part of the task. "I believe my job is to talk about what's going on in the world but use comedy to help it go down a little bit better," he explained. "I see myself as someone who generally is a great connector of people . . . [who] helps sort of bring about positive change on some level. [It] does not need to be big. It can be really small."

To this end, he plays up his identity as a middle-class family man as a way of preemptively reassuring white audiences, who might otherwise make assumptions about him based on his race. At the same time, he is not shy about denouncing racism. In the first episode of his CNN show in 2016, he traveled to the South, where he met with leaders of the KKK and got them to talk openly about their white supremacist views. Several years earlier, in 2013, Bell had been preparing for his late-night show, FX's *Totally Biased*, when he heard the news that the vigilante George Zimmerman had been acquitted of murder charges for his slaying of seventeen-year-old Trayvon Martin the previous year. Bell then worked the news into his show to voice his anger and pain at the decision. "I knew I had to say something, and I didn't have a joke about it," he explained. "But I knew, I was like, 'If I don't . . . I'm not the person I claim to be.'"

Bell's work to address discrimination shares some important qualities with that of Joey Soloway, the creator of the show *Transparent*. The show centers on an older white transgender woman named Maura and her adult children who are working through accepting her late-in-life transition. Soloway explained that they created the show in part to address their own internalized shame about their own gender nonconformity. Soloway was also committed to centering the lives of the marginalized—it was particularly important to them, for instance, that the show include a trans protagonist, rather than just a minor character. By prominently representing this group, Soloway hopes to make clear to everyone, especially cisgender audiences, that trans people are ordinary and relatable. "We need to make a world where people focus on love for the other rather than ridiculing the other," they explained. "It [can be] done by creating TV shows."

Compared to the narrow conception of normalcy that dominated American TV shows as recently as a decade or two ago, recent shows such as *Transparent* and *Pose* offer fuller, more nuanced depictions of the lived reality of LGBTQ+ people, making visible what was once unknown and out of sight for straight and cis audiences. This is true of many other traditionally marginalized groups, as well. In fact, TV depictions of these groups, and whether they are extended recognition and dignity, are determined in part by creatives in the entertainment industry. At their best, they actively challenge stereotypes by representing members of these groups as the complex, multidimensional figures that all humans are. Over time, these more nuanced depictions can gradually shift our perceptions and destigmatize the traditionally stigmatized.

In our conversations with the many different comedians and Hollywood creatives we interviewed, we gained valuable insight into the distinct strategies they use for fighting stigmatization and extending recognition to all groups. One of these is a strategy we call "reflecting reality," which means, essentially, telling stories that avoid reinforcing stereotypes and stay true to the realities of life for nondominant groups. This is, for instance, what both W. Kamau Bell and Joey Soloway described. The goal is to change society's understanding of marginalized groups by expanding ideas of who they are and what their lives look like—by describing the world as it really is.

Another popular strategy is "emotional modulation"— appealing to audiences' emotions to change their perceptions of a certain group. The hope is that these emotional connections can generate empathy, which in turn can foster a deeper understanding of unfamiliar perspectives and experiences. Consider, for example, Tanya Saracho, the executive producer and showrunner of the TV series *Vida*, which tells the story of two Mexican American sisters who become reconnected after their mother dies and learn that she had been married to a woman. After this revelation, the sisters get to know their mother's wife, and one sister grapples with her own queerness. The characters experience both the joys of queer life and the brutal homophobia that is still prevalent in so many corners of our society. For queer audiences who recognize aspects of these highs and lows from their own lives, such stories can produce a powerful sense of emotional resonance and validation. But the emotional appeals are also universal enough to give cisgender and heterosexual people a limited—but still very powerful—sense of the experiences that queer people face in real life.

One of the less popular strategies we identified is "the Trojan horse," or the subtle inclusion of social messages in seemingly neutral entertainment. One example is *Shameless*, a Showtime series that tells the story of a family living in poverty on Chicago's South Side. The father of the family deals with addiction and a variety of chronic health issues, and through his story, we are exposed to the stark realities of the American health care system. The show explores the many ways poverty affects the Gallagher family, but stories of their heartbreaking struggles are punctuated and interrupted by absurd and humorous moments. When my team spoke to the show's executive producer and showrunner, John Wells (whose previous shows include *ER* and *The West Wing*), he underscored how this mix of emotion and humor is useful for connecting with audiences on complex, serious issues.

Another strategy that Hollywood creatives use involves rethinking not just their artistic choices but the organizational hierarchy of their field, and the way that opportunities within it are extended to different groups. This is what we called "see it to be it"—by which we mean efforts to proactively open career pathways in creative industries for members of marginalized groups. This not only allows members of marginalized groups to demonstrate their own excellence but also shows them what's possible when people who look like them are in those roles. And it gives the broader industry—and the viewing public—the chance to learn from their life experiences and perspectives. One example is Cristela Alonzo, the star and creator of a semiautobiographical show called *Cristela*. The show follows her character as she works to achieve the American dream, balances family obligations, and navigates microaggressions in her workplace. While Alonzo discusses being "the first Latina with a sitcom" or "the only woman doing stand-up" at a particular club, she is committed to changing things for new writers and comics. When she entered the field, "the mentorship that I had was from anybody that I could get." While she was ultimately able to find good mentors, the scarcity of Latinx women in the field meant it was difficult for her to get advice on the challenges she faced. "I think my main objective right now it to actually make sure that people have more power to be able to create their own projects," she said. "I'm really into mentorship . . . my friend Dolores [Huerta] tells me . . . 'I love teaching people [that] they're powerful. I love seeing them run with that power and teaching others that they have power.' . . . That's the same feeling I get."

By and large, many of the change agents whom my team and I interviewed—Hollywood creatives and the comedians alike—used these strategies of "reflecting reality," "emotional modulation," "the Trojan horse," and "see it to be it." But if we compare the Hollywood creatives and the comedians, it's clear that their working conditions influence how they approach promoting recognition. By virtue of their medium, creatives in film and television have access to a wider range of strategies for building recognition than comedians do: they can, for instance, craft immersive narratives about nondominant groups, challenge stereotypes through empathetic characters, and increase the visibility of previously "unseen" stories. But despite these opportunities, Hollywood creatives must contend with the risk-averse companies that employ them, and therefore have less autonomy in some ways than comedians, who in many cases work independently, answering only to themselves. So even though Hollywood creatives have more artistic possibilities available to them, they are often less free to pursue those possibilities. And they are also fearful that a reactionary backlash may restrict their future freedom. They therefore develop strategies to make sure that change lasts beyond the current moment.

The situation for comedians is different. Because of their independence and the more limited range of strategies available to them, comedians who work to expand recognition largely do so through self-presentation. Those who come from underrepresented groups, in particular, do so by making themselves visible, by claiming a rightful spot for themselves in a field that has traditionally been homogeneous. Of course, plenty of comedians come from overrepresented groups in the industry—that is, white men. These comedians often work to expand recognition, too, and use a variety of the different strategies we covered above. Some, however, are skeptical of that goal, arguing that creating social change is outside the boundaries of comedy. For instance, comedians my team spoke to denounced what they called "clapter," or placing more emphasis on popular social messages than on humor. One comedian who shared this skepticism was Jim Norton. "My job is not to educate people," he explained. "My job is not to change the way they feel. . . . My job is not to use a platform to change. I mean I'm not arrogant enough to think that's what it is. If someone changes their opinion because of something I said, fine. But I don't expect them to. I don't deserve credit if they do. And I don't deserve blame if they change their opinion to something shitty."

Celebrities are another important group of change agents. Consider, for instance, the singer Lizzo, who, in her music and in the way she crafts her public image, works to expand recognition for people of all body types, particularly those of heavy Black women. In an interview with BET, Lizzo explained that as a "big Black woman," her goal is to help little girls who look like her to see themselves and "see what is possible . . . the crowds should feel the love, feel the self-love, feel the positive vibes."

Celebrities use their role as change agents to expand recognition for many different groups, of course. Consider, for instance, the TV moguls Martha Stewart and Oprah Winfrey. Martha Stewart, with her magazine *Martha Stewart Living* and its companion TV show (both established in the early 1990s), modernized the role of the homemaker after feminist gains in the 1970s and '80s and new economic pressures had made it something of an anachronism. Through her TV show in particular, which debuted in 1993, she taught the

American public—often working-class women—how to perform "middle classness" through homemaking skills, ranging from "cooking and gardening to ironing, pet-keeping, flower arranging, collecting, and decorating for Christmas." In teaching these women to perform domesticity "with distinction," Stewart was, in a way, aiming to expand recognition for these working-class, stay-at-home women, elevating their status, even if also reinforcing traditional, regressive gender roles. This was achieved as she "cultivated an entrepreneurial identity via storytelling that resonated profoundly with millions of consumers in the 1990s." Oprah Winfrey, too, has worked to expand recognition of marginalized groups, including African American women and victims of domestic violence, in part by offering herself as an ambitious model of material success for others to emulate. Although change agents, both women have also contributed to some less positive trends, overidealizing entrepreneurship and disseminating neoliberal "scripts of self" focused on material success, self-reliance, and individual achievement. So do other influential cultural producers—influential self-help gurus such as Tony Robbins and televangelist Creflo Dollar, who preaches prosperity theology or "gospel capitalism." Their reckoning of economic inequality is ambiguous at best, as is the case for many of the change agents discussed in this book. Resisting this ambiguity can be seen as a tall order in hypermaterialist America, where no other marker of success makes unanimity as decisively as material success.

Many change agents are, of course, focused more explicitly on social justice and policy than celebrities tend to be. As participants in the rough-and-tumble world of civic organizing, these activists create and share new narratives through social media, traditional news media, entertainment, advertising, and education. And as pragmatists, they judge the effectiveness of their strategies based on only one measure: results.

Rashad Robinson is one such activist; he works to recognize and advocate for the Black community. An energetic Black man in his forties, Robinson exudes an unshakable faith in our ability to transform the world—a faith that guides his work as president of the progressive nonprofit organization Color of Change. With roughly 1.7 million members, the organization's work centers on, as Robinson puts it, mobilizing "Black folks and their allies to push decision-makers to create a more human and less hostile world." This is accomplished by "moving systems so that they work better for us," by talking with the media, building coalitions, and creating an organization that is "truly Black-led and has high standards." Robinson himself is focused on building a strong "infrastructure" for the movement, scaling it up, and using it to fight for social change. That often means meeting directly with politicians to inform them about the challenges that African Americans face and to make clear to them that Black communities are an important political constituency. The key, Robinson said, is to make them "nervous about disappointing you."

Robinson's work also includes expanding voter access and participation among people of color. He zeroes in on crucial districts with prominent Black constituencies and mobilizes local partners to raise awareness and get out the vote. He wants people of color, and Black people in particular, to have more weight and "matter more" to our society in the twenty-first century. This includes supporting progressive candidates running for district attorney and similar offices and engaging young Black voters. For him, this is how hope is kept alive, one step at a time. Although his immediate focus is on voting, his ultimate goals are much broader—working toward empowerment, visibility, and recognition in the political and public sphere.

Another such activist is Ami McReynolds, a member of the leadership team at Feeding America, the largest organization fighting hunger in the US. While this nonprofit has historically framed its action as "charitable giving," McReynolds described why it is now shifting the language of its mission to focus on "equity and social justice." The "charity frame," she explained, is an inherent paternalistic view, since it assumes that low-income people are needy and lacking in brains, morals, or willpower. She and her coworkers, however, are not afraid to talk about racism and the structural forces that help perpetuate poverty and racial inequality. Their work feeds a broader discussion about fighting for social justice and shifts the narrative toward what humans collectively owe one another—rather than what pulls them apart.

Examples of inspiring activists fighting to expand recognition abound. Another is Jee Kim, a New Yorker who led a Ford Foundation–funded organization called Narrative Initiative for several years, which he explained is focused on "creating opportunities for hope." For years, Kim taught young activists how to create alternative narratives to the American dream, with a focus on what Americans can accomplish together by promoting solidarity. For instance, the Narrative Initiative organized a major endeavor to foster social solidarity in Minnesota by supporting unions and advocating on public billboards for more solidarity through welfare spending.

Still another is Phillip Atiba Goff, a Yale social psychologist who researches and advocates for policing equity. Goff is adamant in his rejection of "false narratives"—including one that he sees as among the most pernicious, a narrative that he calls "let's return the US to what it was." In recognition of Goff's important work, Warner Bros. TV Group hired him to help develop content to "promote equity, inclusion, and social justice," praising him as a "leading voice of moral clarity." In this new role, Goff uses the network to deliver messages of recognition at a broader scale.

Political activists, politicians, and the political media are also crucial agents of change. Increasingly, many are appealing to young people who are critical of the excesses of capitalism and support a rising movement for democratic socialism. This movement is significant given that the United States has historically been inhospitable to socialism, especially when compared to other advanced industrial societies.

In recent years, support for socialist values rapidly gained in popularity. In 2018 Alexandria Ocasio-Cortez (AOC) won the Democratic primary for a seat in the US House of Representatives, defeating Joseph Crowley, an influential member of the party establishment in Queens, New York. Since taking office in 2019, she has brought a youthful, social media–savvy energy to DC. Soon, with several other progressive women of color who were elected that same year, she formed a group of lawmakers known as "the squad." Defying decades of socialist bashing in American politics, she proudly touted her membership in the Democratic Socialists of America (DSA). US senator Bernie Sanders of Vermont has also identified as a democratic socialist (though he is not affiliated with DSA) and has built an enormous following, especially among younger voters by criticizing the failures of capitalism. Riding this wave of popularity, he came close to winning the Democratic party's presidential nomination in 2016, and again was a serious contender in 2020.

Although the DSA was founded decades ago, in the 1980s, the recent popularity of these politicians has provided the party with a significant boost in membership, which rose to nearly one hundred thousand members by July 2021. With members who average thirty-three years of age, this movement's radical message and critique of capitalism is central to how a portion of American youth view a desirable future. According to a Gallup poll, 50 percent of millennials and Gen Z were supportive of socialism in 2019. At the same time, capitalism has been rapidly losing popularity with young people—only 51 percent had a positive view of it in 2019, down from 66 percent in 2010.

The 2008 financial crisis, the Occupy movement, and the runaway costs of housing and higher education have also contributed to this shift. While socialists have historically been most known for their work fighting against economic inequality, the DSA has become more deeply attuned to a broad range of social justice issues which include abortion, immigration, voting rights, racial justice, and housing discrimination. Leftist publications like *Jacobin*, *The Intercept*, and *The Baffler* are rising in popularity in part because they adopt a lively and provocative tone that contrasts with the style of the more serious and older publications like *The New Left Review*, *Dissent*, and *The Nation*. However, the line between "old guard" and "new guard" is becoming blurred.

Bhaskar Sunkara is an illustrious representative of this new generation, who is now the president of *The Nation*. He started the socialist magazine *Jacobin* in 2010 in his dorm room when he was still a student at George Washington University in Washington, DC. He was motivated by his dissatisfaction with other progressive media outlets. When my team spoke with him, Sunkara pointed out how online magazines could work around the constraints of the traditional mainstream media—like printing costs and distribution—to target niche audiences.

These media express young people's disconnect from the American dream. This is the case of Patreon-based socialist podcasts, such as *Chapo Trap House* and *Red Scare*. They are somewhat irreverent and use vivid polemical and often vulgar language, which add to their popularity with millennials. *Chapo* was able to reach half a million people a month at the time of our interview in 2020. My research team talked with one of its hosts shortly after Bernie Sanders lost the Democratic primary during his presidential run in 2020. The show's listeners had put in over a thousand hours texting and phone banking for Sanders. The audience, he said, is composed of the "temporarily embarrassed overeducated professional middle class, and [those] who just can't find decent entertainment or political opinions anywhere else." The show, he continued, "is a safe harbor for people who have views outside the mainstream, CNN, MSNBC, viewpoints I get every day."

Cornel West, the influential political philosopher and theologian, has been a leading figure of the DSA and the American left who has consistently advocated for the African American community and other groups. In the many speeches West gave during the pandemic and the Trump presidency, he argued that hope is essential to action, an act of imagination and moral courage needed to maintain the momentum to fight back. In past decades, his moral convictions led him to produce two hip-hop albums in 2001 and 2007 with a variety of musical collaborators focused on messages about "change, awareness, and solidarity." Wanting to scale up his message of moral urgency beyond academia via hip-hop earned him a rebuke from then Harvard president Lawrence Summers, who did not understand how a hip-hop album fit with West's intellectual agenda of influencing the public sphere.

Beth Huang is one of the local leaders of the DSA in Boston. She is deeply influenced by the work of my colleague Marshall Ganz, who has been promoting the use of narratives for social change for decades. Beth's attraction to democratic socialism goes back to her days as a student during the 2008 financial crisis, when the money she and her parents had saved for her to attend college shrank significantly as the stock market plunged, forcing her to reconsider her plans and priorities. Ultimately, this experience drew her toward a career focused on addressing social instability through advocacy and civic participation. Like many young people, Huang believes that today's resurgent progressive energy is most useful at the local level: "My state representative is a DSA member and is leading the charge on rent control in the Massachusetts State House. . . . I think that we have a tremendous opportunity to grow in the next five years, twenty years. The pandemic really has shown how unsustainable the political and economic systems are. . . . By mobilizing narratives, we have used the election as a vehicle, winning the actual election, but also [for] changing people's expectations about how the government's institution should work for working people."

These leftist change agents stand in contrast to others who seek to reform capitalism in a less confrontational way. Through their advocacy, these agents hope to make capitalism more inclusive, equitable, and attentive to the needs of all groups. For instance, the nonprofit lobbyist association Business Roundtable issued a widely publicized declaration in 2020 that it would focus less exclusively on delivering returns for business shareholders and more on providing value to all stakeholders in the community—including workers, consumers, and others. Additionally, organizations such as the B-Lab and GIIN aim to certify corporations that are committed to attenuating the negative impacts of capitalism on equity, sustainability, and governance. Their work is reinforced by investors such as

Geeta Ayier of the Boston Common Asset Management Company and many others who use their funds to encourage companies to embrace similar principles.

Business Roundtable's network includes powerful economists who advocate for such an approach. One is Heather Boushey, the director of the progressive think tank Washington Center for Equitable Growth, who has also served on President Joe Biden's Council of Economic Advisers. Although in the past, most progressive economists have been men, including such luminaries as Amartya Sen, Paul Krugman, Joseph Stiglitz, and Dani Rodrik, the presence of women economists in these circles is noteworthy. Recently, several progressive foundations, including the Omidyar Network and the Hewlett Foundation, have provided major funding to expand the work on renewing capitalism to make it less about profit-making and more about inclusion and ethics.

All these capitalism-oriented change agents are, of course, focused more on the politics of distribution than the politics of recognition. In other words, their primary goal is not to expand recognition but rather to fight inequality within the framework of capitalism. They consist of businesspeople and entrepreneurs who advocate for social change both materially and by pushing for institutional change with new narratives. Some are working on President Biden's plans to grow the social infrastructure, for instance, and many are focusing on vigorous state intervention into the economy. Unlike their socialist counterparts, they unabashedly embrace capitalism, but with a more inclusive twist.

Hopefully, by now, the enormous diversity of change agents is becoming clear. From Hollywood creatives and stand-up comics to celebrities, political activists, democratic socialists, and progressive economists and entrepreneurs, what unites change agents is their commitment to closing the recognition gap. Across professions and areas of influence these individuals use a range of strategies to convince others that a different world is possible. While their work may be invisible to the average person, together, slowly but surely, they are forming new narratives that focus on recognizing and extending dignity to all groups. And these narratives play a direct role in determining whom we value as a society.

CHAPTER 7

THE NEXT GENERATION

HOW GEN Z FIGHTS FOR THE FUTURE

Carlos, a self-described "small-town guy going places," is the son of immigrants from Ecuador. His parents raised him while working in restaurants on the East Coast and in Chicago. Like many children of immigrants, Carlos embraces the traditional version of the American dream, focusing on achieving some measure of professional success. As of 2019, when my research team spoke with him for the first time before the pandemic, he was in his twenties and working two jobs to support himself, while also attending a public university in the Chicago metropolitan area.

Like many students, Carlos believes that, as a society, we should proactively recognize the experiences, validity, and dignity of all groups. For instance, the Black Lives Matter protests of 2020, he said, were a long time coming. He bitterly recalled encounters with classism and racism in his own life as a working-class, brown-skinned Latino. He explains that he sees himself as an "ally" in the movement for Black lives: "What's the point of going on if I'm going to be treated differently and not be given the same opportunities?"

Managing his time, he said, can be challenging, and juggling so many commitments leaves little time for relaxing or going out with friends. But in spite of these challenges, Carlos is committed to the idea that we all need to support one another. In our second interview conducted in July 2020, he said that the COVID-19 pandemic "opened my eyes to how we can help each other and be more careful." The pandemic also shifted how he thinks about future success. While he still believes that "if you set yourself up today, you can do well in the future," he has become less critical of those who don't live up to their full potential. He's also more sensitive to how people's circumstances can be outside their control. "This definitely made me think about how I can still do something about changing the system and making sure people [around me] have a good foundation for themselves," he told us.

Carlos resembles many other young people today, in that he hovers between two different sets of objectives: achieving upward mobility for himself on the one hand and, on the other, contributing to the community so that everyone—across all groups—can make their way through life from a position of acceptance and dignity. Carlos's generation, Gen Z, offers particularly valuable insight into our current problems because they have been forced to wrestle with the different—and at times, contradictory—philosophies they have encountered during their upbringing in a profoundly divided society.

I have seen up close how uncertain the road ahead is for young people, through my three adult children, their friends, and the graduate students I work with. But to better understand the unique challenges facing this group, and how this affects their thinking about value and dignity, my research team interviewed eighty college students (aged eighteen to twenty-three) from the Northeast and the Midwest regions of the United States.

We talked with them just a few months before the start of the COVID-19 pandemic, mostly in the fall of 2019, and were able to reinterview more than half of them in the summer of 2020 to capture how that turbulent period may have influenced their views.

These young people attended thirty-two different institutions of higher education, ranging from community colleges, Catholic schools, Ivy League universities, and everything in between. Of course, choosing to interview only college students meant that our group was not fully representative of this age group. Only about half of eighteen- to twenty-three-year-olds in the US are college students—and that half is disproportionately middle class. To partially correct for this, only half of the people we talked to were middle class (we labeled them "privileged"). The remainder were working class (we labeled them "less-privileged") (see Appendix B for details). Slightly more than half were people of color, reflecting the fact that this cohort is more racially and ethnically diverse than previous generations.

I compare the views of these college-educated people with national surveys. Ideologically, the group leaned toward the liberal/progressive end of the political spectrum, which is true of Gen Z generally, and may also be a product of their status as college students, given the well-documented tendency of universities to feed left-of-center social and political attitudes.

Below, we will hear from young people directly, gaining valuable insight into their views, the kind of life they want to live, their ideals, and their aspirations.

What are the ideals that Carlos's generation embraces? As is the case for many other Americans, young people embrace aspects of the neoliberal measures of worth, with a focus on work ethic, self-reliance, and the pursuit of professional success and material wealth. Yet for this group facing growing inequality and various crises, these values are combined with a focus on personal balance that dampen the risk of failure and protect their mental health: especially postpandemic, they also value a more collectivist vision of success, that is, contributing to the community. In lieu of color-blind uniformity that many prized in the fifties, they celebrate differences. For these young people, being non-white, low-income, immigrant, or queer doesn't push people outside the circle of belonging. That is to say, they also embrace recognition, the idea that everyone, just by virtue of their humanity, is worthy of dignity and respect. "Humans are humans," they say—regardless of national origin, sexual orientation, disability, or income. "I see you" and "I feel seen" stand as emblematic expressions of this generation, adorning T-shirts and coffee cups, and showing up in a wide variety of memes.

And for Gen Z, these ideas are more than just an abstraction—they are a *motivation* for how they lead their daily lives and may engage in political action. Indeed, this age group has developed an articulated story about who they are as a group (what sociologists call a "cohort narrative") and speak as such on social media. Instead of buying wholesale into the world of boomers and the American dream, many believe they are envisioning entirely new ways of thinking about where our society should be going and what we should get out of it. They defined themselves as aiming to create the kind of world they hope to live in. In fact, in many cases they make up "their own story" as they work to replace this American dream with a dream of inclusion.

Of course, bold new ideas are bound to create conflict—and

Gen Z's views and values have certainly sparked intergenerational disagreements about what's next. While some may think that they are reinventing the world, they are far from the first generation to have messianic aspirations. Given their history, baby boomers and Gen Xers may be skeptical about whether Gen Z's new vision truly represents a radical break from what their own generations fought for. Throughout time and across countries, young people have always been at the forefront of social movements and social change. They are the least invested in the status quo, and so are the likeliest to have innovative solutions to address societal crises. They also understandably feel that they have the most at stake when it comes to our planetary future.

Who are the Gen Zs, also called zoomers? Originally, the term mostly referred to the first cohort made of true "tech natives"—those who had never experienced a world without internet. But today, they are portrayed as those who came of age under the shadow of a pandemic, which has brought not only isolation and health worries, but also a host of psychological and economic difficulties, making it exceedingly difficult for them to gain momentum at the start of their adult life. At the same time, their futures are darkened by multiple other crises, including political polarization, growing inequality, threat to democracy, climate change, social-media-generated peer pressure, and heightened levels of racism and xenophobia.

In some respects, Gen Zs resemble their elders, the millennials, who entered the job market under the cloud of the 2008 housing crisis and recession. Many in this earlier cohort had false starts as they tried to pursue careers or gain financial stability. They have experienced precarity, and were the first generation that had to contend with the gig economy as they also faced rising costs for higher education and housing. These factors have led them to have an ambivalent relationship with the American dream and to prioritize their private life. With their situation aggravated by the COVID-19 crisis, they are less likely to experience upward mobility than their parents or their contemporaries in many European countries. Unsurprisingly, even in their thirties and forties, fewer marry and many have found it difficult to buy homes, build equity, and afford to raise a family. Gen Zs are following in their footsteps given their uncertainty concerning where they are heading in the future. But they are also more hopeful than their elders.

While in the past, some experts who study young people often emphasized how the decline of communities and institutions held them back in the labor market, I find that many among those we talked to come up with a more positive scenario about where we are heading. This is in part because they embrace *recognition* as their own particular brand of progressivism, which is different from the demands of feminists and racial justice activists characteristic of the civil rights era: the latter were concerned with second-wave feminism issues (e.g., Equal Rights Amendment [ERA], reproductive rights, and pay equity for women) and gave no thought to declaring their gender pronouns, fighting for access to gender-neutral restrooms, and other aspects of intersectionality and LGBTQ+ politics. Also, today's youth are demanding respect for a wider range of groups with historically stigmatized identities. They explicitly connect the fate of ethno-racial groups with those of Indigenous people, people living with disabilities, those who have sexual and gender nonconforming identities, and other forms of marginalization and intersectionalities that were less salient in the sixties. Beyond inclusion, they also emphasize sustainability and authenticity (living your "whole" or "best" self)—though the latter was also valued by the sixties generation (by the beatniks and the hippies in particular).

Recognition is important not only for the subset of young people we interviewed, but for a broader population of that age group, including some who are not in college. This is suggested by a 2018 Pew national survey of Gen Zs where 59 percent (more than the percentage who are college students) said that administrative forms should offer gender options other than "man" and "woman." Even those who identified as Republican were more open to this (and to fighting racial discrimination in particular) than older Republicans. Embracing recognition functions as a lever and a buffer against the impact of economic stagnation on individual lives. It creates the possibility of social progress in the form of a more inclusive future, even in a period of economic contraction.

This focus on recognition may account for the fact that a significant number of the young people we interviewed expressed a renewed sense of hope. Opinion surveys have also captured this trend. According to one, 56 percent of eighteen- to twenty-nine-year-olds in the US said they would describe themselves as hopeful in 2021, compared to 31 percent just four years earlier, in 2017—and, notably, there was no significant difference based on political party affiliation. Among Black and Hispanic Americans, the swing was even more dramatic, with the number of people describing themselves as hopeful increasing from 18 percent to 72 percent and 29 percent to 69 percent, respectively. For white people, notably, the change was much less significant, with the number of hopeful people increasing only from 35 percent to 46 percent. These changes are probably associated with the defeat of President Trump during the 2020 presidential election and the 2020 Black Lives Matter demonstrations, which, while sparked by deeply troubling instances of police brutality, ultimately created space for optimistic, forward-looking projects of inclusion and justice. The heightened levels of hopefulness may prove short-lived as circumstances change, but the rapid change is notable nevertheless.

How do these young people understand their challenges and find hope in the future? For them, worth is not measured exclusively by socioeconomic success or by emulating the lifestyles of professionals and managers. Instead, it is assessed in several dimensions that allow people to shine under different lights.

We already saw how neoliberal ideas gained influence over the last decades, celebrating those who are competitive, entrepreneurial, self-reliant, and focused on social and economic success. Some young people we spoke with still embraced some of these ideas. This came up in our interviews, as Gen Zs identified hard work, entrepreneurship, and success as the keys to salvation in these unsettled times. However, they frame these traits as contributing to their self-actualization and their trajectory of personal development. One such interviewee was Louise, a student from Detroit, who said that working hard allows you to "live your passion," and that it is available to all. But hard work cannot solve the problems of our individualist society. As we have seen, meritocracy too often obscures the privileges and resources that some groups enjoy while others are left to face steeper and steeper challenges on their own.

The combined effect of growing inequality and the compounded crises they experience mean that young Americans are also increasingly skeptical of the American dream. Among those we talked to, three out of four considered it to be unattainable, too materialistic, or too narrow, given the diversity of American society. As a distant goal, it has lost its appeal: as my daughter Chloe pointed out to me, it puts us on a "hedonistic treadmill" where we are never satisfied and always want more. To quote her, "It's not like you will be okay once you 'get there,' wherever that is."

Young people are also skeptical of consumerism. Half of those we interviewed, for instance, said they were "anti-materialists," largely motivated by acute environmental concerns. My two daughters also share these views: they make a point of buying clothes at secondhand shops. Others choose not to own a car, in an effort to limit their carbon footprints, while still others opt for vegan or vegetarian diets.

Breaking out of the materialist mindset that defines the American dream, Ashley, a Black student who attends a public university on the East Coast, said that while many people see the world in terms of money, "there are so many other things you can use to gauge or add value. Does that person have talents, or do they have certain skills that they can offer or share and teach and spread?"

The question of how to imagine an alternative future weighs heavily for this group, as they experience ambivalence toward ambition and careers, in part due to their concern with mental health. For Dani, a Black middle-class student from Massachusetts, ambition creates "a lot of pressure on you because people have different circumstances and the more you see people your age doing things the more you're like, 'Oh, I should do that . . .' You're trying to measure up to what is being shown to you by people your age."

A number of young people are suffering from mental illness at much higher rates than previous generations, as they come under pressure to engage in "competitive individualism." The situation worsened with the pandemic: In March 2021, a long-standing poll of eighteen- to twenty-nine-year-olds (conducted by Harvard University) found that more than half had been "feeling down, depressed, and hopeless" in recent weeks. Shockingly, nearly a third reported that they had considered self-harm.

In the face of pressures, many reject the focus on competition to develop a life more in sync with their personal needs. Ryan, a Midwestern white nonbinary student, critiqued overly narrow definitions of success. Instead, they said, success "should be about 'feeling fulfilled in your life.' The focus of the American dream is usually on career, and I would like to see it be more [about] fulfillment and what feeling successful means to you."

Many say they want to (or have to) prioritize mental health and inner peace over ambition and the "hedonistic treadmill." They aspire to be "well-rounded" people, a mindset they contrast with that of their workaholic parents and the blind pursuit of success. Half criticize people who focus narrowly on ambition at the expense of meaningful relationships, and four out of five describe relationships as major sources of support. They say that building connections with others helps them achieve a sense of balance, well-being, and worthiness in a competitive culture. They support "anything that makes you happy" and "fulfilled," inspired by the therapeutic culture, which promotes an ethos centered on self-care, positive thinking, happiness, self-actualization, authenticity, and personal balance. This focus is not surprising given that the therapeutic culture is supported by a multibillion-dollar business sector that makes well-being an omnipresent expectation, prioritizing an inner self and a body that can be optimized. The broader social forces that affect well-being (like poverty, discrimination, food deserts, and segregation) are generally not part of the picture.

Another alternative narrative to neoliberal values that these college students came up with was to combine personal professional aspirations with the promotion of collective well-being. One out of four cited collective advancement and social impact as crucial components of their future professions. This was particularly frequent among students we interviewed a second time, during the pandemic, perhaps because the COVID-19 crisis made our collective interdependence unmistakable. As Rada, a student of Middle Eastern descent from Michigan, puts it: "My American dream is less about my own success. I don't think that's unique to me. I want to have an impact and create change." Her embrace of personal success fuses with a strong desire to build a better society.

Thus, while embracing neoliberal goals, many young people are also sensitive to the ways in which our fate as human beings is connected to that of others. Some academics call this having "a sense of linked fate." This way of thinking emphasizes collective identity, solidarity, empathy, and a sense of belonging. It means defining one's worth based on what we can contribute to the community, in a way that is compatible with professional and material success.

It is remarkable that two-thirds of the young people we talked to believe that growing inequality is incompatible with their ideals of communal connectedness, belonging, and greater social solidarity. Making more people matter may be the only path to improving our society in their eyes, even in the face of unequal economic resources. This shift helps move us away from defining success by one's wealth and class mobility. As Ashley puts it, a person's value should be measured in "how much they're able to contribute their time and volunteer [and give] in other ways to a community." This alternative matrix is compatible with recognition because it "democratizes" worth, making it available to everyone (unlike measuring a person by how much he or she makes).

This generation also distinguishes itself by its generosity, especially when compared with their elders: 32 percent donate to causes they believe in, and 50 percent are looking for jobs in nonprofits. During the COVID-19 crisis, 66 percent of Gen Z people and 74 percent of millennials provided financial aid to nonprofits or other people, in comparison to 53 percent of boomers. Spurred by an effective grassroots campaign on TikTok and Twitter, many young people donated from their COVID-19 relief checks to pay for bail bonds for Black Lives Matter demonstrators arrested during the summer of 2020.

Students from privileged backgrounds in particular often imagine themselves playing a leadership role in fostering change, which some deride as a "messianic complex" to improve the lives of the less fortunate. Even if they aspire to prestigious and lucrative careers, these students often saw their objective as valuable because they help others. For instance, for Shelby, another white Midwestern student: "I can use what I've been given to give back . . . to build up communities. . . . I feel a sense of purpose from that, that I'm doing something valuable and important by making a difference in people's lives."

Given how Gen Z supplement neoliberal ideals with a focus on recognition and community betterment, it is not surprising that they also articulate a "cohort narrative" about the special political and social mission of their generation, which they contrast with what they perceive as the political complacency of boomers. This is captured by Neil, a white Chicagoan, when he says, "We are in the cockpit now." Expressing the political stance of his generation, Carlos wonders, "Someone has to do it, so why not me?"

In many instances, members of Gen Z define themselves in contrast to baby boomers and Gen Xers, whom they view as passive, inept, or complicit in wrongdoing. For instance, they blame these generations for failing to act earlier to fight climate change, and for ultimately creating the crisis we are now facing. They also tend to downplay or ignore how these generations contributed to the fight for gay rights, women's rights, and civil rights. Jasmine, a Black woman from the Northeast, described her generation's enthusiasm for social change in contrast to boomers, who she said are "used to just going with the flow of things." She adds, "Now we're finally talking about issues in schools, about the LGBTQ+, gender, race, what it means to be able-bodied and all this stuff." As Enrique, a Latino student from suburban Chicago, put it: "We're a lot more open-minded [about] issues like equality . . . a little more realistic and we've caught flaws whereas other generations didn't think about them." Attitudes like this may be, in part, a way of finding agency in the face of uncertainty. Half of the young people interviewed mentioned that generational turnover will facilitate social change.

As is the case for their commitment to recognition, their political activism can act as a buffer or an alternative to the pressures of competitive individualism and the pursuit of the American dream. Thus it is not surprising that surveys of Gen Z have described them as an "activist generation" focused on social justice and equality. And indeed, the majority of eighteen- to twenty-nine-year-olds surveyed in 2021 describe themselves as politically active, as do 36 percent of a group of Gen Zs surveyed the same year. Moreover, the media frequently describe them as "changemakers" who hold our collective future in their hands—and became especially fixated on this idea during the global demonstrations in the summer of 2020.

As you might expect, the level of political engagement is particularly high among college students. For more than fifty years, a team of researchers at UCLA has conducted a national survey of first-year college students, asking about their experiences, preferences, and attitudes on a multitude of different issues. The 2016 survey reported that students that year were more likely to participate in a protest than any other cohort since the survey began, including the radical cohorts of the 1960s, whose activism focused on civil rights and the Vietnam War. Some are concerned with reparations for slavery, trans issues, police violence, mass incarceration, immigration reform, and other topics that were far less salient for 1960s student activists. This priority is reflected in Gen Z's explicitly inclusive practices, like their attention to using the correct pronouns. Signaling this shift, the popular dictionary Merriam-Webster chose the singular pronoun *they* as 2019's "word of the year." For their part, *woke* and *cisgender* were among the "top ten" words in 2021.

Overall, they are more liberal or progressive than conservative: Many young people we talked to place great importance on efforts to fight climate change and look to figures like the Swedish climate activist Greta Thunberg for hope. Several of them supported the Democratic Socialists of America, and Senator Bernie Sanders was one of their most frequently cited sources of inspiration. Only eight of them (most in the Midwest) self-described as conservative. In this, their political leanings are not unlike other young Americans'. A January 2020 Pew Research Center survey found that 61 percent of voters ages eighteen to twenty-three said they were definitely or probably going to vote for the Democratic candidate for president in the 2020 election, as compared to less than a quarter (22 percent) who said they were planning to vote for Trump. Also, the 2019 UCLA freshman survey revealed that "just over two in five (44 percent) students entering college in 2019 identified as politically middle-of-the-road. . . . Nearly one-third (32 percent) identified as liberal and 4 percent as far left." This compares to 18 percent who identify as conservative and 2 percent who identify as far right.

Many young people we talked to are deeply committed to social justice—and even brought the subject up unprompted. When we reinterviewed some of them in the wake of the Black Lives Matter protests, they were often critical of those who do not embrace racial justice, speak up, or use their social media for activism. Two-thirds spontaneously wanted to discuss "systemic racism." Jasmine, a Black student from the East Coast, reported that "white supremacy [is] the biggest issue that we have."

These young people value optimism, which they see as a prerequisite to social change, and eschew negativity, pessimism, and cynicism, which they see as standing in the way of progress. This is part of their broader commitment to inclusion and social change. They are critical of "doomers," by which they mean their peers who abstain from having children or investing in the future due to fears of impending global disaster due to global warming. Ian, a white student from Chicago, explains, "The outlook of 'doom and gloom' is not going to help anyone when you're trying to achieve a better society." He believes this attitude feeds the status quo and that it is better to "continue the fight."

Many young people are also hyperaware of the downsides of political activism, which ranges from feeding alleged "political correctness" to being sucked into political "bubbles." This creates serious peer pressure. In the second round of interviews, college students discussed hyperpoliticization, which encourages impression management on social media. Dani, a Black student, describes this as "exhausting," while Dean, another Black student, says it's "traumatizing." Moral pressures to follow the "woke" party line are rejected by several of the young people the team spoke to. Some talk about "activism fatigue." These pressures were felt particularly keenly by African Americans during the 2020 Movement for Black Lives, especially given the intensity of Black Twitter.

Students are often disappointed with how their values are coopted into empty slogans by employers and corporations, and with diversity trainings and other policies that too often turn out to be insufficient and largely symbolic, intended to protect institutions from complaints or lawsuits more than to actually help people of color. They can also see that many of their own peers are superficial in their beliefs. As Elaina puts it, "everyone loves to preach about how open they are but [most are not as] open as they want everyone to see them. . . . I feel like it's just a lot of talk and no action." Sofi goes further when she says, "a lot of people [feel] that they were excused from the movement just because they did a superficial thing like post the blackout square or put the hashtag of Black Lives Matter on their bio [on social media]."

This skepticism contributes to the fact that a third of our interviewees do not participate in the political process. However, in the 2020 presidential election, 50 percent of all eligible Americans between the ages of eighteen and twenty-nine voted, compared to 67 percent overall. They participated in larger numbers that year than they had in the past: in the 2016 presidential election, the participation rate for young people was only 39 percent. For Shelby, a Midwestern white student, "Disillusionment with the political system is a big problem . . . people [feel like we] don't matter and what we do doesn't matter." Many interviewees, for example, expressed impatience with the incompetent government response to the pandemic. Being cynical or skeptical about national electoral politics and the major parties, some prefer to be politically engaged at the local level, where they believe they can have more impact and where political change is more likely.

Of course, we need to remember that generations are not monoliths, and Gen Z in particular exhibits a remarkable diversity of viewpoints and attitudes. There are numerous differences, for example, between students whose parents are middle-class professionals and those who come from working-class backgrounds.

We saw that privileged students often described their future in terms of playing a leadership role in creating social change. They often ground their visions of collective life in political projects of inclusion, empathy, and kindness. Their narratives of change remain largely divorced from structural discussions of power, although many denounce systemic racism and promote social change.

Working-class (or first gen) students' college experiences can be radically different from the middle class's, busy as many are to support themselves and help their family pay their bills. This is especially true for the many students whose friends and families had been disproportionately affected by sickness and unemployment during the pandemic years. As a student named Dean put it, "giv[ing] back to my parents" was a priority for him. While they also embrace creating social change, they must simultaneously attend to other immediate concerns, which is often incompatible with taking on leadership roles. Middle-class students seem largely unaware that their emphasis on collective pursuits may be out of reach to less privileged students. As a consequence, ironically, their concern with the promotion of hope and social justice may not easily include those they aim to empower.

There also seems to be some difference in "political styles" across classes. Working-class youth we talked to are perhaps more attuned to confrontation as essential to social change, whereas their middle-class counterparts are slightly more likely to emphasize "being a kind human" as the foundation of greater tolerance and inclusion. Relying on utopian images of harmonious imagined futures can detract from the brutal power struggles that have historically fed social change. History has shown that kindness does not deliver social justice. Living with racism, precarity, and injustice feeds anger, which may not be compatible with a genteel emphasis on kindness and empathy expressed largely by the middle-class students and presented as an alternative to the dog-eat-dog pursuit of upward mobility.

Since the team interviewed only those in college, a cross-class comparison is particularly urgent, especially given that younger workers below twenty-five were particularly hit by the pandemic. These developments are seen as feeding xenophobic, far-right, and populist attitudes, often attributed to the loss of status among the white working class. Also, like their parents, many young workers are not sure of what they think and keep their distance from politics. They may be less "undecided" than cynical or alienated.

Indeed, working-class students often expressed far less trust in social institutions, like government, schools, or employers. Surveys show that working-class youth is more likely than their middle-class peers to become socially disengaged, which can lead some to embrace political cynicism and extreme beliefs (including conspiracy theories). This is particularly the case among those who have dropped out of high school or vocational training and those who feel hopeless. These include those with mental health difficulties and those who feel paralyzed by precarity. As fewer and fewer young people can afford health care, higher education, rent, and other necessities, more and more feel that society's problems are intractable. Many young people of color also feel pessimistic, fearing that the systemic obstacles they face are unlikely ever to change.

Whether these young people feel "seen" or "enabled" by our institutions to take charge of their lives is crucial to our future and to their capacity to "aspire." If they feel recognized, they are more likely to engage with politics, civil society, religion, the labor market, and more. Schools, politicians, social movements, employers, and the media need to act as engines of hope for them, too. Rather than dismissing these voters, it is crucial to better capture what motivates them and what type of alternative narratives (and humor) could attract and speak to them. If President Trump's taped comments on grabbing women "by the pussy" made him more popular among a certain category of men who appreciate sexist and vulgar humor, it is urgent to consider what alternatives are available at the progressive end of the political spectrum.

After having considered how Gen Z embrace some neoliberal ideals—hard work and success—while combining them with other priorities—recognition, mental health, community improvement, political mobilization—we have to consider where these young people find the narratives that inspire them. Who do they listen to when it comes to imagining alternative futures? Does the work of change agents I discussed in previous chapters matter to them? Who else do they listen to? Answering these question helps us understand how exposure to new narratives inspires recognition and other sources of hope.

The interviews point to three main sources of influence: change agents, institutions, and peers. Among change agents, activists, politicians, and entertainers loom large in the world of media-focused Gen Zs. And unsurprisingly, many of them lean left and feed Gen Z's passion for inclusion and social justice.

When asked who inspires them, as we have seen, students most often spontaneously mentioned the environmental activist Greta Thunberg, whose influence is bolstered by social media and movements popular among youth—such as the Sunrise Movement and the Extinction Rebellion. As Neil, a student from the Midwest, puts it, "When [Greta] canoed from Europe to America, the actual environmental impact of her doing that is relatively minor . . . [but] she's inspiring people to do the change." As a hyper-visible link in recognition chains, Greta is helping young people challenge consumerism, give voice to the needs of younger generations, and write their own scripts about our future society.

Senator Bernie Sanders was widely seen as a radical generational ally when we conducted our interviews, and he comes second. Also mentioned are self-professed democratic socialist congresswoman Alexandria Ocasio-Cortez, and former First Lady Michelle Obama, who is viewed as an important role model. It is telling that only one Republican politician is mentioned by the young people we talked to: former governor of California and media star Arnold Schwarzenegger.

Entertainers were also a source of inspiration for many. These included pathbreaking singers Lady Gaga and Billie Eilish, and also mostly non-white artists and celebrities such as Yara Shahidi, Bruce Lee, Chance the Rapper, Beyoncé, and Oprah Winfrey. Also salient are sports stars such as football player Tom Brady and non-white athletes such as Lamar Jackson, boxers Mike Tyson and Manny Pacquiao, and baseball players David Ortiz and Eric Hammond.

It is striking that while none of the students found businesspeople inspiring, a few mentioned writers such as the antiracist author Ta-Nehisi Coates and the Instagram-famous poet Rupi Kaur, who writes about sexual violence. There were also political commentators ranging from the conservative show host Ben Shapiro to "The Young Turks" (TYT), a popular group of YouTube progressives. Overall, the latter far outnumber conservatives, which is consistent with Gen Z's embrace of social inclusion and their ambivalence toward neoliberal values.

Unexpectedly, given their suspicion toward large organizations, institutions are also mentioned as sources of inspiration and hope. Students value higher education as an institution that provides knowledge and contributes to inclusion by broadening worldviews. Some mention their faith in innovation, science, and technology as sources of progress and resources in shaping our uncertain future.

While some conservatives and liberals may believe that nonprofits, the US government, and other organizations are working to address social problems, young progressives are far more critical of their role and generally pessimistic about the ability of these organizations, and of the United States, to improve the world.

A small group of our interviewees mentioned religion as a source of inspiration and reassurance—mostly children of immigrants and the upwardly mobile. For example, one student, Sidney, said that religion "inspires me because that's where I place my hope. Maybe that's why I don't feel doomed in life: I don't really place my hope even in this world necessarily, but I place it in my faith." Religion acts as a buffer against uncertainty, as suggested by Frederica: "I still do what I can in terms of educating myself, fighting different injustices, and stuff like that," she said. "But at the end of the day, I personally feel like a lot of things are out of my hands."

In contrast to change agents and institutions, the group most often mentioned by students as a source of inspiration are people in their everyday lives: their friends and peers, as well as their family. In fact, more than two-thirds described their peers as a source of hope. Many said that this support gives them a sense of agency and blunts the anxiety of facing the unknown. For instance, Elaine from Rhode Island said: "I'll talk to my friends about it, and we'll make it like, 'Hey, we can do a protest or we can start cutting out plastic.' We are coming up with solutions that can happen right away. Not everything is outside of my control." Black students in particular find fortitude in interpersonal support and understanding, especially when experiencing racism. Their need for solidarity finds expression in the phenomenon of so-called Black Twitter, where African American young people support each other at a time when conversations about racism and Black Lives Matter are omnipresent and often described as emotionally exhausting.

What kind of world do these young people want to live in? Given their inability to achieve the traditional American dream that has animated the United States since World War II, those we talked to propose a number of new and different visions of how our society should work. They are critical of a life of competition leading to a predefined path of economic and professional success. They are combining old values like hard work with a new emphasis on contributions to the community, recognition, equity, and social change. They embrace the goal of creating a more pluralistic world grounded in ethical and political choices that enables a wider range of types of successes and makes more room for personal well-being. They also favor personal projects that allow people to "do their thing," as they seek personal balance and prioritize authenticity and self-actualization. They self-identify as change makers in their political commitment to creating a better, sustainable world. They are particularly preoccupied with lifting up people of color and sexual minorities. Yet not many mention the plight of the downwardly mobile working class, low-income people, and rural people.

We saw that young people in 2016 were more likely to participate in protests than any other cohort surveyed over the last fifty years. Commentators are still assessing whether these protests will be effective in making change. We have many reasons to believe that the current trend will persist, especially as we turn increasingly into a "social movement society" in which protest has become a normal part of politics.

Some have argued that the postmaterialist values expressed by our college students are characteristic of all middle-class youth who have seen their material needs satisfied. The landscape in which this generation evolves today is radically different from the conditions that prevailed when postmaterialist theorists formulated this approach in the seventies, and when the sixties generation was protesting. For instance, formal diversity, equity, and inclusion (DEI) efforts have become a mainstay of most bureaucratic organizations in the United States and beyond, and therapy is a constant point of reference in middle-class culture. Moreover, the meaning of "progressivism" has evolved considerably over time. Supporting the Civil Rights Movement did not mean supporting trans rights; questions of identity (ethnicity, immigration, sexuality, gender) are now much more salient across all generations than a few decades ago.

I wager that the political views of younger people are being shaped by this new cultural context and by change agents and their peers at least as much as by their distance from material necessity. Also, whether their progressivism is entirely due to their youth or to the pandemic is doubtful given the broad moral features of this cultural context in which they are coming of age. We will have to assess how their long-term political commitments change in light of the massive cultural transformation they are experiencing and will experience in the future. However, there is some evidence that progressive "old boomers" maintained progressive self-identity and political orientations as they advanced in age. I would expect that the same will happen with left-of-center Gen Zs, with political variations within this group considered at large.

How they will put their aspirations into practice (whether they say "inclusion" while partaking in privilege) remains an open question. The new values and narratives shaping their expectations may become more and more influential as their cohort age into positions of greater power in the decades to come. If, like Carlos, they embrace inclusion and believe that "we have to be our own futures," we have yet to see how their ideals of inclusion can resonate more broadly.

CHAPTER 8

DIFFERENT YET THE SAME

SOLUTIONS FOR BUILDING AN INCLUSIVE SOCIETY

How else can we promote the social inclusion of those who are often viewed as second-class citizens in our divided world? Young people, with their novel insights and energy, give us some degree of hope. So do the change agents who promote inclusion. But if we are to truly transform the way we think about who matters, we should consider how all of us can amplify these voices by the choices we make in who we hang out with, how to live our lives, and how institutions (such as the government, the law, and schools) can play a role in extending recognition and dignity to everyone.

I have said this before, but it bears repeating that the gap between the "winners" and the "losers" of our current system is growing, separating a minority of college-educated professionals and managers, who have the credentials needed for upward mobility, from the "people below," workers without a college degree who make up a whopping two-thirds of the American workforce. For this group, life expectancy has declined since 2010, while the general trend was for life expectancy to increase. Their horizons have drastically narrowed over the last decades: they have lost their footing in many occupations where they used to be hired. They were displaced from 7.4 million jobs in the United States since 2000. Most of these jobs were their way into the middle class, and many now require a college degree. Occupations such as software developer, business manager, sales supervisor, administrative assistant, and purchasing agents didn't used to require a college degree, but they increasingly do. This growing class polarization is a dead end. Producing more wealth and distributing it better are crucial. But equally important is devising new narratives about more expansive understanding of who matters. This practice needs to be baked into daily life.

Other researchers have given the topic some thought. In *The Sum of Us*, racial justice advocate Heather McGhee focuses on redistributing resources by mobilizing narratives of solidarity. Duke sociologist Chris Bail works to increase tolerance across differences, conducting experiments where citizens exchange their views anonymously on social media to gain greater understanding of different perspectives. Francesca Polletta, one of the leading experts on the impact of narratives on social cohesion, analyzes moral norms, civility, emotions, rituals, and advocacy and their social effects. She concludes that to overcome divisions and inequality, people need to build relationships over time as they do activities and projects together. In *The Tyranny of Merit*, political philosopher Michael Sandel also denounces societies that worship success and merit too exclusively. His solution is to celebrate work and togetherness as conditions for democratic life.

There is much to like about these approaches, and some certainly overlap with what I propose. However, I go further by pointing to the need to produce and diffuse more narratives that broaden recognition: How can we multiply the standards we use to define someone as worthy, to include not only neoliberal ideals, but also spirituality, morality, altruism, creativity, and civic-mindedness? How can we more often and better celebrate our shared humanity? The answer may lie in how we have reduced stigmatization of certain groups in the past. This is not about individuals learning to become kinder, but about figuring out how to transform our societies to produce and diffuse different messages about who matters.

Institutions can play an important role in creating these changes. Employers can help lift up the too-often-invisible or taken-for-granted care work of (typically female) parents, friends, community members, educators, spiritual leaders, and others. Think of human resources policies favoring work/family balance (family leave, flex time) that implicitly acknowledge both our contributions as bread-winners and caregivers. These make a difference, as shown in a study of nursing home employees who were given more autonomy and flexibility in their time management. The implicit message of these policies is that employers recognize that their employees' personal lives are important. This simple fact resulted in less absenteeism and greater work satisfaction. Such flexibility remains somewhat rare in the lower rungs of the American labor market, which offers poor conditions to working mothers, who continue to do most of the family's care work. The working conditions for the majority of US mothers are particularly harsh when compared to those in Italy, Sweden, and France, each of which provides extensive state-subsidized childcare.

Individuals can also play central roles in achieving these goals. We know this is possible because we can already see these practices in action. We saw that the group of Gen Z students we interviewed are already judging worth through a wide range of social contributions. And many Hollywood creators we interviewed work to expose audiences to more diverse and complex representations of different groups. Promoting broader criteria of worth is also something that we can and should do in our daily lives. Instead of a winner-take-all contest, we can value traits that are available to all. These would include spirituality, morality, and altruism—and activities such as creating, educating, and entertaining—which can be valued without subordinating them to material production, consumption, and the profit motive.

We can all cultivate a wider range of friends and relationships across class and racial boundaries, decide to reside in more integrated neighborhoods, and send our kids to more diverse schools. Broad exposure to a wide range of people encourages pro-diversity attitudes, including more openness toward immigrants. Moreover, frequent interactions with people of different racial backgrounds may help reduce racism. So will frequent exposure to narratives that valorize diversity. In other words, we can structure our lives so that we are all more exposed to diversity every day.

For our families, we can also lower pressures to achieve, which makes for less stressful lives across the social ladder. This can also contribute to sustainability and equality by lowering consumption, as well as resources and opportunity hoarding. Instead of pushing children toward instrumental activities, we could instead encourage them to gain a broad range of life experiences. We can direct them away from the "excellent sheep" pathway. Viewing such solutions as unrealistic is certainly a measure of the powerful hold that neoliberal thinking has on our worldviews. Being able to imagine a different world is only a first step.

It is important to keep in mind what changing our thinking about worth can and cannot do. New and more expansive standards of worth cannot eliminate insecurity and suffering. But they can change how people understand their place in society to help bolster their sense of agency and improve their overall well-being. Consider that in countries like Denmark and Sweden, which have strong social safety nets and more protections for workers, lower-income people are less stigmatized than in the US. Whereas more privileged Americans see their lower-income peers as lazy and undeserving, Danes and Swedes tend to see those in need as victims of broader economic pressures. This makes quite a difference in how low-income people experience their lives in these countries.

Alternative criteria of worth help explain how one's quality of life can be experienced strikingly differently across social contexts. Anthropologist Bhrigupati Singh shows how the dwellers of one of the poorest villages in India experience hardship less acutely than researchers initially expected. This is because, in a context of acute deprivation, scarcity is normalized as part of daily life, which affects social expectations. Also, when people had prior exposure to crises, they had improved faith in their ability to navigate challenges. This strengthened social resilience: past experiences of dealing successfully with change can bolster our belief that we will be able to do so again.

While dignity and alternative standards of worth do not make insecurity, scarcity, and material constraints go away, they affect how people understand who they are and their place in society. These alternative standards help bolster their sense of worth and agency, which are associated with subjective dignity, which in turn promotes lower levels of depression and higher subjective well-being.

Moreover, cross-national studies show that happiness is not linearly correlated with income. The impact of income on happiness plateaus after a certain level of economic security is reached, which is why happiness and economic prosperity are often less related than we might think. Developmental economist and Nobel laureate Amartya Sen has written extensively about this and has helped the discipline of economics move away from focusing exclusively on material prosperity and to better consider quality of life, sustainability, and well-being. Inspired by his work, the United Nations' annual Human Development Report defines well-being not only in terms of material wealth, but also in terms of "capacity to aspire," which refers to people's ability to plan, hope, and dream.

In the current context of political polarization, we urgently need to lift up "ordinary universalism"—which I define by what we all have in common as people, what makes us similar or compatible. This perspective can influence how people bridge boundaries with those who are different. This was clear to me in the early nineties, as I was interviewing a group of immigrant workers from Morocco and Algeria living in France, studying how they categorize people either by similarities or by differences. When asked about how they are similar to and different from the French, they pointed to our physical similarities ("we all spend nine months in our mother's womb and have ten fingers"), our shared human nature ("there are good and bad people in all races"), our shared needs ("we all get up in the morning to buy our bread at the baker"), our shared spiritual origin ("we are all children of God"), and our shared cosmological humility ("we are all insignificant grains of sand in the universe"). Similarities between different groups need to be more visible if we are to escape our current cultural impasse of polarization and political sectarianism. But, paradoxically, this can—and must—be achieved while appreciating the differences that define various groups.

This idea of "ordinary universalism," of emphasizing similarities over differences, is central to the work of many change agents. Take, for instance, Desmond Meade, the activist in Florida who leads the Florida Rights Restoration Coalition, where he fights to restore voting rights to formerly incarcerated people and emphasizes the many ways in which "we are all the same." Or consider Sister Barbara Staley, the mother Superior of the Missionary Sisters of the Sacred Heart, whose religious order promotes human solidarity through projects around the globe, and who spoke to me about our shared humanity. Faith-based organizing mobilizes people by making salient all that we have in common across our differences.

The power of ordinary universalism can be seen all across the world. A recent study of female janitors working in a Mumbai mall showed how their focus on commonalities produced a strong sense of solidarity and resilience, which helped them deal with mistreatment on the job. They showed compassion for coworkers, visiting them when they were sick and advocating for them when needed. They also shared food and used terms of kinship ("aunty" and "sister") to downplay status differences and forge community.

Similar patterns were found in other settings, including between students and janitors at a university in Malaysia. Older women janitors were observed giving advice to students about their health and nutrition, behaving as "surrogate aunties" rather than as low-status service workers. These women made salient their role as caring human beings instead of low-status service workers.

Creating common ground and unity has become more urgent since the Trump years, as discussions of political polarization, echo chambers, and filter bubbles are crowding online spaces. Change agents promote different methods of creating a shared sense of community. Social psychologists Matthew Feinberg and Robb Willer argue that forcing Republicans and Democrats, or conservatives and progressives, to converge around a single set of positions or policies is doomed to failure. When citizens try to agree on policies, the framing of the conversation encourages opponents to maintain their stance and impose their views on others. These authors believe it is more productive to engage in "moral reframing," by focusing on commonalities and shared sacred values ("dignity" or "family") instead of differences.

Ordinary universalism can also be seen increasingly in youth culture. Young people embrace global popular culture, which often celebrates antiracism, feminism, and LGBTQ+ rights, along with other more traditional themes, such as sex and violence. Low-income Parisian youth often distance themselves from their dead-end jobs and broaden their horizons by embracing hybrid and multiracial global hip-hop culture. This includes a form of "aesthetic cosmopolitanism" that mixes hybrid genres ("*banlieue* rap," for example, which includes references to North African musical traditions). For their part, middle-class Turkish immigrants in Berlin emphasize their cosmopolitan literacy, including their bilingualism and biculturalism, to contest the stigma they experience from some of the more provincial and less educated nationalist German citizens.

Ordinary universalism refers not only to what we all have in common, but also to embracing ethnic, religious, national, and other differences. Nationalist populism, Islamophobia, and xenophobia are on the rise in many countries, and ordinary universalism can be a vital counterweight. It weakens the boundaries between groups, making them more flexible and crossable. The turn toward "superdiversity" and a more "cosmopolitan canopy" contribute to this. So does the use of the category "people of color," or that of "Latinx," an umbrella term for a "supra-ethnic" category. These changes in terminology are part of a broader minority rights revolution. Equally important is the (contested) presence of affirmative action in universities and nonprofits, and the creation of affinity groups in the corporate sector.

One way that some corporations and other large organizations promote ordinary universalism is through what are called diversity, equity, and inclusion (DEI) initiatives. These have been criticized in some circles as "happy talk" or empty, symbolic gestures, rather than serious attempts to reckon with the marginalization of certain groups. They are also criticized as a hollow marketing ploy to increase profit, a corporate sleight of hand to appease workers, and an additional burden on employees of color who are asked to educate their peers. But while these criticisms are all valid, thinking seriously about how to emphasize our similarities and value our differences is worthwhile—small decisions do create change and can slowly transform broader patterns, one step at a time.

In fact, while the United States has frequently failed to live up to its ideals, there is a long American tradition of interpersonal altruism that characterizes the civic and religious culture and permeates everyday interactions, even while in tension with a culture of racism. Nevertheless, solidarity appears to be weaker in the United States than in many other advanced industrial societies, in part because of high levels of political polarization. Americans have stronger negative views toward those who don't share their political views, compared with their counterparts in other wealthy countries. This dynamic has worsened in recent years as inequality and unemployment have continued to rise. When groups feel they are competing with one another for resources, people are more likely to focus on who gets what, instead of on broadening recognition.

Few acknowledge that there is a common quest for recognition between the white working class who support right-wing populist candidates and progressive groups of LGBTQ+ people and antiracist advocates. That these camps often see recognition as zero-sum certainly hinders this acknowledgment. Many resist the view that both groups deserve dignity, or that one group's suffering is commensurate with the other's. But by recognizing how their claims overlap, we may be better able to bridge boundaries and lower polarization. Progressive finger-wagging can only stoke working-class resentment toward professionals and managers, just as much as the claims of right-wing populists to represent the values of America irk progressives. Changing these attitudes may be an insurmountable challenge, but it is one that we all must contemplate.

The quest for recognition can bring together those at the extreme poles of American politics. We need to have a collective conversation across various corners of the public sphere about what it is, how to broaden it, and why it matters to people across the political spectrum. Many people understand the need to address economic inequality, but they fail to see why recognition of dignity is so important.

So what else should we *do* about broadening recognition? Ordinary people can work to reduce the stigma of marginalized groups, as well. To see how this works in practice, let's consider two different groups that have, to varying degrees, become less stigmatized in recent decades: those living with HIV or AIDS and people labeled obese. In each instance, to understand the process of destigmatization, we must first identify who the main social actors involved in reducing stigma were, the cultural tools they drew on, and the destigmatizing actions they are engaged in.

For people living with HIV or AIDS, the main figures driving destigmatization were experts (doctors, lawyers, and social scientists), journalists, and activists—all of whom drew on the cultural resources available to them to reframe how this group was perceived. For example, they used language centered on equality, human rights, and dignity—and ultimately shifted the narrative from one of blame and judgment to one about a medical condition that can affect anyone. They had to counter a dominant narrative that HIV and AIDS arose from sexually promiscuous, and thus shameful and blameworthy, gay men. They also used the law to promote human rights and equal protections.

For destigmatization to take place, the knowledge produced by experts had to be credible and conclusive. Medical researchers were able to show that HIV and AIDS was an illness that could affect anyone. They demonstrated the potential for "linked fate" or "common destiny" with members of the stigmatized group.

Prominent agents of change from politicians to celebrities also started to provide support. For instance, in the nineties, basketball megastar Magic Johnson revealed that he was HIV-positive. And several years earlier, in 1987, Lady Diana was photographed shaking hands with an unidentified AIDS patient without wearing gloves to demonstrate that the disease could not be transmitted by touch.

In contrast, people labeled obese had fewer of these forms of support. Some advocates supported the "health at every size" movement, to counter the arguments that shaming of heavier people was justified as a matter of promoting health. But medical researchers were not ready to support the view that body mass index does not matter. Activists working to reduce fat-shaming often found it difficult to overcome the stereotype that obese people are uneducated, lazy, self-indulgent, and irresponsible. While there is now more support for body positivity, destigmatization was much slower than it was for those living with HIV, and it is still facing enormous resistance.

Comparing these two cases, my colleagues and I concluded that destigmatization required a recognition chain that included support from prestigious public figures, a wide broadcast of messaging, and activists borrowing effective strategies from other successful movements to gain traction.

From these cases we can draw some key insights about how to reduce the stigmas cast upon all marginalized groups locally, and eventually, beyond national boundaries. While the groups involved vary from case to case, many of us can contribute through our own involvement as experts or participants in social movements. We can all work to change the conversation about who belongs in our daily lives. The first lesson we should remember is that instead of simply appealing to individual kindness, empathy, or charity, we need to promote new narratives to support positive representations of all groups, so that they become taken for granted and part of our daily lives.

But reducing stigma isn't easy, given the certainty of backlash. Activists must overcome a "clash of background assumptions," where opposing views don't often even have a shared language for constructive dialogue. A second lesson, then, is that recruiting allies is crucial. For members of stigmatized groups, support from "outsiders" is validating and acts as a buffer against assault.

Recognition chains play an essential role. Consider cultural producers who operate at a large scale in sectors like advertising, who complement the efforts of citizens to reduce stigma. By broadening who appears in ads, these producers can have a positive impact on how certain groups are seen. To better understand how this works, my team spoke with Molly Kennedy, who works in advertising and developed some of the beauty brand Dove's marketing campaigns. She explained how, for over ten years, Dove has promoted self-esteem and featured "real women" in their ads. Whereas other similar brands have tended to feature disproportionately white and skinny women in their ads, Dove has prioritized including women of color and women with larger and varied body types. Jessica Weiner, who consults with Dove, explicitly ties these changes to broadening recognition. Weiner also assisted Mattel in launching Barbie dolls "with diverse hair, face, and body types" in 2016, and in modeling new Barbie dolls on inspiring women like the filmmaker and producer Ava DuVernay.

Many observers have dismissed this "branding diversity," calling it a crass marketing gimmick. But this approach has been an effective means for diffusing at scale more inclusive messages about who is worthy. According to Maria Garrido, a senior executive at Paris-based Vivendi International, and Katie Eng, from the minority-owned marketing agency PACO Collective, acknowledging the buying power of minority groups and appealing to them specifically are at odds with traditional assimilationist approaches to marketing. In the past, marketers worked to convince minority groups that they needed to become like the dominant group. While many continue to debate the value of the assimilationist ideal that animated American society for most of the twentieth century, the forthcoming demographic shift toward a multiracial minority-majority society calls for broadening recognition.

As we saw in the previous chapter, young people are working hard to change perceptions at an individual level—but there is only so much they can accomplish. Their bottom-up efforts must be supplemented by change agents and activists who strategize to shift organizations and the law in order to make structural change at a national scale. If advocates want to increase welfare resources distributed to the poor, promote the voting rights of the formerly incarcerated, raise the minimum wage, and improve access to health insurance, they have to mobilize the power of the law. Top-down and bottom-up strategies complement one another. It is worth considering these top-down strategies in a bit more detail.

Governments play an important role in the promotion of cultural policies and diversity programs that celebrate the culture of various groups and spread recognition. Sociologist Jeffrey Reitz has argued that governments promote multiculturalism by rallying popular support for diversity. In Canada, for instance, such efforts were vital in transforming the country's national identity to include ethnic minorities. In 1971, in response to a movement for Quebec's independence, Canadian prime minister Pierre Elliott Trudeau launched an innovative federal policy that recognized the culture of all immigrant groups. In 1988, the federal government passed the Multiculturalism Act to deal with the growing diversity of the population and committed substantial funding to promote the art, culture, and traditions of various ethnic and Indigenous groups. Many French Canadians were critical of this policy for not acknowledging their historical place as a founding nation of the Canadian polity and favored "interculturalism" over multiculturalism. Nevertheless, even today, many programs exist to facilitate the integration of immigrants into the Canadian polity. This has led Canadian immigrants to be more involved in national politics compared to their American counterparts.

Policies can sustain dignity or create stigmatization. The governmental preference for means-tested policies, such as the Temporary Assistance for Needy Families (TANF) program, is viewed by low-income people as feeding stigmatization. This program funds monthly cash assistance payments to low-income families with children, as well as a range of services. It was widely perceived by recipients as a handout, and some feel stigmatized for benefiting from this program. This is unlike the more universal Earned Income Tax Credit (EITC) through which low- to moderate-income workers and families get a tax break. The latter "work bonus" program is perceived as a "just reward for work" and as a path to upward mobility.

The law also plays a significant role in enforcing official privileges, handicaps, and pecking orders, dictating how resources are distributed among different groups. In the United States, the law supports the well-to-do with favorable estate laws and mortgage deductions for primary residences and second homes. It also legitimizes claims—for instance, when victims of racism use legal recourse. Or laws can enact segregation, as when Israel enforces laws that segregate Arab-Palestinian children in K–12 education.

But legal rights are an expression of the relative legitimacy of groups, and they send messages about which groups are favored. The ongoing battle over abortion rights in the US, Latin America, and elsewhere is not solely about the question of when life begins; rather, it is also a matter of whether the law recognizes women's agency over their own bodies or whether men should have the power to dictate standards. In brief, the law and the institutions that enforce it play an important role in either supporting or weakening recognition and dignity.

Another example comes from the education sector (public or private) where top-down, organizational level efforts to strengthen recognition can do more than just help certain groups feel deserving and worthy—they can also shape their upward trajectories. Sociologist Prudence Carter compared eight schools in South Africa and the United States, focusing (among other things) on the schools' differing policies regarding natural hairstyles. Girls in schools that were more culturally flexible, where Black girls could wear their hair in natural styles rather than straighten it to accommodate white beauty standards, had higher self-esteem and academic placement. By acknowledging these girls' self-presentation as acceptable, the schools extended to them the dignity of recognition, which contributed to their academic success.

If organizations are going to extend recognition to all groups, then policy experts and lawmakers need to be asked and trained to consider the messaging power of the changes they want to enact. Each legal decision, whether they concern abortion, hairstyles, or trans kids, transforms how groups perceive their position and relative worth in society—whether their dignity is being honored. This dimension of identity is intrinsic to the political process and policy experts should be systematically trained to think about the implications of laws and policies for recognition.

While new narratives are necessary for cultural change, they cannot be successful on their own. We all have to be carriers, just as change agents, Gen Z, knowledge workers, social movement participants, and various institutional sectors already play this role.

The time for considering alternatives is right now. The solutions I have discussed can be practices at the individual, group, and the national level—embracing several criteria of worth, ordinary universalism, and stigma reduction, combined with the use of the law and institutions to promote changes, including narrative changes. They are an essential complement to the many efforts of civic action and imagination that already animate many neighborhoods and communities.

While the vision offered here may be too idealist for some, we have to remember that ideals have moved the world many times before. Much of what defines our reality today could not be imagined a few decades ago. It is with this in mind that we must continue to work toward the future we want to foster. Defining what is possible too narrowly will irremediably reduce our universe of alternatives. Much will depend on how urgently we perceive the need to develop new collective orientations.

CONCLUSION

STRENGTHENING OUR CAPACITY TO LIVE BETTER TOGETHER

In 2004, Massachusetts became the first US state to legalize same-sex marriage—but it was only eleven years later, in 2015, that the practice became legal nationwide. This was accomplished through a range of different tactics, including ballot referenda, laws passed by state legislatures, and court rulings—including the Supreme Court's ruling in *Obergefell v. Hodges.* But none of this would have happened but for the herculean efforts of countless activists and ordinary people who joined forces to realize their shared vision of justice and fairness. These people were fighting to create the type of society they hoped to live in. In many cases, they were inspired or guided by change agents, who created the narratives that showed us all that another world was possible. Their success demonstrates that significant changes are possible, and it also shows the way for broadening recognition to other marginalized groups.

This book is for people—of all ages—who are wondering what lies ahead, how to move forward, and what kind of society our children will inherit. It is written to help all of us think through the last several decades and the current moment. It is about where to find the glimmers of hope for the road ahead, and what we can do to feed the type of society we are yearning for. This is particularly crucial after decades of growing inequality and a pandemic.

While millennials and Gen Z are often dismissive of boomers, they are walking in the footsteps of a generation that led the Civil Rights Movement and the second-wave feminist movement, the effects of which are still being felt to this day. Even if younger generations are dissatisfied with what they perceive as their elders' complacency about the destruction of the environment, I can think of many political points of intergenerational convergence that can be built upon and expanded further.

Like these young people, I believe that individuals can make a difference, as I did in my youth. But what I hope I have communicated with this book is the crucial role of narratives in enabling us to do so. Narratives orient and magnify the consequences of our actions. They can operate as scaffolding that strengthens our impact. They are a condition for our social resilience. Ultimately, they strengthen our capacity to create the world we wish to live in.

Hope has clear implications for social change. Anthropologist Arjun Appadurai says that hope is tied to our "capacity to aspire," to project ourselves into the future as a citizen, creator, professional, parent, partner, worker, earner, and more. Unlike optimism, hope is not an expression of our temperament, but a plan for the future. That plan is shaped by narratives, which can help us overcome challenges in our lives and open new possibilities.

Of course, hopes and dreams are not the same: Dreams (like the American dream) are typically not anchored in what is possible. In contrast, hope is a projection from one's current state, constrained by feasibility. Still, as the economist Albert Hirschman argued, being too tied to what is probable can curtail one's "horizons of possibility." Because there is so much we cannot predict, we must work constantly to keep our minds open to unexpected possibilities.

Hope can animate any number of life-changing decisions. The decision to migrate, for instance, is motivated in most cases by a hopeful sense of what the future will hold once one "gets there." Even the decision to partner with someone for life is a leap of faith, as is the decision to procreate. One's basic notions about agency (are individuals masters of their fate? Or simply lucky or unlucky?) can also affect our social trajectories and contribute to shaping experiences of inequality.

The election of Donald Trump in 2016 reminded many of us that the long "arc of the moral universe" that Martin Luther King Jr. and Barack Obama spoke of should not be taken for granted. Progress can easily be reversed, and patterns of backlash can be dramatic. In recent years, we have seen renewed threats to LGBTQ+ rights, immigrants' rights, and reproductive rights—including the stunning overturning of the Supreme Court's 1973 decision in *Roe v. Wade*. Surely, this is not the last time we will face backlashes, but the future is unwritten and we need to be active in shaping it.

We engineer our world together by mobilizing narratives that expand recognition about who is worthy. As today's younger generations teach us, the choices we make, how we vote with our feet every day, matter. A more inclusive society is within our reach, but making it a reality means being the change we envision for our world.

Why is living in more diverse circles going to make a difference? Recent research has shown that when a privileged student has a college roommate from a less-privileged background, it has a significant impact on their understanding of inequality. This exposure can help a privileged person understand the challenges that come with not having class privilege, and to revise meritocratic and individualist accounts of success. Befriending someone from a low-income background makes them less likely to believe that the poor are poor because of moral failings. More generally, increasing contact between groups of different backgrounds contributes to a decline of prejudice and discrimination.

This remains one of the most effective approaches to forging connections between groups that are typically isolated from one another. Inclusion isn't just a platitude that powerful people promote to be politically correct, or to feather their own nest. Affirmative action, corporate employee resource groups, and related practices can be effective only if integration occurs at a social level. That requires all of us to take ownership of the problem. This broad embrace has everything to do with social resilience—instead of celebrating individual grit as a virtue, let's create institutions and cultural scripts that can act as support to normalizing inclusion and fostering solidarity.

For middle-class white people, for instance, this might mean supporting local school desegregation efforts. White parents can decide to move to more racially diverse neighborhoods and send their children to schools with more racially diverse populations, which encourages friendships across racial lines and helps young people prepare to participate in a more inclusive society.

For the many working-class white people who value "treating people as people" and extending respect to everyone, this may mean increasing their exposure to those they perceive as unlike themselves and living up to these principles more fully—and this holds for middle-class people as well. For everyone, these collectivist attitudes should be applied not only to those who are already familiar, but also to those who may be less familiar.

We should remember, too, that it is worth trying to understand even people we may strongly disagree with. White working-class people who support populist conservative politicians are also seeking recognition. Liberals, progressives, and even anti-racists need to consider how to connect with them. By reframing these groups as people in search of dignity and respect, it may be possible to develop a constructive dialogue that can contribute to mending our flailing democracy. While some methods they use to seek dignity are abhorrent, we can still recognize that their search for a scapegoat stems from struggles with their loss of a sense of worth and precarity. The Democratic Party could make significant gains by regaining working-class voters with not only redistributive policies, but also with messages of solidarity and dignity, as an alternative to the Republican Party's populist messages of division and blame. Redirecting working-class anger toward the one percent is more likely to sustain fruitful alliances than driving wedges between diverse categories of workers who have so much in common.

Middle-class white people need to recognize our own role in reproducing stigmas, not only by keeping low-income people and other marginalized groups at bay, but also through opportunity hoarding. White people need to develop understanding and emotional intelligence in order to go beyond conditioned "white fragility." Many avoid conversations about race and live in fear of being accused of racism. This avoidance, euphemistically called "color-blindness," perpetuates harms against people of color by ignoring each group's unique challenges.

Future generations matter as well: what we tell our kids about the value of diversity shapes their perceptions of the environment from an early age. We are responsible for the kind of world we inspire them to work toward. We need to learn to connect with a wide range of people by desegregating our own social circles, neighborhoods, schools, workplaces, and more.

Baby boomers and Gen Xers need to cross generational divides. In particular, they should do more to prioritize environmentalism, as pollution and climate change are already harming younger people's hopes for their future. Some younger people feel they cannot ethically plan to have children when sustainability remains a low priority for governments, companies, and many older citizens. Building greater awareness of such issues is essential to bridging generational tensions.

Expanding worth to stigmatized groups does not require deep understanding. But it does require a willingness to support other groups when they seek recognition. Learning to think in these terms may not bring about rapid or radical change. But I wager that having the language to think about these options can help us envision a world where more people feel valued. What do we have to lose?

Some countries, such as Germany, have put in place "civic education" high school curricula to teach children the art of communal living in a multicultural environment. In Massachusetts, where I live, civic education is largely focused on learning about government, voting, local associations, volunteering, and human rights. American schools can do more to teach multicultural values as American values—which will mean going beyond efforts that are limited to a specific time period, like Black History Month or Latinx Heritage Month. We have to invent other paths for becoming an inclusive society. All our cultural institutions must take the lead in spreading narratives about linked fates and our collective responsibilities. Significant efforts are already being made in this direction.

In the workplace, diversity trainings and supposedly inclusive hiring practices have often had disappointing results. Research on what helps increase diversity in organizations tells us that mentoring, teaching by example, providing support when needed, and making managers responsible for diversifying the workforce will help much more than one-off or intermittent diversity trainings.

When it comes to solutions, we saw that today's marketplace of ideas—self-reliance, personal efficacy, and willpower—are grossly inadequate to meet the challenges we face. We are told that it is our responsibility, and ours alone, to look deep within ourselves, into our own psyche, to find "grit"—the internal strength and resilience needed for individuals to act upon the world through sheer determination. This goes hand in hand with a fashionable focus on the trends of mindfulness, positive psychology, and other "quick fixes." This focus on individual solutions is at odds with a broader understanding of the dynamics that drive the problems we aim to address. In contrast, the solutions that I propose generate change by creating and diffusing new narratives—by organizing our environment differently.

This book's solutions are also at odds with currently trendy ideas about "tribalism," which assume that humans have a permanent and innate tendency to hoard resources in favor of our ingroup members. But political polarization is driven by much more than what happens in our heads. It is influenced by outside factors such as high levels of unemployment, economic competition, and economic inequality, as well as by electoral rules.

I prefer to think that our sense of community waxes and wanes across different times and contexts. We may feel differently depending on how much weight we put on our shared identity as members of a given group, how often group members interact, and how tight our bonds are. These dimensions influence how much "groupness" a group experiences, and whether they define themselves in opposition to other groups. In arguing that humans have an inherent instinct to protect ingroups, proponents of "tribalism" downplay the many social factors that drive this groupness. We need a broader approach to make sense of what is going on and to understand how boundaries between groups can change.

Some members of dominant groups can view the recognition of subordinate groups as an indication of their own group's demise. In response, some redouble their efforts to ensure that their own group remains dominant. While President Barack Obama's election was a prominent victory in African Americans' fight for recognition, many white people perceived his presidency as a threat to their group. Later, many white voters acted on their resentment by electing Donald Trump.

This has implications for how we go about promoting solidarity and fighting discrimination. A lot of corporations and universities put their faith in making people aware of their unconscious or implicit biases, as if awareness would reduce bias. But biases are developed over a lifetime and don't easily adapt to awareness. Instead, we should be reducing stigma, by transforming the lenses through which groups are perceived.

In order to feed solidarity, advocates need to promote narratives that extend equal worth to marginalized groups, including by promoting diverse networks. This makes fostering inclusion less dependent on random acts of kindness and empathy. Instead, by making narratives of inclusion widely available, advocates can ensure that diversity is baked into our society's shared background assumptions. Cuing can help, but it is a limited solution.

While this book is largely concerned with the United States, understanding the value of recognition and dignity is equally important around the world. Indeed, other countries have their own versions of the American dream. For many people emigrating from the Middle East, Asia, and Africa, the European dream offers the promise of a better life. Chinese president Xi Jinping, meanwhile, has promoted a distinctive and popular "China dream," which emphasizes the possibilities of economic upward mobility.

Some of the US's problems are also present in other societies. Many have also seen skyrocketing income inequality and experienced a decline in upward mobility. Everywhere, young people have faced setbacks and are mobilizing politically to fight for their futures. At the same time, unsurprisingly, the suicide rate in several strongly neoliberal countries (Australia, Canada, the UK, and the US) has increased, particularly among young people. This may be connected to a greater feeling of isolation which is fed by individualism.

America's reckoning for racial justice inspired progressive movements elsewhere: after the massive Black Lives Matter mobilizations in the summer of 2020, similar movements proliferated in Europe, Asia, and beyond. Countries such as France, which had been reluctant to deal with domestic anti-Black racism, are now addressing it like never before. Other groups are now mobilizing more visibly and intensely, including First Nations in Canada, Indigenous people in Latin America, the Roma in Europe, and women in Iran. As such groups gain visibility, others around the world feel more empowered to expand recognition. For instance, Asians in France launched an anti–Asian hate hashtag campaign

"#jenesuispasunvirus" ("I am not a virus"). Still, many young people are feeding the base of right-wing movements in Germany, Poland, and other countries.

Even though circumstances are different in every country and region, some solutions I have identified still apply. Many wealthy countries face persistent challenges with xenophobia and racism, and with integrating immigrants and refugees. Challenges to democracy are also becoming even more threatening around the world, as nationalists are gaining influence on both sides of the Atlantic.

While many Americans believe they live in the best country, we must remember that, as of 2020, one is better off living in twenty-eight other advanced industrial countries than the United States, if one considers personal safety, health and wellness, environmental quality, personal freedom, and choice. There is much work to be done. To sustain hope, let's remember that much has changed in the last decades and many more changes are ahead.

Reimagining the kind of society we want to live in is necessary, and change agents and young people we talked to help all of us see what alternative narratives might look like—what new models and ideas are emerging. They tell us that a focus on recognition should be at the center of how we think about the future moving forward.

Fortunately, divisions are not fixed. Much is within our power as we consider how to organize our daily lives, including deciding where we send our kids to schools and in which neighborhoods we live. We can all feed or fight social and spatial segregation, that is, create more opportunities for contacts between groups as we make decisions about our daily lives.

Again, we must remember that dignity is no luxury. Rather, it has a direct impact on well-being. This is why recognition needs to be factored explicitly into lawmakers' thinking as they advocate on behalf of their communities. This is also why citizens need to produce a society with stronger bonds of solidarity. Everyone will win from such a shift. The downwardly mobile working class is in search of respect just as much as ethno-racial and religious minorities and LGBTQ+ groups. These common needs must be recognized by all; many can claim dignity at once, even if their suffering is greater than others'. Bringing together the struggles of these groups is perhaps the most essential step for healing our divided world. More change is possible—and indeed necessary—as attitudes toward marginalized groups have continued to change over the last decades. The same cannot be said about attitudes toward the working class, who are often perceived as the losers of the system. Their horizons of possibilities have drastically narrowed over the last decades, as their wages have declined, together with their sense of worth. Trump provided an empowering narrative for these people, but liberals and progressives have largely failed to counter that narrative. Explicitly acknowledging how workers are penalized by the cultural dominance of the upper-middle class, instead of indulging in self-congratulatory smugness and class ethnocentrism, would be a first step.

Over the course of this book, I have sketched various strategies for extending dignity and recognition to all groups, broadening our definitions of worth, celebrating our common humanity, and reducing stigma. People must think about how their own search for recognition will contribute to shaping the life they want and allow them and those they love to flourish. With this in mind, perhaps we can all live better together.

ACKNOWLEDGMENTS

I have been studying how people define their worth and that of others for almost forty years, and I've shared my findings in my books *Money, Morals, and Manners*, *The Dignity of Working Men*, *How Professors Think*, and *Getting Respect* (coauthored). As these titles suggest, these academic books are about what people value, whom they choose to respect, and how they fight for their own dignity. They also concern how people draw boundaries and contribute to segregation and inequality. This new book, *Seeing Others*, is the culmination of this research agenda. It is an attempt to make sense of it all and to bring my perspective to a wider audience. I hope the book will prove useful as we all work to find meaningful paths forward.

Seeing Others would not have become a reality without a generous two-year fellowship from the Andrew Carnegie Foundation, a yearlong residential fellowship from the Russell Sage Foundation, and grants from the Harvard University Faculty of Arts and Science, the Weatherhead Center for International Affairs at Harvard University, and the GlobalMentalHealth@Harvard Initiative, a joint effort of the Harvard Medical School, Harvard T. H. Chan School of Public Health, and the Harvard Global Health Institute. The support of such organizations makes research possible.

Equally crucial were those whose words and thoughts are at the center of this book, both the "change agents" who agreed to be interviewed for this project, as well as the American college students who welcomed an invitation to participate in the study. Words do not suffice to express my gratitude that they agreed to participate in the study in the midst of the pandemic.

But many other people have accompanied me on the road that has led to this book, from its early conception, to the conducting and coding of interviews during the peak of the pandemic, to the challenging process of learning to write for a wide audience.

In 2014 one of the most seminal contemporary philosophers writing on the topic of recognition, Axel Honneth, invited me to deliver the annual Adorno Lectures at Institut für Sozialforschung, in Frankfurt, Germany. This was a first opportunity to draw connections between my writings on worth, dignity, and respect to recognition conceived as a cultural process. Although I never published these three lectures, they led to my 2016 Presidential Address to the American Sociological Association delivered a few months before the election of Donald Trump. "Addressing Recognition Gap: Destigmatization and the Reduction of Inequality" was the first iteration of the argument that is more fully developed in *Seeing Others*. It also led to my 2017 Erasmus Prize essay "Prisms of Inequality: Moral Boundaries, Exclusion, and Academic Evaluation." This was followed by another pivotal invitation from the leading British sociologist of inequality, Mike Savage, who asked me to give the 2018 *British Journal of Sociology* (*BJS*) lecture at the London School of Economics titled "From Having to Being: Self-Worth and the Current Crisis of American Society." This lecture expanded on both the Presidential Address and the Erasmus essay. I am grateful to Axel and Mike for these invitations, as well as to the colleagues who published thoughtful essays responding to this *BJS* lecture, which inspired its further development: Andrew Cherlin (Johns Hopkins University), Margaret Frye (University of Michigan), Eva Illouz (Hebrew University), Giselinde Kuipers (KU Leuven), Adia Wingfield (Washington University in St. Louis), as well as Mike Savage himself.

While working on this book, I benefited from the research assistance of several exceptionally capable graduate students and collaborators, particularly Nicole Letourneau, Derek Robey, Mari Sanchez, and Shira Zilberstein, who played a crucial role in recruiting respondents and conducting and coding interviews with change agents and students. This book would not exist without them. We developed together papers that are the basis for sections on how change agents and college students produce social change. Other graduate and undergraduate research assistants who contributed to the data collection and analysis include Laura Adler, Elena Ayala-Hurtado, Stefan Beljean, Adrienne Chan, Johnny Cook, Nino Cricco, Maleah Fekete, and Priya Thelapurath. I thank the Harvard students who contributed terrific comments on the manuscript: Victoria Ashbury, Elena Ayala-Hurtado, Adrienne Chan, Johnny Cook, Derek Robey, Mari Sanchez, Priya Thelapurath, and Shira Zilberstein, as well as former students Laura Adler (Yale University), Nina Ghcihman (University of California, Berkeley), and Bo Yun Park (University of Richmond). Finally, I benefited from exceptional staff and administrative support from Lisa Albert in the Department of Sociology and Kathleen Hoover in the Weatherhead Center for International Affairs.

My thinking was also influenced by the members of the program Successful Societies of the Canadian Institute for Advanced Research, an organization that generously supported my work for eighteen years. This band of loyal friends and colleagues had a big impact on my thinking and influenced the argument developed here. I thank in particular Gérard Bouchard (Université du Québec a Chicoutimi), Wendy Espeland (Northwestern University), Peter Gourevitch (University of California, San Diego), David Grusky (Stanford University), Peter Hall (Harvard University), Patrick Le Galès (Science Po), Hazel Markus (Stanford University), Paul Pierson (University of California, Berkeley), Biju Rao (World Bank), Francesca Polletta (University of California, Irvine), William Sewell Jr. (University of Chicago), Anne E. Wilson (Wilfrid Laurier University), as well as other early program members, James Dunn (McMaster University), Ron Levi (University of Toronto) and Ann Swidler (University of California, Berkeley). Other program members Irene Bloemraad, Leanne Son Hing, and Will Kymlicka also influenced my thinking as we coauthored a 2019 *Daedalus* paper that shaped chapter 2 of *Seeing Others*.

My terrific collaborators from the *Getting Respect* team were also on my mind as I developed my argument, which is informed in many ways by our shared understanding of experiences of groupness, stigmatization, and discrimination in the United States, Brazil, and Israel: Joshua Guetzkow (Hebrew University), Hannah Herzog and Nissim Mizrachi (Tel Aviv University), Elisa Reis (Federal University Rio), Graziella Moraes Silva (Graduate Institute for International and Development Studies), and Jessica Welburn (Rand Corporation).

The following colleagues and friends took time to comment on chapters of the book or on the book as a whole. I am deeply indebted to them for their generosity, especially given that they are all way too busy. They include Suzanne Berger (MIT), Bart Bonikowski (New York University), Clayton Childress (University of Toronto), Matthew Clair (Stanford University), Frank Dobbin (Harvard University), Shai Dromi (Harvard University), Jan Willem Duyvendak (University of Amsterdam), Wendy Espeland (Northwestern University), Lisa Glazer (Pine Street Inn), Mary Ann

Glynn (Boston College), Peter Hall (Harvard University), James Jasper (CUNY Graduate Center), Paul Lichterman (University of Southern California), Cathie Jo Martin (Boston University), Jonathan Mijs (Boston University), Michelle Nicholasen (Harvard University), Helga Nowotny (University of Vienna), Francesca Polletta (University of California, Irvine), Leah Price (Rutgers University), Violaine Roussel (Université de Paris 8), Abigail Saguy (UCLA), Mike Savage (London School of Economics), Amelia Thelen, and Natasha Warikoo (Tufts University).

At Harvard, I received inspiration from many friends, colleagues, and students from the departments of sociology and African and African American Studies, the Weatherhead Center for International Affairs, and the Center for European Studies. I benefited from exchanges with colleagues from other departments such as political scientists Jennifer Hochschild, Michael Sandel, and Brandon Terry; experts of mental health such as Arthur Kleinman, Laura Kubzanski, Cindy Liu, and Vikram Patel; education experts such as Anthony Jacks and Jal Mehta; and many more. But I want to single out members of the research cluster on Comparative Inequality and Inclusion at the Weatherhead Center for International Affairs who helped me think about stigma, recognition, dignity, respect, status, solidarity, unsettled times, and social resilience over the last few years through their own work on the transformation of boundaries toward immigrant and refugees, low-income groups, ethnoracial, religious, national, and sexual minorities, and more—in particular Lorenza Antonucci (University of Birmingham), Cetin Celik (Koç University), Poulami Chakrabarti (Queens University), Yuval Feinstein (University of Haifa), Jason Ferguson (Harvard Society of Fellows and University of California, Los Angeles), Lorenza Fontana (University of Glasgow), Kobe De Koere (University of Amsterdam), Matthias Koenig (University of Heidelberg), Ron

Levi (University of Toronto), Arturo Rodriguez Morató (University of Barcelona), Sandra Portocarrero (Columbia University), Kristina Bakkaer Simonsen (Arhuus University), Anna Skarpelis (Wissenschaft Zentrum Berlin), Ioana Sendroiu (University of Hong Kong), Talia Schiff (Tel Aviv University), Cécile Van de Velde (Université de Montréal), Thijs van Dooremalen (KU Leuven), Gökce Yurdakul (Humbolt University), Kate Williams (University of Melbourne), and Elke Winter (University of Ottawa).

Students in my undergraduate course "Culture and Inclusion in a Divided America," which I taught at Harvard in the spring of 2022, were a useful sounding board as I was finishing the book. Their insights and experiences helped me sharpen arguments and anticipate objections.

In addition to those mentioned above, a number of friends and colleagues were useful interlocutors as I developed the book. Some helped me identify and reach out to interviewees across multiple milieux. At the risk of forgetting someone, I want to thank Nancy Ammerman (Boston University), Chris Bail (Duke University), Julie Battilana (Harvard University), Sheri Berman (Barnard College), Amy Binder (University of California, San Diego), Luc Boltanski (Ecole des Hautes Etudes en Sciences Sociales), danah boyd (New York University), Robert Boynton (New York University), Xavier de Souza Briggs (Brookings Institute), Angèle Christin (Stanford), Pedro Conceição (United Nations Human Development Programme), Shelley Correll (Stanford University), David Craig (University of Southern California), Dana Fischer (University of Maryland), Marshall Ganz (Harvard University), Doug Hartmann (University of Minnesota), Diane Isenberg (Ceniarth), Riva Kastoryano (Sciences-Po), Shamus Khan (Princeton University), Giselinde Kuipers (KU Leuven), Nicholas Lemann (Columbia University),

Ya-Wen Lei (Harvard University), Sarah Lewis (Harvard University), Jane Mansbridge (Harvard University), Reece Peck (College of Staten Island), Walter Powell (Stanford University), Andrea Press (University of Virginia), Cecilia Ridgeway (Stanford University), Michael Schudson (Columbia University), Rachel Sherman (New School), Iddo Tavory (New York University), Dorian Warren (Center for Community Change), and Andreas Wimmer (Columbia University).

My desire to communicate to readers beyond the academy became more urgent during the Trump years. Margo Beth Fleming at the Brockman Agency persuaded me that I should and could write a trade book and that now was the time. She encouraged me through thick and thin. Through our regular exchanges around shared interests ranging from stand-up comics to our intimate friends, our Peloton coaches, she became a trusted sounding board, for which I am so grateful.

At Atria/One Signal Publishers, an imprint of Simon & Schuster, Julia Cheiffetz and early on, Nicholas Ciani, helped me develop my argument and improve it in most significant ways. I also thank the whole Atria team for their engagement with the project. I benefited from the uber-competent editorial work of Connor Guy and Emi Ikkanda.

I also want to acknowledge the crucial support of my siblings Vincent and Natalie, as well as that of several close friends (near and far) who contributed to my sanity during the isolation of the pandemic years and/or much needed post-COVID adventurous and fun trips—Ben Schneider, Kathleenn Thelen, Michael Pekowski, Lisa Glaser, Diane Isenberg, Cathie Jo Martin, Jim Milkey, Susan Eckstein, Paul Osterman, James Jasper, Sarah Rosenfield, Bruce Carruthers, Wendy Espeland, Neil Fligstein, Heather Haverman,

Liz Cohen, Herrick Chapman, Jenny Mansbridge, Sandy Jencks, Riva Kastoryano, as well as others I stayed connected with via Zoom or other means—you know who you are.

Last but not least, this book would not exist without the engagement, entertainment, steady presence, and affection of my terrific family (and our pandemic she-dog Youpi/Max/Poupi). The project benefited from conversations with and feedback from my adult children Gabrielle and Pierre, as well as Chloe who commented on the manuscript. I also want to thank my partner in crime, husband and sociologist extraordinaire Frank Dobbin, whose own deadlines, interest, love, and support were crucial in helping me complete this project.

Finally, the book is dedicated to Pierre and Chloe, because their own life experiences and hopes made me want to write this book, for them and for their friends, in celebration of their collective future. And because it is their turn and because I love them so very much.

APPENDIX A: CHANGE AGENTS

My research team and I conducted interviews with 185 change agents over roughly eighteen months. We sampled for breadth and diversity, with the goal to identify a wide range of people who could best inform us on the various facets of the contemporary public sphere. Only three interviewees requested anonymity as a condition for participating in the research project.

With the goal of identifying change agents with a relatively high level of cultural influence, my assistants and I used various networks to gain entry into some fields. We also asked respondents for referrals. We reached far and deep to capture various segments of this world that do not overlap with our networks. But we also asked friends, colleagues, and acquaintances working in various milieux to help us identify potential interviewees and facilitate contacts. While political orientation was not a criteria of eligibility for the study, many turned out to be liberal or progressive. Due to time and resource limitations, the sample is not comprehensive. For instance, we did not conduct interviews with change agents working in the fields of fashion or gastronomy.

The overall sample includes seventy-five interviews with individuals working in comedy and entertainment. In many cases, their content is viewed by millions, giving them unique influence over public discourse. These interviews were conducted to gain a more detailed understanding of the recognition strategies used in these professional fields, which produce particularly rich narratives concerning the representation of various groups. These respondents include current showrunners, producers, directors, actors, and staff writers, with the majority having worked in multiple roles during their careers. For the purposes of this study, we categorized them based on their primary role in the creation of the TV series or film of interest (see Appendix A).

The research assistants for this part of the project, Nicole Letourneau and Derek Robey, contacted the entertainers through public relations representatives, managers, agents, and personal contact information, when available. As response rates in this group were low, recruitment criteria were expanded to include comics featured on the Netflix comedy series *The Standups.* This portion of the sample consists of popular stand-up comics, comedy writers (for scripted television, late-night television, or movies), and improvisational comics. We used snowball sampling to increase the diversity and breadth of our sample until we reached saturation.

Nicole Letourneau and Derek Robey conducted the bulk of the interviews with this group and coded the data. We coauthored a few papers which inform the section of chapter 5 that concern the strategies of destigmatization used by entertainment workers. They took the lead with these papers.

Data collection took place between March 2020 and March 2021. The context of the pandemic facilitated reaching out to influential change agents who may not have given us time under normal circumstances. It also influenced what we heard since it is quite possible that this common existential and health trauma made many respondents worry about the quality of our collective life and where we are heading as a society. But then, most contexts have peculiarities and it is difficult to speculate about what we would have learned from interviews conducted under different circumstances.

Interviews were typically conducted via video calls on Zoom or via telephone. But for one exception, they were audio recorded and transcribed. The interviews covered topics such as: 1) professional life; 2) social and cultural contributions and audiences; 3) American society and social change; and 4) identity and biography. Participants were asked questions pertaining to how they conceive of their work and its impact, objectives and motivations when creating their work, achievements and failures, and perceptions of others in their industry. They were asked about methods through which they reach their audience, social messages in their work, and changes in their field. They were also asked to reflect on contemporary American society, the American dream, and its challenges. Finally, they were asked to reflect on themselves in terms of identity, family background, and assessment of themselves compared to others. The interview schedule is available upon request.

Using NVivo, research assistants coded the original interview transcripts after inductively developing a coding key based on a subset of interviews. These codes capture the main challenges facing American society; their professional trajectory; professional goals and contributions; professional challenges, views of the future, and so forth. Ten percent of the interviews have been double-coded for intercoder reliability. Only minor discrepancies were found. They were discussed and adjustments were made.

APPENDIX A

Change Agents Interviews

Category	Interviewee	Organization/Affiliation
Academia		
	Chignell, Andrew	Princeton University
	Craig, David	University of Southern California
	Gates, Henry Louis	Harvard University
	Lewis, Sarah	Harvard University
	West, Cornel	Union Theological Seminary
Advertising		
	Eng, Katie	PACO Collective
	Garrido, Maria	Havas Group, Vivendi
	Weiner, Jessica	Talk to Jess
Art and Creation		
	Diaz, Natalie	Poet
	Ewing, Eve L.	Poet, University of Chicago, Marvel
	Harris, Lyle Ashton	Photographer, New York University
	Ludwig, Justine	Creative Time
	Opie, Catherine	Photographer, UCLA
	Steinman, Megan	The Underground Museum
	Willis Thomas, Hank	Photographer
	Willis, Deborah	Curator and photographer, New York University
Climate Justice		
	Blackford, Loren	Sierra Club
	Eder, Katie	Future Coalition, March For Our Lives
	Goldtooth, Dallas	Indigenous Environmental Network
	Gunn-Wright, Rhiana	Green New Deal/Roosevelt Institute
	McKibben, Bill	365.org
	Noisecat, Julian Brave	Indigenous movements, Green New Deal
	Rabb, Nick	Sunrise Movement
	Rathor, Skeena	Extinction Rebellion, UK
Community Organizing		
	Buchman, Ellen	The Opportunity Agenda
	Ganz, Marshall	Kennedy School of Government, Harvard University
	Gomez, Alejandra	LUCHA (Arizona)

Category	Interviewee	Organization/Affiliation
Community Organizing (cont.)		
	Han, Hahrie	Democracy Center, Johns Hopkins
	Kunreuther, Frances	Building Movement Project
	Reyes, Arturo	We the People (Michigan)
	Spillane, Ashley	Rock the Vote
Corporate Sector		
	Brown, Tim	Allbirds
	Culmone, Kim	Mattel
	Dreger, Monica	Mattel
	Gelobter, Lisa	tEQuitable
	Jepsen, Mary Lou	Openwater
	Kennedy, Molly	Dove
	Price, Mandy	Kanarys
	Smith, Elise	Praxis Labs VR
Feminism/Gender		
	Crenshaw, Kimberlé	Columbia Law School
	Gay, Roxane	Author
	Sarsour, Linda	Women's March, Arab American Association
	Stimpson, Catharine	New York University
Hollywood		
	Berk, Bobby	*Queer Eye*
	Bloom, Rachel	*Crazy Ex-Girlfriend*
	Brown, Karamo	*Queer Eye*
	Cappiello, Heather	*Madam Secretary*
	Chaiken, Ilene	*The L Word*
	Chavkin, Rachel	*Hadestown*
	Cole, Joe Robert	*Black Panther*
	Cooper, Akela	*Luke Cage, The 100*
	Daniels, Lee	*Empire*
	Di Nonno, Madeline	Geena Davis Institute
	Drucker, Zackary	*Transparent*
	Dungey, Channing	Netflix, Warner Brothers
	Evans, Bridgit Antoinette	Pop Culture Collaborative
	Feldman, Liz	*Dead to Me*

Category	Interviewee	Organization/Affiliation
Hollywood (cont.)		
	Fogelman, Dan	*This Is Us*
	Gamble, Sera	*You, The Magicians*
	Hader, Bill	*Barry*
	Jefferson, Cord	*Watchmen, Succession, The Good Place*
	Kang, Angela	*The Walking Dead*
	Karolinski, Alexa	*Unorthodox*
	Calderón Kellett, Gloria	*One Day at a Time*
	King, Michelle	*The Good Wife*
	King, Robert	*The Good Wife*
	Konner, Jenni	*Girls*
	Leonard, Franklin	*The Black List*
	McDougal Jones, Naomi	writer, producer
	Messer, Erica	*Criminal Minds, Charmed*
	Miller, Bruce	*The Handmaid's Tale*
	Noblezada, Eva	*Yellow Rose, Hadestown*
	Nunn, Laurie	*Sex Education*
	Plec, Julie	*The Vampire Diaries*
	Rodriguez, Dailyn	*Queen of the South*
	Saracho, Tanya	*Vida*
	Schur, Michael	*The Office, Parks and Recreation*
	Soloway, Joey	*Transparent*
	Starrbury, Michael	*When They See Us*
	Strong, Danny	*Empire*
	Swafford, Erika Green	*How to Get Away with Murder, New Amsterdam*
	Tigelaar, Liz	*Little Fires Everywhere, Once Upon a Time*
	Tramble Spellman, Nichelle	*Truth Be Told*
	Urman, Jennie Snyder	*Jane the Virgin*
	Wells, John	*Shameless*
	Anonymous 1	Showrunner
	Anonymous 2	Showrunner
Hollywood/Comedy		
	Alonzo, Cristela	Netflix Special: *Cristela Alonzo: Lower Classy*
	Barthwell, Ali	The Second City; *Last Week Tonight with John Oliver*

Category	Interviewee	Organization/Affiliation
Hollywood/Comedy (cont.)		
	Bell, W. Kamau	*United Shades of America*; Netflix Special: *Private School Negro*
	Brennan, Neal	Netflix Special: *Neal Brennan: 3 Mics*; *Chappelle's Show*
	Carney, Brittany	Featured on Comedy Central Stand-Up
	Cole, Deon	Netflix Special: *Deon Cole: Cole Hearted*; *Black-ish*
	Das, Vir	Netflix Special: *Losing It*; Netflix Special: *Abroad Understanding*
	Glass, Todd	Special: *Todd Glass Talks About Stuff*
	Gold, Judy	*Comedy Central Presents: Judy Gold*
	Gulman, Gary	HBO Special: *The Great Depresh*
	Jay, Kavin	Netflix Special: *Kavin Jay: Everybody Calm Down!*
	Kroll, Nick	*Kroll Show*; *Big Mouth*; Special: *Thank You Very Cool*
	List, Joe	Netflix's *The Standups*; Special: *I Hate Myself*
	Lucas, Keith	Netflix Special: *Lucas Brothers: On Drugs*
	Lucas, Kenny	Netflix Special: *Lucas Brothers: On Drugs*
	MacFarland, Kelly	Comedy Album: *I Woke Up Today*
	Mahbubani, Vivek	*Stand Up, Asia!* for Comedy Central Asia
	Mittal, Aditi	Netflix Special: *Things They Wouldn't Let Me Say*
	Morin, Brent	Netflix Special: *I'm Brent Morin*
	Nathan, Vijai	Solo Show: *Good Girls Don't, But Indian Girls Do*
	Nevins, Andrea	*Hysterical*
	Norton, Jim	Netflix Special: *A Mouthful of Shame*; *The Jim Norton Show*
	Pepitone, Eddie	Special: *For the Masses*
	Povitsky, Esther	Comedy Central Special: *Hot for My Name*; *Alone Together*
	Ryan, Katherine	Netflix Special: *Katherine Ryan: Glitter Room*
	Shlesinger, Iliza	Netflix Special: *Unveiled*; Netflix Special: *Elder Millennial*

Category	Interviewee	Organization/Affiliation
Hollywood/Comedy (cont.)		
	Sosa, Daniel	Netflix Special: *Daniel Sosa: Sosafado*
	Thurston, Baratunde	*The Daily Show*; *The Onion*
	Watts, Reggie	*Comedy Bang! Bang!*; *The Late Late Show with James Corden*; Comedy Central Special: *A Live in Central Park*
	Anonymous 2	Stand-up comic
Immigration		
	Jiménez, Cristina	United We Dream
	Vargas, Jose Antonio	Define American
Journalism/Writing		
	Filipovic, Jill	Journalist
	Hannah-Jones, Nikole	*The New York Times*
	Legro, Michelle	Gen by Medium
	Martin, Courtney	Public Speaker
Labor Journalism		
	Greenhouse, Steven	*The New York Times* Labor Journalist
Labor Organizing		
	Jayaraman, Saru	One Fair Wage
	Karvelis, Noah	RedforED
	Miller, Michelle	Coworker.org
	Poo, Ai-jen	National Domestic Workers Alliance
LGBTQA Activism		
	Dunham, Cyrus Grace	Trans activist
	Fleischer, David	LA LGBT Leadership Lab
	Vaid-Menon, Alok	Artist
	Willis, Raquel	Trans activist
New Technology		
	boyd, danah	Data & Society, New York University
	Conte, Jack	Patreon
	Kong, David	MIT Media Lab's Community Biotechnology Initiative
	Humphreys, Bonnie	Crisis Text Line

APPENDIX A

Category	Interviewee	Organization/Affiliation
New Technology (cont.)		
	Lublin, Nancy	Crisis Text Line
	Roy, Deb	MIT Media Lab
	Venkatesh, Sudhir	Columbia University, Twitter
	Zuckerman, Ethan	Center for Civic Media, Massachusetts Institute of Technology
Philanthropy/Foundation		
	Briggs, Xavier de Souza	Brookings Institution
	Hunt-Hendrix, Leah	Solidaire Network, Ways to Win
	Kleinfeld, Rachel	Carnegie Endowment for International Peace
	Pennington, Hilary	Ford Foundation
	Plough, Alonzo L.	Robert Wood Johnson Foundation
	Yang, Chi-hui	Ford Foundation
Poverty		
	McReynolds, Ami	Feeding America
	Warren, Dorian	Center for Community Change
Racial/Social Justice		
	Carruthers, Charlene	Black Youth Project
	Dove, Shawn	Campaign for Black Male Achievement
	Goff, Phillip Atiba	Yale University
	Meade, Desmond	Florida Rights Restoration Coalition
	Robinson, Rashad	Color of Change
Religion		
	Herring, Rev. Alvin	Faith in Action
	Morn, Rev. Mary Katherine	Unitarian Universalist Service Committee
	Pesner, Jonah	Religious Action Center of Reform Judaism
	Suleiman, Imam Omar	Faith Forward Dallas at Thanks-Giving Square
	Wilson-Hartgrove, Jonathan	Poor People's Campaign
Social Impact		
	Aiyer, Geeta	Boston Common Asset Management
	Bouri, Amit	GIIN
	Kassoy, Andrew	B-Lab
	Staley, Sister Barbara	Missionary Sisters of the Sacred Heart
	Whittaker, Martin	JUST Capital

APPENDIX A

Category	Interviewee	Organization/Affiliation
Social Policy		
	Boushey, Heather	Washington Center for Equitable Growth
	Exley, Zack	New Consensus, Justice Democrats
	Greenberg, Leah	Indivisible
	Levin, Ezra	Indivisible
	McElwee, Sean	Data for Progress
	Wong, Felicia	Roosevelt Institute
Socialist Revival		
	Hsiao, Andrew	Verso Books
	Huang, Beth	Democratic Socialists of America (Boston)
	Robinson, Nathan	*Current Affairs Magazine*
	Sunkara, Bhaskar	*Jacobin Magazine, The Nation*
	Anonymous	Chapo Trap House
Technology and Narrative Change		
	Allardice, Nick	Change.org
	Collings, Naureen	More in Common
	Heimans, Jeremy	Purpose
	Jenkins, Alan	Harvard Law School, The Opportunity Agenda
	Kendall-Taylor, Nat	FrameWorks Institute
	Kim, Jee	Narrative Initiative, Roosevelt Institute
	Dixon, Tim	More in Common
	Pariser, Eli	Civic Signals
	Slezak, James	Swayable
	Uhls, Yalda	Center for Scholars & Storytellers, UCLA
	Wong, Robert	Google Creative Lab

APPENDIX B: COLLEGE STUDENTS

Chapter 6 draws on original analyses presented in papers coauthored with Mari Sanchez and Shira Zilberstein, who conducted the interviews with American college students, together with Derek Robey. Produced in the context of the broader book project, these papers provide a more detailed analysis of the data, from which I draw inspiration.

Respondents were recruited using snowball sampling from multiple points of entry. To create diverse samples, the research assistants mobilized a range of contacts at public and private colleges and universities in the Midwest and the Northeast (including elite universities and community colleges). The name and place of origin of the respondents have been changed to protect confidentiality.

We do not aim to generalize findings to a larger population but to improve our understanding of the worldviews of our respondents. This is why the use of theoretical sampling focused on class is justified.

While recruiting interviewees, we did not aim to include an equal proportion of politically progressive, moderate, and conservative youth. However, our sample is somewhat politically diverse—particularly in the Midwest, reflecting the greater political diversity of this region as compared to the Northeast, which strongly leans Democratic, liberal, or progressive.

The semi-structured interviews were conducted via video calls on Zoom or via telephone. The questionnaire concerned the collective challenges respondents and American society face and how they respond to them, how much they believe they can influence what is happening now, how and where they find hope and inspiration, and what they view as their pathways for reaching their goals. We also looked into their perception of their generation and its challenges, their views on criteria of worth and belonging, and how they imagine their ideal futures.

We conducted two rounds of in-depth interviews with students, before and during COVID-19. Forty-seven of our original eighty respondents agreed to be reinterviewed in June and July 2020. This subset cannot be distinguished from the other members of the sample on any relevant dimension.

For Round One, conducted between September 2019 and February 2020, we used vignettes where we asked respondents their views on a range of young people with different leisure/work profiles (more or less ambitious, career-oriented, etc.). These averaged ninety minutes and explored respondents' self-concept, what they perceive as their expected selves, objectives, and life choices, how they understand what is possible, the challenges they face, the resources they have at their disposal, and how they imagine their future, envisage a better society, and find hope (if relevant).

Round Two interviews averaged around twenty minutes and were conducted in June and July 2020. They aimed to capture how respondents reacted in response to the increase in uncertainty generated by COVID-19 and to the recent Black Lives Matter (BLM) movement against police violence that followed the killing of George Floyd on May 25, 2020. We explore whether they frame differently their identity, objectives, perceived challenges, resources, agency, and future, compared to Round One interviews. We considered respondents' subjective resilience, that is, what students tell us they have done to address challenges and maintain hope. Both interview schedules are available upon request.

Tables A and B describe our two samples. Participants are between eighteen and twenty-three years of age. Middle-class and upper-middle-class students represent half of our interviewees in Wave 1 (forty out of eighty individuals) and Wave 2 (twenty-three out of forty-seven individuals).

In the Northeast, 54 percent of respondents have parents who are college-educated professionals, managers, or businesspeople. Twenty-three percent have semiprofessional parents with some college, and 14 percent have blue-collar/low-status white-collar parents who are not college educated. In contrast, 44 percent of the Midwest interviews have college-educated parents who are professionals, managers, or businesspeople; 13 percent have semiprofessional parents with some college; and 37 percent have blue-collar/low-status white-collar parents who are high school graduates. This represents almost three times the number of less privileged youth than in our Northeastern sample.

While we note some class and ethnic differences within the cohort, we do not conduct a systematic comparison between class or ethnic groups. Fifty-eight percent belong to racialized groups—mostly Asians and African Americans. The Midwesterners are more diverse than students from the Northeast, as are the working-class as compared to the upper-middle-class students.

Using NVivo, we coded the original interviews after inductively developing a coding key based on a subset of interviews. These codes capture 1) cultural repertoires individuals draw on to make sense of the future; 2) scripts of self; 3) views on conditions that foster social resilience as defined above. Coding involved determining whether their statements about their self-concept, challenges, and views on the future fit within each category and what repertoires their statements drew on. Ten percent of the interviews have been double-coded for intercoder reliability.

TABLE A: Northeast and Midwest College Students by Parent Education and Current Occupation*

		NORTHEAST	MIDWEST	TOTAL
Privileged	Professionals, managers, business owners (college-educated)	30	10	40
Less privileged	Semi-professionals (some college or college degree)	12	8	20
	Low status white-collar workers and blue-collar workers or single-parent households (some college or HS degree)	9	11	20
Total		51	29	80

*Twenty-one of the privileged respondents are white (14 from the Northeast and 7 from the Midwest), while only 13 of the less privileged are white (6 from the Northeast and 7 from the Midwest).

APPENDIX B

TABLE B: Northeast and Midwest College Students* Aged 18-23 by Gender, Race/Ethnicity***, and Type of Higher Education Institution Attended******

		NORTHEAST	MIDWEST	TOTAL
Gender and Ethnicity	Male White	9	7	16
	Female White	11	7	18
	Subtotal White	*20 (39%)*	*14 (48%)*	*34 (43%)*
	Male Black	8	2	10
	Female Black	3	3	6
	Male Latinx	2	5	7
	Female Latinx	3	1	4
	Male Asian	3	0	3
	Female Asian	12	4	16
	Subtotal POC	*31 (61%)*	*15 (42%)*	*46 (57%)*
Type of Higher Education Institution	Ivy-league	9	0	9 (11%)
	Private research universities (including regional institutions)	7	3	10 (13%)
	Public research universities	25	9	34 (43%)
	Liberal arts colleges and universities (including regional institutions)	10	14	24 (30%)
	Community College	0	3	3 (4%)
TOTAL		51	29	80

* Classified based on region of origin (Northeasterners come primarily from Massachusetts while Midwesterners come from Illinois, Indiana, Minnesota, and Missouri).
** Two respondents identified as non-binary.
*** Four East Coasters and two Midwesterners self-identified as biracial, but were categorized by the race/ethnicity they most identified with (Note: POC stands for "person of color").
**** Categories: 1) Ivy (e.g., Harvard, Cornell, Columbia); 2) Public research (e.g., UMass-Amherst, U of Illinois at Urbana-Champaign, U of Wisconsin at Whitewater); 3) Private research (e.g., Boston University, U of Rochester, DePaul); 4) Liberal arts college (e.g., Union, Elmhurst College, St. Mary's); 5) Community colleges (e.g., Oakton, Kankakee, Truman).

NOTES

INTRODUCTION: The Power of Recognition

1 ***Hannah-Jones's opening essay*** "The 1619 Project," *New York Times*, August 14, 2019, https://www.nytimes.com/interactive/2019/08/14/magazine/1619-america-slavery.html; *The 1619 Project: A New Origin Story* (New York: Random House Publishing Group, 2021).

2 ***With support from the Pulitzer Foundation*** Naomi Schaefer Riley, "'The 1619 Project' Enters American Classrooms," *Education Next* (blog), May 28, 2020, https://www.educationnext.org/1619-project-enters-american-classrooms-adding-new-sizzle-slavery-significant-cost/.

2 ***That same year, then-president Donald Trump*** Philip S. Gorski, Samuel L. Perry, and Jemar Tisby, *The Flag and the Cross: White Christian Nationalism and the Threat to American Democracy* (New York: Oxford University Press, 2022). Chap. 2.

2 ***conservative lawmakers attempted to bar teachers from any 1619 Project*** Adam Serwer, "The Fight Over the 1619 Project Is Not About the Facts," *The Atlantic*, December 23, 2019, https://www.theatlantic.com/ideas/archive/2019/12/historians-clash-1619-project/604093/; Naaz Modan, "What's behind the 1619 Project Controversy?," *K-12 Dive*, February 12, 2021, https://www.k12dive.com/news/whats-behind-the-1619-project-controversy/594965/.

4 ***Dignity affects quality of life*** Daniel A. Hojman and Álvaro Miranda, "Agency, Human Dignity, and Subjective Well-Being," *World Development* 101 (2018): 1–15; Matthew A. Andersson and Steven Hitlin, "Subjective Dignity and Self-Reported Health: Results from the United States before and during the Covid-19 Pandemic," *SSM - Mental Health*, May 7, 2022, 100113.

4 ***Bolstering this claim, economists recently found*** Milena Nikolova and Femke Cnossen, "What Makes Work Meaningful and Why Economists Should Care about It," IZA Institute of Labour Economics, April 2020.

5 ***Consider, for instance, the narrative of meritocracy*** Michael Sandel, *The Tyranny of Merit: What's Become of the Common Good?* (New York: Farrar, Straus and Giroux, 2020).

5 ***structural obstacles that have long held back*** Melvin Oliver and Thomas M. Shapiro, eds., *Black Wealth / White Wealth: A New Perspective on Racial Inequality* (New York: Routledge, 1995).

5 ***psychologists, governments, and policy makers*** Angela Duckworth, *Grit: The Power of Passion and Perseverance* (New York: Scribner, 2016); "Strategic National Framework on Community Resilience," Community Resilience Programme (London: UK Cabinet Office, March 2011).

5 ***But grit is not determined by individual will*** Peter A. Hall and Michèle Lamont, eds., *Social Resilience in the Neoliberal Era* (New York: Cambridge University Press, 2013).

5 ***to engage in civic life*** Eric Klinenberg, *Palaces for the People: How Social Infrastructure Can Help Fight Inequality, Polarization, and the Decline of Civic Life* (New York: Crown, 2018).

5 ***But the lines that divide us are not immutable*** Michèle Lamont et al., *Getting Respect: Responding to Stigma and Discrimination in the United States, Brazil, and Israel* (Princeton, NJ: Princeton University Press, 2016), 35–58; Richard Fletcher, Alessio Cornia, and Rasmus Nielsen, "How Polarized Are Online and Offline News Audiences? A Comparative Analysis of Twelve Countries," *International Journal of Press/Politics* 25, no. 2 (2020): 169–95; Noam Gidron, James Adams, and Will Horne, "American Affective Polarization in Comparative Perspective," *Elements in American Politics*, 2020, https://doi.org/10.1017/9781108914123.

5 ***In 1973, for instance, 90 percent*** Amy Adamczyk and Yen-Chiao Liao, "Examining Public Opinion About LGBTQ-Related Issues in the United States and Across Multiple Nations," *Annual Review of Sociology* 45, no. 1 (July 30, 2019): 401–23, https://doi.org/10.1146/annurev-soc-073018-022332.

5 ***Another study showed that*** Jacob Poushter and Nicholas Kent, "The Global Divide on Homosexuality Persists," Pew Research Center's Global Attitudes Project, June 25, 2020, https://www.pewresearch.org/global/2020/06/25/global-divide-on-homosexuality-persists/.

6 ***(DEI) initiatives has become enormously popular*** Eunmi Mun and Jiwook Jung, "Change above the Glass Ceiling: Corporate Social Responsibility and Gender Diversity in Japanese Firms," *Administrative Science Quarterly* 63, no. 2 (June 1, 2018): 409–40; Heidi Gottfried and Laura Reese, eds., *Equity in the Workplace: Gendering Workplace Policy Analysis* (Lanham, MD: Lexington Books, 2004).

6 ***But they are clearly not enough*** Frank Dobbin and Alexandra Kalev, *Getting to Diversity: Changing Workplaces for Good* (Cambridge, MA: Harvard University Press, 2022).

6 ***When I say "recognition,"*** "[Recognition is] the affirmation of positive qualities of human subjects and groups." Axel Honneth, *The I in We: Studies in the Theory of Recognition* (Cambridge, UK: Polity Press, 2014). I am referring to a vast range of criteria and contesting dimensions of worth (including

whether and how much socioeconomic status is valued). It also takes into consideration the cultural schemas that underpin definitions of worth, which are typically overlooked by social psychological approaches to status. See also Charles Taylor et al., *Multiculturalism: Examining the Politics of Recognition*, ed. Amy Gutmann (Princeton, NJ: Princeton University Press, 1994); Nancy Fraser, "Rethinking Recognition," *New Left Review* 3 (2000): 107–20.

7 ***which psychologists came to call the "Obama effect"*** Seth K. Goldman and Diana C. Mutz, "The Impact of the Obama Campaign on White Racial Attitudes," in *The Obama Effect: How the 2008 Campaign Changed White Racial Attitudes* (New York: Russell Sage Foundation, 2014), 1–14; Luis M. Rivera and E. Ashby Plant, "The Psychological Legacy of Barack Obama: The Impact of the First African-American President of the United States on Individuals' Social Cognition," *Social Cognition* 34, no. 6 (December 2016): 495–503.

7 ***something other than "social status,"*** Michael Sauder, Freda B. Lynn, and Joel Podolny, "Status: Insights from Organizational Sociology," *Annual Review of Sociology* 38 (2012): 267–83, https://www.annualreviews.org/doi/10.1146/annurev-soc-071811-145503; Cecilia L. Ridgeway, "Why Status Matters for Inequality," *American Sociological Review* 79, no. 1 (February 2014): 1–16, https://journals.sagepub.com/doi/10.1177/0003122413515997. People who study interpersonal status recognize that status often requires respect. Steven L. Blader and Siyu Yu, "Are Status and Respect Different or Two Sides of the Same Coin?," *Academy of Management Annals* 11 (2017): 800–824, https://doi.org/10.5465/annals.2015.0150.

7 ***But this is not necessarily so for the working class*** Michèle Lamont, *Money, Morals, and Manners: The Culture of the French and the American Upper-Middle Class* (Chicago: University of Chicago Press, 1992); Michèle Lamont, *The Dignity of Working Men: Morality and the Boundaries of Race, Class, and Immigration* (Cambridge, MA: Harvard University Press, 2000); Antony S. R. Manstead, "The Psychology of Social Class: How Socioeconomic Status Impacts Thought, Feelings, and Behaviour," *British Journal of Social Psychology* 57, no. 2 (April 2018): 267–91, https://doi.org/10.1111/bjso.12251; Lauren Valentino, "The Heterarchy of Occupational Status: Evidence for Diverse Logics of Prestige in the United States," *Sociological Forum* 36, no. S1 (2021): 1395–1418, https://doi.org/10.1111/socf.12762.

7 ***Having one's sense of worth affirmed.*** Hojman and Miranda, "Agency, Human Dignity, and Subjective Well-Being."

8 ***Republican Party has been more successful than the Democratic Party*** "In Changing U.S. Electorate, Race and Education Remain Stark Dividing Lines," Pew Research Center, June 2, 2020, https://www.pewresearch.org/politics/2020/06/02/in-changing-u-s-electorate-race-and-education-remain-stark-dividing-lines/.

8 ***her opponent Donald Trump*** Michèle Lamont, Bo Yun Park, and Elena Ayala-Hurtado, "Trump's Electoral Speeches and His Appeal to the American White Working Class," *British Journal of Sociology* 68, no. S1 (2017): S153–80.

8 ***the plethora of recent studies on them*** Cynthia Miller-Idriss, *Hate in the Homeland: The New Global Far Right* (Princeton, NJ: Princeton University Press, 2020); Gorski, Perry, and Tisby, *The Flag and the Cross*; Amy J. Binder and Jeffrey L. Kidder, *The Channels of Student Activism: How the Left and Right Are Winning (and Losing) in Campus Politics Today* (Chicago: University of Chicago Press, 2022); Yuval Feinstein, *Rally 'round the Flag: The Search for National Honor and Respect in Times of Crisis* (New York: Oxford University Press, 2022).

8 ***worsened during the pandemic*** Alison Brunier and Carla Drysdale, "COVID-19 Pandemic Triggers 25% Increase in Prevalence of Anxiety and Depression Worldwide," World Health Organization, March 2, 2022, https://www.who.int/news/item/02-03-2022-covid-19-pandemic-triggers-25-increase-in-prevalence-of-anxiety-and-depression-worldwide.

9 ***divert us from more pressing matters*** Francis Fukuyama, *Identity: The Demand for Dignity and the Politics of Resentment* (New York: Farrar, Straus and Giroux, 2018); Mark Lilla, *The Once and Future Liberal: After Identity Politics* (New York: Harper, 2017).

10 ***about 50 percent of Americans their age attend college*** Erin Duffin, "U.S. Higher Education Enrollment Rates, by Age Group 1970-2019," *Statista*, June 2, 2021, https://www.statista.com/statistics/236093/higher-education-enrollment-rates-by-age-group-us/.

10 ***the media often use the label "Gen Z"*** Journalists regularly refer to Gen Zs and millennials with generational labels, with references to the first group peaking in 2019 and those to the second group peaking in 2014 (according to our LexisNexis analysis). For their part, social scientists note that the label "Gen Z" was made up by the media as well as by the marketing industry and that it does not designate an actual demographic group. (Philip N. Cohen, "Generation Labels Mean Nothing. It's Time to Retire Them," *Washington Post*, July 7, 2021, https://www.washingtonpost.com/opinions/2021/07/07/generation-labels-mean-nothing-retire-them/.) Throughout the book I refer to cohorts by these labels, especially when I cite surveys that use the terms, but I do so while recognizing that we cannot distinguish between patterns that are characteristic of a time period, a cohort, or age group. This is known as the "age-cohort-period" (ACP) effect. For details, see Ethan Fosse and Christopher Winship, "Analyzing Age-Period-Cohort Data: A Review and Critique," *Annual Review of Sociology* 45, no. 1 (July 30, 2019): 467–92. This debate is beyond the scope of my book.

10 ***those born between 1997 and 2012*** Michael Dimock, "Defining Generations: Where Millennials End and Generation Z Begins," Pew Research Center, accessed June 2, 2022, https://www.pewresearch.org/fact-tank/2019/01/17/where-millennials-end-and-generation-z-begins/.

11 ***What is the point of living with purpose*** Michèle Lamont, "From 'Having' to 'Being': Self-Worth and the Current Crisis of American Society," *British Journal of Sociology* 70, no. 3 (June 2019): 660–707.

13 ***correlated with a rapid decline in the number of attempted suicides*** Julia Raifman et al., "Difference-in-Differences Analysis of the Association between State Same-Sex Marriage Policies and Adolescent Suicide Attempts," *JAMA Pediatrics* 171, no. 4 (2017): 350–56.

13 ***the American Supreme Court's June 2022 decision*** Nina Totenberg and Sarah McCammon, "Supreme Court Overturns Roe v. Wade, Ending Right to Abortion Upheld for Decades," NPR, June 24, 2022, https://www.npr.org/2022/06/24/1102305878/supreme-court-abortion-roe-v-wade-decision-overturn.

13 ***have been threatened by conservative lawmakers*** "Legislation Affecting LGBTQ Rights Across the Country," American Civil Liberties Union, October 7, 2022, https://www.aclu.org/legislation-affecting-lgbtq-rights-across-country.

13 ***Backlashes like these may slow down social progress*** Yasemin Nuhoglu Soysal, *Limits of Citizenship: Migrants and Postnational Membership in Europe* (Chicago: University of Chicago Press, 1994); John W. Meyer, Patricia Bromley, and Francisco O. Ramirez, "Human Rights in Social Science Textbooks: Cross-National Analyses, 1970–2008," *Sociology of Education* 83, no. 2 (2010): 111–34.

16 ***those who condemn so-called identity politics*** Lilla, *The Once and Future Liberal.*

17 ***feel like an "outsider within"*** Patricia Hill Collins, "Learning from the Outsider Within: The Sociological Significance of Black Feminist Thought," *Social Problems* 33, no. 6 (1986): s14–32, https://doi.org/10.2307/800672.

19 ***lenses through which stigmatized groups are perceived have changed*** In 2000, the Netherlands was the first country to fully recognize same-sex marriage, and as of 2017, twenty-nine countries adopted the provision. Poushter and Kent, "The Global Divide on Homosexuality Persists."

Chapter 1: THE VIEW FROM ABOVE: The Upper-Middle Class and the Failures of the American Dream

22 ***Lower-income families*** Juliana M. Horowitz, Ruth Igielnik, and Rakesh Kochhar, "Most Americans Say There Is Too Much Economic

Inequality in the U.S., but Fewer Than Half Call It a Top Priority," Pew Research Center, January 9, 2020, https://www.pewresearch.org/social-trends/2020/01/09/most-americans-say-there-is-too-much-economic-inequality-in-the-u-s-but-fewer-than-half-call-it-a-top-priority/. Middle-income Americans are adults whose annual household income is two-thirds to double the national median, after incomes have been adjusted for household size. Lower-income households have incomes less than 67 percent of the median, and upper-income households have incomes that are more than double the median.

22 ***their hard work and personal sacrifices will never be rewarded*** Raj Chetty et al., "The Fading American Dream: Trends in Absolute Income Mobility since 1940," *Science* 356, no. 6336 (April 28, 2017): 398–406.

22 ***One result has been a major mental health crisis*** Holly Hedegaard, Sally C. Curtin, and Margaret Warner, "Suicide Mortality in the United States, 1999-2019," National Center for Health Statistics, February 19, 2021, https://doi.org/10.15620/cdc:101761; Catherine K. Ettman et al., "Prevalence of Depression Symptoms in US Adults Before and During the COVID-19 Pandemic," *JAMA Network Open* 3, no. 9 (2020): e2019686, https://doi.org/10.1001/jamanetworkopen.2020.19686.

22 ***The 2008 Great Recession left many*** Those higher on the income ladder generally fare best in terms of relative subjective well-being when they compare themselves to others lower in the pecking order. See Arthur S. Alderson and Tally Katz-Gerro, "Compared to Whom? Inequality, Social Comparison, and Happiness in the United States," *Social Forces* 95, no. 1 (September 1, 2016): 25–54. However, between 2005 and 2015, increases in past-year depression have been particularly high among those in the lowest and highest annual household income groups in the United States. See Andrea H. Weinberger et al., "Trends in Depression Prevalence in the USA from 2005 to 2015: Widening Disparities in Vulnerable Groups," *Psychological Medicine* 48, no. 8 (2018): 1308–15.

22 ***They opened the gates to*** Anne Case and Angus Deaton, "Life Expectancy in Adulthood Is Falling for Those without a BA Degree, but as Educational Gaps Have Widened, Racial Gaps Have Narrowed," *Proceedings of the National Academy of Sciences* 118, no. 11 (March 16, 2021): e2024777118, https://doi.org/10.1073/pnas.2024777118; Robert H. Frank and Philip J. Cook, *The Winner-Take-All Society: Why the Few at the Top Get So Much More Than the Rest of Us* (New York: Penguin Books, 1996).

23 ***the archetypal corporate white male worker*** Erin L. Kelly and Phyllis Moen, *Overload: How Good Jobs Went Bad and What We Can Do about It* (Princeton, NJ: Princeton University Press, 2020). See esp. chap. 3.

23 ***upward mobility generally out of reach*** Xi Song et al., "Long-Term Decline in Intergenerational Mobility in the United States since the 1850s," *Proceedings of the National Academy of Sciences* 117, no. 1 (2020): 251–58.

23 ***especially since the Trump presidency*** Andrei S. Markovits, *Uncouth Nation: Why Europe Dislikes America* (Princeton, NJ: Princeton University Press, 2007). See esp. chaps. 3–4.

23 ***this country is in steady decline*** Devon Haynie, "Report: American Quality of Life Declines Over Past Decade," *US News & World Report*, September 11, 2020, //www.usnews.com/news/best-countries/articles/2020-09-11/a-global-anomaly-the-us-declines-in-annual-quality-of-life-report. Also, Richard Wike et al., "America's Image Abroad Rebounds With Transition From Trump to Biden," Pew Research Center, June 10, 2021, https://www.pewresearch.org/global/2021/06/10/americas-image-abroad-rebounds-with-transition-from-trump-to-biden/.

23 ***have multiplied in recent years*** Dana R. Fisher, *American Resistance: From the Women's March to the Blue Wave* (New York: Columbia University Press, 2019).

23 ***the 2020 Black Lives Matter (BLM) movements*** Jen Kirby, "George Floyd Protests Go Global," *Vox*, May 31, 2020, https://www.vox.com/2020/5/31/21276031/george-floyd-protests-london-berlin.

23 ***though certainly not all*** Jason L. Ferguson, "'There Is an Eye on Us': International Imitation, Popular Representation, and the Regulation of Homosexuality in Senegal," *American Sociological Review* 86, no. 4 (August 1, 2021): 700–27.

23 ***To understand what future is possible*** This chapter draws on Lamont, "From 'Having' to 'Being.'"

24 ***this tiny group holds 32 percent of the national wealth*** David Huyssen, "We Won't Get out of the Second Gilded Age the Way We Got out of the First," *Vox*, April 1, 2019, https://www.vox.com/first-person/2019/4/1/18286084/gilded-age-income-inequality-robber-baron; The Federal Reserve, "Distribution of Household Wealth in the U.S. since 1989," The Federal Reserve System, June 21, 2021, https://www.federalreserve.gov/releases/z1/dataviz/dfa/distribute/chart/index.html.

24 ***studied by social scientists*** Miles Corak, "Income Inequality, Equality of Opportunity, and Intergenerational Mobility," *Journal of Economic Perspectives* 27, no. 3 (September 2013): 79–102; Thomas Piketty and Arthur Goldhammer, *Capital in the Twenty-First Century* (Cambridge, MA: Belknap Press of Harvard University Press, 2014); Branko Milanovic, *Global Inequality: A New Approach for the Age of Globalization* (Cambridge, MA: Harvard University Press, 2018); Michael Savage, *The Return of Inequality: Social Change and the Weight of the Past* (Cambridge, MA: Harvard University Press, 2021).

24 ***move up the social ladder*** Chetty et al., "The Fading American Dream"; Debraj Ray and Garance Genicot, "Measuring Upward Mobility," Working Paper,

Working Paper Series (National Bureau of Economic Research, February 2022), https://doi.org/10.3386/w29796.

24 ***By 2020, the ratio had ballooned*** Lawrence Mishel and Jori Kandra, "CEO Pay Has Skyrocketed 1,322% since 1978: CEOs Were Paid 351 Times as Much as a Typical Worker in 2020," Economic Policy Institute, August 10, 2021, https://www.epi.org/publication/ceo-pay-in-2020/.

24 ***US had greater income inequality than any of the other G7 countries*** Organisation for Economic Cooperation and Development, "Income Inequality (Indicator)," 2021, https://doi.org/10.1787/459aa7f1-en.

25 ***As these policies gained momentum*** Peter B. Evans and William H. Sewell, "Neoliberalism: Policy Regimes, International Regimes, and Social Effects," in *Social Resilience in the Neo-Liberal Era*, eds. Peter A. Hall and Michèle Lamont (Cambridge, UK: Cambridge University Press, 2013), 35–68.

25 ***Their "market fundamentalism" implemented austerity policies*** Fred Block and Margaret R. Somers, *The Power of Market Fundamentalism: Karl Polanyi's Critique* (Cambridge, MA: Harvard University Press, 2016).

25 ***They encouraged the maximization of competition*** Wendy Nelson Espeland and Michael Sauder, *Engines of Anxiety: Academic Rankings, Reputation, and Accountability* (New York: Russell Sage Foundation, 2016).

25 ***This accelerated the concentration of wealth*** Lawrence Mishel and Josh Bivens, "Identifying the Policy Levers Generating Wage Suppression and Wage Inequality," Economic Policy Institute, *Economic Policy Institute* (blog), May 13, 2021, https://www.epi.org/unequalpower/publications/wage-suppression-inequality/.

25 ***growing inequality is correlated with worsening health*** Ichiro Kawachi and Lisa F. Berkman, "Social Ties and Mental Health," *Journal of Urban Health* 78, no. 3 (2001): 458–67.

25 ***promised to remove barriers to personal achievement*** James T. Adams, *The Epic of America* (Boston, MA: Little, Brown & Co., 1931), 404.

26 ***continues to feed the aspirations of many*** James M. Jasper, *Restless Nation: Starting Over in America, Restless Nation* (Chicago: University of Chicago Press, 2009). Chap. 1.

26 ***that animate our national myths*** Gérard Bouchard, *Les Nations Savent-elles Encore Rêver? L'avenir des Nations et des Mythes Nationaux à l'ère de la Mondialisation* (Montreal, QC: Boréal, unpublished, 2019).

26 ***As many surveys have shown*** "George Washington University Battleground Poll," George Washington University, 2018, https://smpa.gwu.edu/about-poll.

26 ***The vast majority believe that inequality*** Leslie McCall, *The Undeserving Rich: American Beliefs about Inequality, Opportunity, and Redistribution* (Cambridge, UK: Cambridge University Press, 2013); Bartels finds that more than 85 percent of the respondents to a 2004 national survey (the Maxwell Poll on Civic Engagement and Inequality) attribute inequality to some people not working as hard as others. Larry M. Bartels, *Unequal Democracy: The Political Economy of the New Gilded Age* (Princeton, NJ: Princeton University Press, 2016).

27 ***In 2022, the final episode of* The Simpsons** Paddy Hirsch and Stacey Vanek Smith, "Bart Simpson's American Dream," *The Indicator from Planet Money*, NPR, May 18, 2022, https://www.npr.org/2022/05/18/1099882160/bart-simpsons-american-dream.

28 ***In this, they resemble younger cohorts*** Forty-seven percent of millennials, 29 percent of Gen X, and 27 percent of baby boomers view "pursuing your passion" as a key component of the American dream. Bank of the West, "The 2018 Millennial Study: What We Found Out," *Means and Matters*, July 19, 2018, https://meansandmatters.bankofthewest.com/article/uncategorized/the-2018-millennial-study-what-we-found-out/.

28 ***The group with the firmest belief*** In one 2016 survey, more than three-quarters of Hispanics (77 percent) believed that most people can get ahead with hard work, compared to 62 percent of the US public. Mark Hugo Lopez, Ana Gonzalea-Barrera, and Jens Manuel Krogstad, "Latinos Are More Likely to Believe in the American Dream, but Most Say It Is Hard to Achieve."

29 ***they'll likely never attain that goal*** Barbara Ehrenreich, *Nickel and Dimed: On (Not) Getting By in America* (New York: Picador USA, 2011), 118.

29 ***Americans who believe the system is fair shrank*** Andrew Dugan and Frank Newport, "In U.S., Fewer Believe 'Plenty of Opportunity' to Get Ahead," Gallup, 2013, https://news.gallup.com/poll/165584/fewer-believe-plenty-opportunity-ahead.aspx.

29 ***believed that life for the next generation will be worse*** Pew Research Center, "Pew Research Center Poll: 2017 Political Typology Survey, June," dataset (Ithaca, NY: Princeton Survey Research Associates International; Cornell University, Roper Center for Public Opinion Research, 2017); Bruce Stokes, "Public Divided on Prospects for the next Generation," Pew Research Center, June 5, 2017, https://www.pewresearch.org/global/2017/06/05/2-public-divided-on-prospects-for-the-next-generation/.

29 ***perceive the dream as attainable for themselves*** Only 37 percent of respondents to the 2018 George Washington University Battleground Poll agreed that the next generation will be better off economically than they are now, but 72 percent agreed that they are optimistic about where they will be financially five years from now. Data compiled by the Enterprise Institute Report, using

publicly available data from the Roper Center (Cornell University), cited by Karlyn Bowman, Jennifer Marsico, and Heather Sims, "Is the American Dream Alive? Examining Americans' Attitudes" (Washington, DC: American Enterprise Institute, 2014).

29 ***choose not to participate in the political process*** Matt Stevens, "Poorer Americans Have Much Lower Voting Rates in National Elections than the Nonpoor, a Study Finds," *New York Times*, August 11, 2020, https://www.nytimes.com/2020/08/11/us/politics/poorer-americans-have-much-lower-voting-rates-in-national-elections-than-the-nonpoor-a-study-finds.html.

29 ***explain the appeal of antistate ideologies*** Miller-Idriss, *Hate in the Homeland.*

30 ***bottom of the labor market*** Bruno Palier, Martin Seeleib-Kaiser, Patrick Emmenegger, and Silja Häusermann (eds.), *The Age of Dualization: The Changing Face of Inequality in Deindustrializing Societies* (New York: Oxford University Press, 2012); Jane Gingrich and Silja Häusermann, "The Decline of the Working-Class Vote, the Reconfiguration of the Welfare Support Coalition and Consequences for the Welfare State," *Journal of European Social Policy* 25, no. 1 (February 2015): 50–75, https://doi.org/10.1177/0958928714556970.

30 ***Many more privileged Americans aren't so aware*** Ann Owens and Peter Rich, "Neighborhood-School Structures: A New Approach to the Joint Study of Social Contexts," *Annual Review of Sociology*, forthcoming; Jonathan J. B. Mijs, "The Paradox of Inequality: Income Inequality and Belief in Meritocracy Go Hand in Hand," *Socio-Economic Review* 19, no. 1 (2019): 7–35.

30 ***wealthy people also tend to underestimate their place*** Elisabeth Bublitz, "Misperceptions of Income Distributions: Cross-Country Evidence from a Randomized Survey Experiment," *Socio-Economic Review* 20, no. 2 (April 1, 2022): 435–62, https://doi.org/10.1093/ser/mwaa025.

30 ***In 2022, a total of 53 percent*** Jeffrey Jones, "Middle-Class Identification Steady in U.S.," Gallup, May 19, 2022, sec. Economy, https://news.gallup.com/poll/392708/middle-class-identification-steady.aspx.

30 ***Poor people are also frequently isolated*** Alford A. Young Jr., *The Minds of Marginalized Black Men: Making Sense of Mobility, Opportunity, and Future Life Chances* (Princeton, NJ: Princeton University Press, 2003).

30 ***it is enormously challenging to keep faith*** Elena Ayala-Hurtado, "Narrative Continuity/Rupture: Projected Professional Futures amid Pervasive Employment Precarity," *Work and Occupations* 49, no. 1 (February 1, 2022): 45–78, https://doi.org/10.1177/07308884211028277.

31 ***many of them are widely shared*** Jennifer Silva, *We're Still Here: Pain and Politics in the Heart of America* (New York: Oxford University Press, 2019);

Sarah Damaske, *The Tolls of Uncertainty: How Privilege and the Guilt Gap Shape Unemployment in America* (Princeton, NJ: Princeton University Press, 2021); Aliya Hamid Rao, *Crunch Time: How Married Couples Confront Unemployment* (Berkeley, CA: University of California Press, 2020); Kathryn Edin, Timothy Nelson, Andrew Cherlin, and Robert Francis, "The Tenuous Attachments of Working-Class Men," *Journal of Economic Perspectives* 33, no. 2 (2019): 211–28.

31 ***Economists, along with the politicians*** Elizabeth Popp Berman, *Thinking like an Economist: How Efficiency Replaced Equality in U.S. Public Policy* (Princeton, NJ: Princeton University Press, 2022).

31 ***The hegemony of the American dream*** Ulrich Beck, Scott Lash, and Brian Wynne, *Risk Society: Towards a New Modernity* (Thousand Oaks, CA: SAGE Publications, 1992); Jim McGuigan, "The Neoliberal Self," *Culture Unbound* 6, no. 1 (2014): 223–40; Emily Martin, "Flexible Bodies: Science and the New Culture of Health in the US," in *Health, Medicine, and Society*, ed. Simon Johnson Williams, Jonathan Gabe, and Michael Calnan (London: Routledge, 2000); Jennifer M. Silva and Sarah M. Corse, "Envisioning and Enacting Class Mobility: The Routine Constructions of the Agentic Self," *American Journal of Cultural Sociology* 6, no. 4 (2018): 231–65; Glenn Adams, Sara Estrada-Villalta, Daniel Sullivan, and Hazel Rose Markus, "The Psychology of Neoliberalism and the Neoliberalism of Psychology," *Journal of Social Issues* 75, no. 1 (2019): 189–216, https://doi.org/10.1111/josi.12305.

32 ***indicators of cultural citizenship and belonging*** Lamont, *The Dignity of Working Men.*

32 ***they have fed considerable social instability*** Ricardo Fuentes-Nieva and Nicholas Galasso, "Working for the Few: Political Capture and Economic Inequality" (Oxfam International, January 20, 2014); James da Costa et al., "How Inequalities Are Driving a Global Youth Mental Health Crisis," The OECD Forum Network, June 6, 2019, https://www.oecd-forum.org/posts/49686-how-inequalities-are-driving-a-global-youth-mental-health-crisis; Leanne S. Son Hing et al., "Failure to Respond to Rising Income Inequality: Processes That Legitimize Growing Disparities," *Daedalus* 148, no. 3 (July 2019): 105–35.

32 ***By 2016, the average incomes*** Pew Research Center, "The American Middle Class Is Losing Ground," December 9, 2015, https://www.pewresearch.org/social-trends/2015/12/09/the-american-middle-class-is-losing-ground/.

32 ***an intensified "fear of falling"*** Barbara Ehrenreich, *Fear of Falling: The Inner Life of the Middle Class* (New York: Pantheon Books, 1989).

32 ***Mental health problems are increasingly*** Weinberger et al., "Trends in Depression Prevalence in the USA from 2005 to 2015"; Ettman et al.,

"Prevalence of Depression Symptoms in US Adults Before and During the COVID-19 Pandemic."

33 ***Maintaining their position requires*** Schieman, Glavin, and Milkie (2009) found that over 70 percent of working individuals experience stress from work interfering with nonwork life. High-status career positions are particularly linked to more work-nonwork interference, indicating more prominent work stressors for educated, upper-middle-class individuals. Scott Schieman, Paul Glavin, and Melissa A. Milkie, "When Work Interferes with Life: Work-Nonwork Interference and the Influence of Work-Related Demands and Resources," *American Sociological Review* 74, no. 6 (2009): 966–88.

33 ***The rates of suicide for those*** Also, Daly, Wilson, and Johnson (2013) found a suicide rate of about 0.085 in their sample for both those with a family income of more than $75,000 a year and individuals with an income of $5,000–$10,000. Mary C. Daly, Daniel J. Wilson, and Norman J. Johnson, "Relative Status and Well-Being: Evidence from U.S. Suicide Deaths," *Review of Economics and Statistics* 95, no. 5 (2013): 1480–1500. For a European comparison, see Ka-Yuet Liu, "To Compare Is to Despair? A Population-Wide Study of Neighborhood Composition and Suicide in Stockholm," *Social Problems* 64, no. 4 (November 1, 2017): 532–57.

33 ***Concerns about money, job stability*** American Psychological Association, "Stress in America: The Impact of Discrimination" (Stress in America Survey, March 10, 2016); Phyllis Moen et al., "Time Work by Overworked Professionals: Strategies in Response to the Stress of Higher Status," *Work and Occupations* 40, no. 2 (2013): 79–114; Juliet B. Schor, *The Overworked American: The Unexpected Decline of Leisure* (New York: Basic Books, 1993); Takashi Amagasa and Takeo Nakayama, "Relationship Between Long Working Hours and Depression in Two Working Populations: A Structural Equation Model Approach," *Journal of Occupational and Environmental Medicine* 54, no. 7 (2012): 868–74.

33 ***their "inability to afford" more children*** Claire Cain Miller, "Americans Are Having Fewer Babies. They Told Us Why," *New York Times*, July 5, 2018, https://www.nytimes.com/2018/07/05/upshot/americans-are-having-fewer-babies-they-told-us-why.html.

33 ***They cannot resist "helicopter parenting"*** Lois Weis, Kristin Cipollone, and Heather Jenkins, "Class, Race, and College Admissions in a Changing US Context," in *Class Warfare: Class, Race, and College Admissions in Top-Tier Secondary Schools*, eds. Lois Weis, Kristin Cipollone, and Heather Jenkins (Chicago: Chicago University Press, 2014); Jacques Steinberg, "Before College, Costly Advice Just on Getting In," *New York Times*, July 19, 2009, https://www.nytimes.com/2009/07/19/education/19counselor.html; Julie Bick, "Navigators for the College Bound," *New York Times*, September 14, 2008, https://www.nytimes.com/2008/09/14/jobs/14starts.html.

33 ***a growing number are hiring independent educational consultants*** Independent Educational Consultants Association, "National Study Shows Dramatic Increase in Hiring Private College Counselors," accessed May 4, 2022, https://www.iecaonline.com/quick-links/ieca-news-center/press/background-information-on-ieca/national-study-shows-dramatic-increase-in-hiring-private-college-counselors/.

33 ***In a 2002 survey that asked students*** Peter Demerath, *Producing Success: The Culture of Personal Advancement in an American High School* (Chicago: University of Chicago Press, 2009), 93.

34 ***A study of privileged students*** Shamus Rahman Khan, *Privilege: The Making of an Adolescent Elite at St. Paul's School* (Princeton, NJ: Princeton University Press, 2012).

34 ***Studies show that these pressures have increased*** Ellen Bara Stolzenberg et al., *The American Freshman: National Norms Fall 2019* (Los Angeles: Higher Education Research Institute, UCLA, 2020), https://www.heri.ucla.edu/monographs/TheAmericanFreshman2019-Expanded.pdf.

34 ***These responses and behaviors are more prevalent*** "Wasting the Best and the Brightest: Substance Abuse at America's Colleges and Universities" (New York: The National Center on Addiction and Substance Abuse at Columbia University [Partnership to End Addiction], March 2007); p.1530 in Suniya S. Luthar, Samuel H. Barkin, and Elizabeth J. Crossman, "'I Can, Therefore I Must': Fragility in the Upper-Middle Classes," *Development and Psychopathology* 25, no. 4 (2013): 1529–49.

34 ***those high-income kids are at most risk*** Suniya S. Luthar and Karen D'Avanzo, "Contextual Factors in Substance Use: A Study of Suburban and Inner-City Adolescents," *Development and Psychopathology* 11, no. 4 (1999): 845–67.

34 ***The "wellness" culture has spread considerably*** Trisha Greenhalgh and Simon Wessily, "'Health for Me': A Sociocultural Analysis of Healthism in the Middle Classes," *British Medical Bulletin* 69, no. 1 (2004): 197–213; Eva Illouz, *Saving the Modern Soul: Therapy, Emotions, and the Culture of Self-Help* (Oakland, CA: University of California Press, 2008).

34 ***treatment or counseling in the US*** John Elflein, "Mental Health Treatment or Counseling among Adults U.S. 2002-2020," *Statista*, May 6, 2022, https://www.statista.com/statistics/794027/mental-health-treatment-counseling-past-year-us-adults/.

34 ***increase in the number of adults who received mental health treatment*** Treatment for mental health has become more available over time, making the rise in the use of mental health services a period trend, rather than attributable only to an increase in psychological distress itself.

34 ***increased by 32 percent (between 1989 and 2016)*** Thomas Curran and Andrew P. Hill, "Perfectionism Is Increasing Over Time: A Meta-Analysis of Birth

Cohort Differences from 1989 to 2016," *Psychological Bulletin* 145, no. 4 (2017): 410–29; Stefan Beljean, "The Pressures of Status Reproduction: Upper-Middle-Class Youth and the Transition to Higher Education in Germany and the United States" (Unpublished dissertation, Department of Sociology, Harvard University, 2019); on how capitalism forms the self, see Eva Illouz, *Consuming the Romantic Utopia: Love and the Cultural Contradictions of Capitalism* (Orlando, FL: University of California Press, 1997).

34 ***Treatment for mental health*** Amy L. Johnson, "Changes in Mental Health and Treatment, 1997–2017," *Journal of Health and Social Behavior* 62, no. 1 (2021): 53–68.

35 ***has pushed the affluent to anxiously compare*** Daly, Wilson, and Johnson, "Relative Status and Well-Being."

35 ***Inside this hyperaffluent bubble*** Adam Thal, "Class Isolation and Affluent Americans' Perception of Social Conditions," *Political Behavior* 39, no. 2 (2017): 401–24.

35 ***underestimate the problems facing the poor*** Jules Naudet, *Stepping into the Elite* (New York: Oxford University Press, 2018).

35 ***As a result, fewer Americans*** Christopher Ingraham, "Three Quarters of Whites Don't Have Any Non-White Friends," *Washington Post*, August 25, 2014, https://www.washingtonpost.com/news/wonk/wp/2014/08/25/three-quarters-of-whites-dont-have-any-non-white-friends/; Douglas S. Massey and Nancy A Denton, *American Apartheid: Segregation and the Making of the Underclass* (Cambridge, MA: Harvard University Press, 1998).

35 ***Figure 1: Income inequality and segregation*** Jonathan J. B. Mijs and Elizabeth L. Roe, "Is America Coming Apart? Socioeconomic Segregation in Neighborhoods, Schools, Workplaces, and Social Networks, 1970–2020," *Sociology Compass* 15, no. 6 (2021): e12884, https://doi.org/10.1111/soc4.12884.

36 ***And their patterns of consumption*** Skidger, "Class & How it is Represented on Television: Class Representation within Sitcoms Since 1950's," May 11, 2013, https://classrepresentationsitcoms.wordpress.com/2013/05/11/class-how-it-is-represented-on-televisionsocial/.

36 ***were upper-middle class*** Richard Butsch, "Class and Gender through Seven Decades of American Television Sitcoms," in *Media and Class: TV, Film, and Digital Culture*, eds. June Deery and Andrea Press (New York: Routledge, 2017).

36 ***In a recent study, the political scientist*** Eunji Kim, "Entertaining Beliefs in Economic Mobility," *American Journal of Political Science*, March 2022, https://doi.org/10.1111/ajps.12702.

38 ***In France, for example*** Jonathan J. B. Mijs, "Why Don't We Care about Growing Inequality?," Centre for Labour and Social Studies, 2018, http://classonline.org.uk/blog/item/why-dont-we-care-about-growing-inequality.

38 ***This belief in meritocracy*** Frank Newport, "Average American Remains OK With Higher Taxes on Rich," Gallup, August 12, 2022, https://news.gallup.com/opinion/polling-matters/396737/average-american-remains-higher-taxes-rich.aspx; McCall, *The Undeserving Rich*.

Chapter 2: THE VIEW FROM BELOW: The Working Class and the Marginalized

39 ***From 1954 to 2022, union membership in the US fell*** Drew DeSilver, "American Unions Membership Declines as Public Support Fluctuates," Pew Research Center, accessed March 21, 2022, https://www.pewresearch.org/fact-tank/2014/02/20/for-american-unions-membership-trails-far-behind-public-support/; Heidi Shierholz et al., "Latest Data Release on Unionization Is a Wake-up Call to Lawmakers: We Must Fix Our Broken System of Labor Law," Economic Policy Institute, January 20, 2022, https://www.epi.org/publication/latest-data-release-on-unionization-is-a-wake-up-call-to-lawmakers/.

39 ***At the same time, fewer joined*** Edin et al., "The Tenuous Attachments of Working-Class Men."

40 ***This fed their growing isolation*** Lorenza Antonucci, Laszlo Horvath, Yordan Kutiyski, and André Krouwel, "The Malaise of the Squeezed Middle: Challenging the Narrative of the 'Left behind' Brexiter," *Competition & Change* 21, no. 3 (June 1, 2017): 211–29, https://doi.org/10.1177/1024529417704135; Gingrich and Häusermann, "The Decline of the Working-Class Vote, the Reconfiguration of the Welfare Support Coalition and Consequences for the Welfare State"; Stevens, "Poorer Americans Have Much Lower Voting Rates in National Elections than the Nonpoor, a Study Finds." However, there was an increase in voting in 2020: "According to the data, about 65 percent of low-income individuals voted, compared to 88 percent of those in the high-income category. In recent election cycles, turnout has been up in every income group, but this disparity between high- and low-income voter turnout persists." Austin Clemens, Shanteal Lake, and David Mitchell, "Evidence from the 2020 Election Shows How to Close the Income Voting Divide," *Equitable Growth*, July 8, 2021, https://equitablegrowth.org/evidence-from-the-2020-election-shows-how-to-close-the-income-voting-divide/.

40 ***Until the US government provided relief*** CBPP Staff, "Robust COVID Relief Achieved Historic Gains Against Poverty and Hardship, Bolstered Economy" (Washington, DC: Center on Budget and Policy Priorities, February 24, 2022).

40 ***In 2020-21, government relief*** Jason DeParle, "Pandemic Aid Programs Spur a Record Drop in Poverty," *New York Times*, July 28, 2021, https://www.nytimes.com/2021/07/28/us/politics/covid-poverty-aid-programs.html.

40 ***The vicious cycle of our current economic model*** A Centers for Disease Control (CDC) 2020 survey found that 26 percent of young adults had considered suicide in the past month, with higher percentages for Black and Hispanic respondents. Anxiety and depression among young adults aged eighteen to twenty-four is 63 percent, which is significantly higher than all other age groups. Perri Klass, "Young Adults' Pandemic Mental Health Risks," *New York Times*, August 24, 2020, https://www.nytimes.com/2020/08/24/well/family/young-adults-mental-health-pandemic.html.

41 ***According to one national study*** Nirmita Panchal, Rabah Kamal, Cynthia Cox, and Rachel Garfield, "The Implications of COVID-19 for Mental Health and Substance Use—Issue Brief—9440-03," February 10, 2021, https://www.kff.org/report-section/the-implications-of-covid-19-for-mental-health-and-substance-use-issue-brief/.

41 ***The opioid crisis, too, provides further evidence*** Edin et al., "The Tenuous Attachments of Working-Class Men"; Arjumand Siddiqi et al., "Growing Sense of Social Status Threat and Concomitant Deaths of Despair among Whites," *SSM - Population Health* 9 (2019): 100449.

41 ***Case and Deaton documented*** Deaths of despair among white people aged forty-five to fifty-four increased from 31 per 100,000 people in 1990 to 92 per 100,000 in 2017. Death rates increased 25 percent for white people without a bachelor's degree and fell 40 percent for college-educated white people. Anne Case and Angus Deaton, *Deaths of Despair and the Future of Capitalism* (Princeton, NJ: Princeton University Press, 2020), 40, 57.

41 ***After all, growing inequality feeds mistrust*** Nicholas R. Buttrick and Shigehiro Oishi, "The Psychological Consequences of Income Inequality," *Social and Personality Psychology Compass* 11, no. 3 (2017): e12304, https://doi.org/10.1111/spc3.12304.

41 ***more likely to think of themselves as "losers"*** Bartels, *Unequal Democracy*, 125; Lamont, *The Dignity of Working Men.*

42 ***These interviews took place*** Lamont and Duvoux show a convergence in patterns between American and French workers, as the latter drew stronger boundaries toward poor and Black people after 2000 than they did in the nineties. Michèle Lamont and Nicolas Duvoux, "How Neo-Liberalism Has Transformed France's Symbolic Boundaries?," *French Politics, Culture & Society* 32, no. 2 (June 1, 2014): 57–75. Stronger boundaries toward the poor have also appeared elsewhere in Western Europe, simultaneously with the diffusion of neoliberal policies. See Jonathan J. B. Mijs, Elyas Bakhtiari,

and Michèle Lamont, "Neoliberalism and Symbolic Boundaries in Europe: Global Diffusion, Local Context, Regional Variation," *Socius* 2 (2016): 1–8.

42 ***workers are hanging on to the notion of self-reliance*** Kate Pride Brown, "The Prospectus of Activism: Discerning and Delimiting Imagined Possibility," *Social Movement Studies* 15, no. 6 (November 1, 2016): 547–60.

42 ***Many analysts suggest that*** Michael Tesler, "How Racially Resentful Working-Class Whites Fled the Democratic Party—before Donald Trump," *Washington Post*, November 21, 2016, https://www.washingtonpost.com/news/monkey-cage/wp/2016/11/21/how-racially-resentful-working-class-whites-fled-the-democratic-party-before-donald-trump/; Noam Gidron and Peter A. Hall, "The Politics of Social Status: Economic and Cultural Roots of the Populist Right," *British Journal of Sociology* 68, no. S1 (2017): S57–84; Justin Gest, *The New Minority: White Working Class Politics in an Age of Immigration and Inequality* (Oxford, UK: Oxford University Press, 2016).

43 ***They were particularly contemptuous of welfare recipients*** Gest, Ibid.; Vanessa Williamson, *Read My Lips: Why Americans Are Proud to Pay Taxes* (Princeton, NJ: Princeton University Press, 2017).

43 ***the 2008 financial crisis made even more workers resentful*** Marianne Cooper, *Cut Adrift: Families in Insecure Times* (Berkeley, CA: University of California Press, 2014).

43 ***Welfare recipients still face intense stigmatization*** Clem Brooks and Jeff Manza, *Why Welfare States Persist: The Importance of Public Opinion in Democracies* (Chicago: University of Chicago Press, 2007).

43 ***Many Americans—particularly Republicans*** A 2016 survey found that close to 60 percent of right-leaning respondents thought that scaling back the government was a good way to improve unequal opportunities, while only 20 percent of left-leaning respondents shared that opinion. Alberto Alesina, Stefanie Stantcheva, and Edoardo Teso, "Intergenerational Mobility and Preferences for Redistribution," *American Economic Review* 108, no. 2 (2018): 521–54. In 1996, on average 75.9 percent of American citizens thought that the government should be responsible for providing a decent standard of living for the poor, whereas only 69 percent of citizens held that belief in 2016. Irene Bloemraad et al., "Membership without Social Citizenship? Deservingness & Redistribution as Grounds for Equality," *Daedalus* 148, no. 3 (2019): 73–104.

43 ***In other Western democracies*** Evidence remains incomplete, but it does appear that people in many Western countries are more likely to say that particular groups of low-income people are responsible for their own fate, and so disavow obligations of solidarity toward them, than before. Bloemraad et al., Ibid.; "ISSP Research Group 2018: International Social Survey Programme: Role of Government V - ISSP 2016" (Cologne: GESIS Data Archive, 2018),

https://doi. org/10.4232/1.13052; Mijs, "Why Don't We Care about Growing Inequality?"

44 ***Groups who benefited*** Bloemraad et al., Ibid.

44 ***attempted to roll back LGBTQ+ rights*** Asad L. Asad, "Latinos' Deportation Fears by Citizenship and Legal Status, 2007 to 2018," *Proceedings of the National Academy of Sciences* 117, no. 16 (2020): 8836–44; Lamont, Park, and Ayala-Hurtado, "Trump's Electoral Speeches and His Appeal to the American White Working Class"; "The Discrimination Administration," National Center for Transgender Equality, April 20, 2017, https://transequality.org/the-discrimination-administration.

44 ***discrimination in the workplace*** "Trump Administration Civil and Human Rights Rollbacks," The Leadership Conference on Civil and Human Rights, accessed July 11, 2022, https://civilrights.org/trump-rollbacks/.

44 ***This often resulted in a hardening of boundaries*** Mijs, Bakhtiari, and Lamont, "Neoliberalism and Symbolic Boundaries in Europe."

44 ***Hispanics, and immigrants*** Richard Alba, *The Great Demographic Illusion: Majority, Minority, and the Expanding American* (Princeton, NJ: Princeton University Press, 2020); Andreas Wimmer, *Ethnic Boundary Making: Institutions, Power, Networks* (Oxford, UK: Oxford University Press, 2013); Lamont, *The Dignity of Working Men*, chap. 2.

44 ***Stigmatized groups, and especially immigrants*** Kristina Bakkær Simonsen and Bart Bonikowski, "Is Civic Nationalism Necessarily Inclusive? Conceptions of Nationhood and Anti-Muslim Attitudes in Europe," *European Journal of Political Research* 59, no. 1 (2020): 114–36; Kristina Bakkær Simonsen and Bart Bonikowski, "Moralizing Immigration: The Impact of Political Framing on Polarization in the United States and Denmark," *Comparative Political Studies*, 58, no. 8 (2022): 1403–36.

45 ***growth in warmth toward several immigrant groups*** The Pew Research Center found that from 2001 to 2018, the number of Americans who favored increasing legal immigration rose 22 percentage points (10 percent to 32 percent) and the number of Americans who favored decreasing immigration fell by 29 percentage points (53 percent to 24 percent). Pew Research Center, "Shifting Public Views on Legal Immigration Into the U.S," 2018, https://www.pewresearch.org/politics/2018/06/28/shifting-public-views-on-legal-immigration-into-the-u-s/.

45 ***Hispanics continue to be presumed "illegal"*** René D. Flores and Ariela Schachter, "Who Are the 'Illegals'? The Social Construction of Illegality in the United States," *American Sociological Review* 83, no. 5 (2018): 839–68; Matthew Clair, *Privilege and Punishment: How Race and Class Matter in Criminal Court* (Princeton, NJ: Princeton University Press, 2020).

45 ***the American National Election Survey showed*** For Republicans the decline was from 66 percent to 59 percent feeling warm between 2004 and 2016; the small decline among Democrats was from 78 to 75 percent between 2011 and 2016.

45 ***In 2017, 55 percent of white Americans*** Harvard T.H. Chan School of Public Health, "Poll Finds a Majority of White Americans Say Discrimination against Whites Exists in America Today," Harvard T.H. Chan School of Public Health, 2017, https://www.hsph.harvard.edu/news/press-releases/poll-white-americans-discrimination; Andrew Daniller, "Majorities of Americans See at Least Some Discrimination against Black, Hispanic and Asian People in the U.S.," Pew Research Center, March 18, 2021, https://www.pewresearch.org/fact-tank/2021/03/18/majorities-of-americans-see-at-least-some-discrimination-against-black-hispanic-and-asian-people-in-the-u-s/.

45 ***the LGBTQ+ community has seen steadier improvement*** Attitudes are more negative (in decreasing order) among Republicans, conservatives, people who attend church weekly, men, and people between fifty and sixty-four years old. Those most supportive of choice are liberals, Democrats, people who attend church less often, people eighteen to twenty-nine, women, etc. Thus, although symbolic boundaries toward LGBTQ+ have weakened, this trend varies in intensity across segments of the population. Justin McCarthy, "Americans Split Over New LGBT Protections, Restroom Policies," Gallup, 2017. Note that attitudes toward LGBTQ+ are more mixed when respondents are asked whether people should use the bathroom of their birth gender or their gender identity.

45 ***the LGBTQ+ community is not clearly associated with the poor*** UCLA School of Law, "LGBT Poverty in the United States," Williams Institute, October 2019, https://williamsinstitute.law.ucla.edu/publications/lgbt-poverty-us/; Matthew Clair, Caitlin Daniel, and Michèle Lamont, "Destigmatization and Health: Cultural Constructions and the Long-Term Reduction of Stigma," *Social Science & Medicine* 165 (2016): 223–32.

46 ***more regularly featured in the media*** Joshua Gamson, *Freaks Talk Back: Tabloid Talk Shows and Sexual Nonconformity* (Chicago: University of Chicago Press, 2009).

46 ***However, the LGBTQ+ community also faces*** "AG Paxton Declares So-Called Sex-Change Procedures on Children and Prescription of Puberty Blockers to Be 'Child Abuse' Under Texas Law," Texas Attorney General, February 21, 2022, https://www.texasattorneygeneral.gov/news/releases/ag-paxton-declares-so-called-sex-change-procedures-children-and-prescription-puberty-blockers-be.

46 ***The wage gap between men and women persists*** Paula England, "The Gender Revolution: Uneven and Stalled," *Gender & Society* 24, no. 2 (March 19, 2010): 149–66.

46 ***By 2021, support for the movement had declined*** Jennifer Chudy and Hakeem Jefferson, "Support for Black Lives Matter Surged Last Year. Did It Last?," *New York Times*, May 22, 2021, https://www.nytimes.com/2021/05/22/opinion/blm-movement-protests-support.html; Deja Thomas and Juliana Menasce Horowitz, "Support for Black Lives Matter Has Decreased since June but Remains Strong among Black Americans," Pew Research Center (blog), September 16, 2020, https://www.pewresearch.org/fact-tank/2020/09/16/support-for-black-lives-matter-has-decreased-since-june-but-remains-strong-among-black-americans/.

46 ***with parallel changes in Europe*** Mijs, Bakhtiari, and Lamont, "Neoliberalism and Symbolic Boundaries in Europe."

Chapter 3: MEETING THE MOMENT: How We Fight for a More Inclusive World

47 ***For their part, psychologists*** Jesse Singal, *The Quick Fix: Why Fad Psychology Can't Cure Our Social Ills* (New York: Farrar, Straus and Giroux, 2021).

49 ***Social scientists have documented*** Dania V. Francis and William A. Darity, "Separate and Unequal Under One Roof: How the Legacy of Racialized Tracking Perpetuates Within-School Segregation," *RSF: The Russell Sage Foundation Journal of the Social Sciences* 7, no. 1 (2021): 187–202.

49 ***individual white families' choices about where they live*** Terry Gross, "Podcast Examines How 'Nice White Parents' Become Obstacles in Integrated Schools," *Fresh Air*, NPR, October 12, 2020, https://www.npr.org/2020/10/12/922092481/podcast-examines-how-nice-white-parents-become-obstacles-in-integrated-schools.

49 ***Americans often judge a person's worth*** Victoria Asbury-Kimmel, "Gradations of Belonging: The Role of Ascriptive and Acquired Characteristics in White Americans' Perceptions of Americanness," Unpublished MS, 2022, Department of Sociology, Harvard University.

49 ***how "American" they are perceived to be (in self-presentation)*** Peter Francis Harvey, "'Make Sure You Look Someone in the Eye': Socialization and Classed Comportment in Two Elementary Schools," *American Journal of Sociology* 125, no. 5 (March 2022): 1417–59.

49 ***In my past work I have argued*** Lamont, *Money, Morals, and Manners.*

50 ***It's easier to distance yourself from*** Ibid.; Lamont, *The Dignity of Working Men.*

50 ***whereas the latter are mentioned more*** Ibid.; Lamont, *Money, Morals, and Manners.*

50 ***The dangers of making such shallow commitments*** Lily Geismer, *Don't Blame Us: Suburban Liberals and the Transformation of the Democratic Party* (Princeton, NJ: Princeton University Press, 2014). See also the *New York Times* podcast *White Nice Parents.*

51 ***Focusing on the Boston*** See also Sylvie Tissot, *Good Neighbors: Gentrifying Diversity in Boston's South End*, trans. David Broder and Catherine Romatowski (London; Brooklyn, NY: Verso, 2015).

51 ***attending a "Title 1" elementary school*** "Title I Part A - Federal Grant Programs," Massachusetts Department of Elementary and Secondary Education, July 28, 2021, https://www.doe.mass.edu/federalgrants/titlei-a/.

51 ***to make sense of the world*** Ann Swidler, "Culture in Action: Symbols and Strategies," *American Sociological Review* 51, no. 2 (April 1986): 273–86.

51 ***When launching his presidential campaign*** Amber Phillips, "'They're Rapists.' President Trump's Campaign Launch Speech Two Years Later, Annotated," *Washington Post*, June 16, 2017, https://www.washingtonpost.com/news/the-fix/wp/2017/06/16/theyre-rapists-presidents-trump-campaign-launch-speech-two-years-later-annotated/.

52 ***In other words, narratives are how we describe reality.*** Strictly speaking, narratives are stories with a beginning, middle, and end, and are clearly identifiable as a chunk of discourse. Francesca Polletta, *It Was Like a Fever* (Chicago: Chicago University Press, 2006); Patricia Ewick and Susan Silbey, "Narrating Social Structure: Stories of Resistance to Legal Authority," *American Journal of Sociology* 108, no. 6 (May 2003): 1328–72, https://doi.org/10.1086/378035. "Frame" refers to "an interpretive [schema] that simplifies and condenses the 'world out there' by selectively punctuating and encoding objects, situations, events, experiences, and sequences of actions within one's present or past environment." David A. Snow and Robert D. Benford, "Master-Frames and Cycles of Protest," *Frontiers in Social Movement Theory* 133 (1992): 137.

52 ***second-wave feminists spread*** Nancy MacLean, *The American Women's Movement, 1945–2000: A Brief History with Documents* (Boston: Bedford/St. Martin's, 2008).

52 ***This capacity is grounded in the environment we inhabit*** Hall and Lamont, *Social Resilience in the Neoliberal Era*; Mari Sanchez, Michèle Lamont, and Shira Zilberstein, "How American College Students Understand Social Resilience during Covid-19 and the Movement for Racial Justice: Toward a Processual Approach," *Social Science & Medicine* 301 (2022): 114890, https://doi.org/10.1016/j.socscimed.2022.114890.

52 **The Dignity of Working Men** Lamont, *The Dignity of Working Men.* See esp. chap. 6.

53 ***as seen during the uproar caused in the early 2020s*** Elizabeth A. Harris and Alexandra Alter, "Book Ban Efforts Spread Across the U.S.," *New York Times*, January 30, 2022, https://www.nytimes.com/2022/01/30/books/book-ban-us-schools.html.

54 ***In fact, eugenics was based*** Evelynn M. Hammonds and Rebecca M. Herzig, eds., *The Nature of Difference: Sciences of Race in the United States from Jefferson to Genomics* (Cambridge, MA: The MIT Press, 2009).

54 ***For instance, an important psychological experiment*** Matthew D. Trujillo and Elizabeth Levy Paluck, "The Devil Knows Best: Experimental Effects of a Televised Soap Opera on Latino Attitudes Toward Government and Support for the 2010 U.S. Census," *Analyses of Social Issues and Public Policy* 12, no. 1 (2012): 113–32.

54 ***In 2014, another important study found*** Jacque Wilson, "Study: '16 and Pregnant,' 'Teen Mom' Led to Fewer Teen Births," CNN, January 13, 2014, https://www.cnn.com/2014/01/13/health/16-pregnant-teens-childbirth/.

54 ***Broadway musical* Hamilton** Mike Scutari, "Can Pop Culture Drive Social Change? These Foundations Think So," *Inside Philanthropy*, July 22, 2016, https://www.insidephilanthropy.com/home/2016/7/22/can-pop-culture-drive-social-change-these-foundations-think.html.

55 ***In addition to expanding many*** Proma Khosla, "'Black Panther' Ticket GoFundMe More than Doubles Goal," *Mashable*, January 9, 2018, https://mashable.com/article/black-panther-gofundme-harlem.

55 ***The GoFundMe page for this effort*** John McCarthy, "How Marvel's Black Panther Marketing Campaign Married Movie and Movement," *The Drum*, February 9, 2018, https://www.thedrum.com/news/2018/02/09/how-marvels-black-panther-marketing-campaign-married-movie-and-movement; Julie Hinds, "'Black Panther' Movie Inspires Crowd-Funding for Ypsilanti Community High Students," *Detroit Free Press*, January 26, 2018, https://www.freep.com/story/entertainment/2018/01/26/black-panther-movie-charity-screenings/1064902001/.

56 ***Which is exactly what the party did*** Heather Cox Richardson, "Letters from an American," *Substack*, accessed June 2, 2022, https://heathercoxrichardson.substack.com/; Reece Peck, *Fox Populism: Branding Conservatism as Working Class* (Cambridge, UK: Cambridge University Press, 2019).

56 ***In her 2010 book* Economists and Societies** Marion Fourcade, *Economists and Societies: Discipline and Profession in the United States, Britain, and France, 1890s to 1990s* (Princeton, NJ: Princeton University Press, 2009).

56 ***In her book* Thinking like an Economist** Berman, *Thinking like an Economist*; Kevin P. Donovan, "The Rise of the Randomistas: On the Experimental Turn in International Aid," *Economy and Society* 47, no. 1 (January 2, 2018): 27–58, https://doi.org/10.1080/03085147.2018.1432153; Justin Fox, "Why Economists Took So Long to Focus on Inequality," Bloomberg.com, January 4, 2016, https://www.bloomberg.com/opinion/articles/2016-01-04/why-economists-took-so-long-to-focus-on-inequality.

56 ***Others may promote more*** Oddný Helgadóttir, "Seeing like a Macroeconomist: Varieties of Formalisation, Professional Incentives and Academic Ideational Change," *New Political Economy* 27, no. 3 (2022): 426440, https://doi.org/10.1080/13563467.2021.1967910.

56 ***Yet, a few prominent economists have*** George A. Akerlof and Rachel E. Kranton, *Identity Economics: How Our Identities Shape Our Work, Wages, and Well-Being* (Princeton, NJ: Princeton University Press, 2010); George A. Akerlof and Dennis J. Snower, "Bread and Bullets," *Journal of Economic Behavior & Organization* 126 (June 1, 2016): 58–71; Robert J. Shiller, *Narrative Economics: How Stories Go Viral and Drive Major Economic Events* (Princeton, NJ: Princeton University Press, 2019); Dani Rodrik, *In Search of Prosperity: Analytic Narratives on Economic Growth* (Princeton, NJ: Princeton University Press, 2003).

57 ***Others have attempted to engage more systematically*** Daron Acemoglu and James A. Robinson, "Culture, Institutions and Social Equilibria: A Framework," Working Paper, Working Paper Series (National Bureau of Economic Research, May 2021), https://doi.org/10.3386/w28832.

57 ***Prominent articles and books on the topic*** Steven Pinker, *How the Mind Works* (New York: W. W. Norton, 1997); Richard H. Thaler and Cass R. Sunstein, *Nudge: Improving Decisions about Health, Wealth, and Happiness* (New Haven, CT: Yale University Press, 2008); Daniel Kahneman, *Thinking Fast and Slow* (New York: Farrar, Straus and Giroux, 2013).

57 ***They gave rise to a new and influential knowledge industry*** Thaler and Sunstein, Ibid.

57 ***In 2015, this area of study assumed*** Michèle Lamont et al., "Bridging Cultural Sociology and Cognitive Psychology in Three Contemporary Research Programmes," *Nature Human Behaviour* 1, no. 12 (2017): 866–72.

57 ***In recent years, many psychologists*** Joshua D. Greene, *Moral Tribes: Emotions, Reason, and the Gap between Us and Them* (New York: Penguin Books, 2013); Jonathan Haidt, *The Righteous Mind: Why Good People Are Divided by Politics and Religion* (New York: Vintage, 2013).

58 ***to explain the growing political polarization*** Amy Chua, *Political Tribes: Group Instinct and the Fate of Nations*, First Edition (New York: Penguin Books, 2018); Eli J. Finkel et al., "Political Sectarianism in America," *Science* 370, no. 6516 (October 30, 2020): 533–36.

58 ***Its proponents often ground it in utilitarianism*** Robert Boyd, Peter J. Richerson, and Joseph Henrich, "The Cultural Niche: Why Social Learning Is Essential for Human Adaptation," *Proceedings of the National Academy of Sciences* 108, no. supplement 2 (June 28, 2011): 10918–25; Cory J. Clark et al., "Tribalism Is Human Nature," *Current Directions in Psychological Science* 28, no. 6 (December 1, 2019): 587–92.

58 ***Not all groups are tribes*** Michèle Lamont et al., *Getting Respect*; Alba, *The Great Demographic Illusion*.

58 ***We know boundaries are changeable*** Rogers Brubaker, "Ethnicity without Groups," *European Journal of Sociology / Archives Européennes de Sociologie / Europäisches Archiv Für Soziologie* 43, no. 2 (2002): 163–89; Michèle Lamont and Virág Molnár, "The Study of Boundaries in the Social Sciences," *Annual Review of Sociology* 28, no. 1 (2002): 167–95; Andreas Wimmer, *Ethnic Boundary Making*.

58 ***there is nothing natural about "seeing race"*** Ellis P. Monk, "Inequality without Groups: Contemporary Theories of Categories, Intersectional Typicality, and the Disaggregation of Difference," *Sociological Theory* 40, no. 1 (March 1, 2022): 3–27; Dieter Vandebroeck and Maaike Jappens, "Some Other 'Primitive Forms of Classification.' Contribution to the Study of Children's Collective Representations," *Poetics*, 91 (April 1, 2022): 101667, https://doi.org/10.1016/j.poetic.2022.101667.

58 ***We have the ability to reimagine the future*** My argument builds on the work of scholars who study the construction of the future. See, for instance: Iddo Tavory and Nina Eliasoph, "Coordinating Futures: Toward a Theory of Anticipation," *American Journal of Sociology* 118, no. 4 (January 2013): 908–42; Elena Ayala-Hurtado, "Narrative Continuity/Rupture." Also Jens Beckert, *Imagined Futures: Fictional Expectations and Capitalist Dynamics* (Cambridge, MA: Harvard University Press, 2016).

Chapter 4: BEING THE CHANGE WE WISH TO SEE: Change Agents and the Quest For Dignity and Recognition

60 ***"portraits of this community that were incredibly noble"*** The Editors of *ARTnews*, "L.A. Story: Catherine Opie on Her Controversial Photographs of Los Angeles Subcultures, in 1998," *ARTnews*, January 22, 2016, https://www.artnews.com/art-news/retrospective/l-a-story-catherine-opie-on-her-controversial-photographs-of-los-angeles-subcultures-in-1998-5700/.

60 ***In another series, she represents*** Avgi Saketopoulou, "Catherine Opie: American Photographer, American Pervert," *Studies in Gender and Sexuality* 14, no. 3 (July 1, 2013): 245–52.

61 ***Her exhibit,* Posing Beauty** Deborah Willis, *Reflections in Black: A History of Black Photographers—1840 to the Present* (New York: W. W. Norton & Company, 2000); Deborah Willis, "Posing Beauty: African American Images from the 1890s to the Present - ProQuest," *Network Journal* 17, no. 1 (2009): 35; Deborah Willis, *Black: A Celebration of a Culture* (New York: Simon & Schuster, 2014).

62 ***the media often centered our attention*** J. Emmett Winn, *The American Dream and Contemporary Hollywood Cinema* (New York: Continuum, 2013); Will

Wright, *Sixguns and Society: A Structural Study of the Western* (Berkeley, CA: University of California Press, 1977).

62 ***These creators are what I call "change agents"*** The change agents are also cultural entrepreneurs. For Lounsbury and Glynn (2001), cultural entrepreneurs produce "entrepreneurial stories [that] facilitate the crafting of a new venture identity that serves as a touchstone upon which legitimacy may be conferred by investors, competitors, and consumers, opening up access to new capital and market opportunities." Michael Lounsbury and Mary Ann Glynn, "Cultural Entrepreneurship: Stories, Legitimacy and the Acquisition of Resources," *Strategic Management Journal* 22 (June 1, 2001): 545–64. These are among many other types of cultural intermediaries who contribute to the creation of organizational fields. On cultural intermediaries, see Gil Eyal and Larissa Buchholz, "From the Sociology of Intellectuals to the Sociology of Interventions," *Annual Review of Sociology* 36 (2010): 117–37. Also on social change more generally, see Julie Battilana and Tiziana Casciaro, *Power, for All: How It Really Works and Why It's Everyone's Business* (Simon & Schuster, 2022).

63 ***They are also concerned with stigmatization*** Goffman distinguishes between three types of stigma: 1) stigma on the basis of physical or external attributes/marks (e.g., obesity); 2) stigma on the basis of internal or personal attributes and character (e.g., mental illness or deviant behavior); and 3) tribal stigma on the basis of racial, ethnic, or religious attributes. Erving Goffman, *Stigma: Notes on the Management of a Spoiled Identity* (Englewood Cliffs, NJ: Prentice Hall, 1963). Also Jo C. Phelan, Bruce G. Link, and John F. Dovidio, "Stigma and Prejudice: One Animal or Two?," *Social Science & Medicine* 67, no. 3 (August 2008): 358–67.

63 ***But recognition is so effective*** While the political philosopher Michael Sandel wrote about how merit feeds stigmatization, recognition work is more encompassing than he suggests as it targets not only class advantages, but also stigmas that are not class-based, such as those based on ethnicity or sexual orientation. See Sandel, *The Tyranny of Merit.*

63 ***Recognition is conferred in different ways*** There is a well-established philosophical literature on recognition. See for instance Taylor et al., *Multiculturalism* and Tariq Modood, "Anti-Essentialism, Multiculturalism and the 'Recognition' of Religious Groups," *The Journal of Political Philosophy* 6, no. 4 (1998): 378–399. In recent years, more empirical approaches have emerged—For instance, a sociology of work perspective on recognition inspired by the scholarship of Arlie Hochschild, such as Allison J. Pugh, "Emotions and the Systematization of Connective Labor," *Theory, Culture & Society* 39, no. 5 (2022): 23–42. From a more experiential perspective in the context of academic life, see Victoria Reyes, *Academic Outsider: Stories of Exclusion and Hope* (Stanford, CA: Stanford University Press, 2022). There is also a growing body of knowledge contributing to the sociology of valuation

and evaluation: Michèle Lamont, "Toward a Comparative Sociology of Valuation and Evaluation," *Annual Review of Sociology* 38, no. 1 (2012): 201–21. A classical reference is: Luc Boltanski and Laurent Thévenot, *De la justification: Les économies de la grandeur* (Paris: Gallimard, 1991). A related contribution is: Nathalie Heinich, *La valeur des personnes. Preuves et épreuves de la grandeur* (Paris: Gallimard, 2022).

63 ***At the broadest level*** Clair, Daniel, and Lamont, "Destigmatization and Health"; Jean Beaman, "Citizenship as Cultural: Towards a Theory of Cultural Citizenship," *Sociology Compass* 10, no. 10 (October 2016): 849–57.

63 ***worthy members of the community*** Lamont, *The Dignity of Working Men*; Bloemraad et al., "Membership without Social Citizenship?"

63 ***The Italian-Scottish political scientist*** Lorenza Fontana, *Recognition Politics: Indigenous Rights and Ethnic Conflict in the Andes* (New York: Cambridge University Press, 2023).

64 ***One feels his two-ness*** W. E. B. Du Bois, "Strivings of the Negro People," *The Atlantic*, August 1, 1897, p. 194, https://www.theatlantic.com/magazine/archive/1897/08/strivings-of-the-negro-people/305446/.

64 ***Together, these two aspects define*** Richard Jenkins, *Social Identity* (London: Routledge, 1996).

66 ***For their part, some Black Brazilians*** Lamont et al., *Getting Respect.* Also, Nissim Mizrachi and Hanna Herzog, "Participatory Destigmatization Strategies among Palestinian Citizens, Ethiopian Jews and Mizrahi Jews in Israel," *Ethnic and Racial Studies* 35, no. 3 (2012): 418–35, https://doi.org/10.1080/01419870.2011.589530. These differences are explained by the history of race relations in each country and other factors, though the situation in Brazil is changing rapidly as racial mobilization and protest are on the rise. Graziella Moraes Silva, "After Affirmative Action: Redrawing Colour Lines in Brazil," in *A Horizon of (Im)Possibilities*, eds. Katerina Hatzikidi and Eduardo Dullo (University of London Press, 2021).

66 ***Activists today are still seeking legal rights and protections*** Rachel B. Vogelstein and Meighan Stone, *Awakening: #MeToo and the Global Fight for Women's Rights* (New York: PublicAffairs, 2021); Noa Milman and Folashade Ajayi, "Black Lives Matter in Europe: Transnational Diffusion, Local Translation and Resonance of Anti-Racist Protest in Germany, Italy, Denmark and Poland," *DeZIM Research Notes* 6, no. 21 (2021): 45. Jasper (1999) distinguishes between citizenship movements (fighting for formal legal rights) and post-citizenship movements (using legal rights to reach other objectives). James M. Jasper, *The Art of Moral Protest: Culture, Biography, and Creativity in Social Movements* (Chicago: University of Chicago Press, 1999).

67 ***Social movement scholar Erica Chenoweth*** Erica Chenoweth, "The Future of Nonviolent Resistance," *Journal of Democracy* 31, no. 3 (July 2020): 69–84. See esp. p. 69.

67 ***In the United States, not only were*** Douglas McAdam, "We've Never Seen Protests Like These Before," *Jacobin*, June 20, 2020, https://jacobinmag.com/2020/06/george-floyd-protests-black-lives-matter-riots-demonstrations; Fisher, *American Resistance*.

67 ***As Badu explained to NPR*** Felix Contreras, "Erykah Badu: Tiny Desk Concert," NPR, August 15, 2018, https://www.npr.org/2018/08/14/638483063/erykah-badu-tiny-desk-concert; Elijah C. Watson, "The Origin Of Woke: How Erykah Badu And Georgia Anne Muldrow Sparked The 'Stay Woke' Era," *Okayplayer*, February 27, 2018, https://www.okayplayer.com/originals/stay-woke-history-georgia-anne-muldrow-erykah-badu-master-teacher.html.

68 ***some moderates have turned against the term*** David Brooks, "This Is How Wokeness Ends," *New York Times*, May 13, 2021, https://www.nytimes.com/2021/05/13/opinion/this-is-how-wokeness-ends.html.

68 ***80 percent of Republicans saw "cancel culture"*** Thomas B. Edsall, "Is Wokeness 'Kryptonite for Democrats'?," *New York Times*, May 26, 2021, https://www.nytimes.com/2021/05/26/opinion/democrats-republicans-wokeness-cancel-culture.html; Charles M. Blow, "The War on 'Wokeness,'" *New York Times*, November 11, 2021, https://www.nytimes.com/2021/11/10/opinion/wokeness-racism-politics.html.

68 ***highly politicized attacks on woke culture*** Ishaan Tharoor, "The U.S. and British Right Ramp up the War on 'Wokeness,'" *Washington Post*, April 9, 2021, https://www.washingtonpost.com/world/2021/04/09/woke-wars-united-states-britain/; Keeanga-Yamahtta Taylor, "'Wokeness' Is Not the Democrats' Problem," *New Yorker*, November 19, 2021, https://www.newyorker.com/news/our-columnists/wokeness-is-not-the-problem; Simon Kuper, "Yes, There Is a Third Way on 'Wokeness,'" *Financial Times*, November 25, 2021, https://www.ft.com/content/39b74435-dbe2-42a8-bbb1-78a3db04137e.

69 ***In sports, football player Colin Kaepernick*** Michèle Lamont, "The Big Picture: Social Solidarity," *Public Books*, 2017, https://www.publicbooks.org/big-picture-social-solidarity.

69 ***have dismissed identity politics as irrelevant*** Lilla, *The Once and Future Liberal*; Sheri Berman, "Why Identity Politics Benefits the Right More than the Left," *The Guardian*, July 14, 2018, https://www.theguardian.com/commentisfree/2018/jul/14/identity-politics-right-left-trump-racism.

70 ***In her 2016 book* Strangers in Their Own Land** Arlie Russell Hochschild, *Strangers in Their Own Land: Anger and Mourning on the American Right* (New York: The New Press, 2016).

70 ***In a separate study, my collaborators and I found*** Lamont, Park, and Ayala-Hurtado, "Trump's Electoral Speeches and His Appeal to the American White Working Class."

70 ***In this context of economic decline*** Feinstein, *Rally 'round the Flag.*

71 ***A 2022 poll conducted by the Southern Poverty Law Center*** Cassie Miller, "SPLC Poll Finds Substantial Support for 'Great Replacement' Theory and Other Hard-Right Ideas," Southern Poverty Law Center, June 1, 2022, https://www.splcenter.org/news/2022/06/01/poll-finds-support-great-replacement-hard-right-ideas.

71 ***A different survey conducted*** PRRI Staff, "Competing Visions of America: An Evolving Identity or a Culture Under Attack? Findings from the 2021 American Values Survey," PRRI, November 11, 2022, https://www.prri.org/research/competing-visions-of-america-an-evolving-identity-or-a-culture-under-attack/.

71 ***the United States will be a majority-minority society*** Alba, *The Great Demographic Illusion.*

71 ***One manifestation of this trend*** Siddiqi et al., "Growing Sense of Social Status Threat and Concomitant Deaths of Despair among Whites."

72 ***the experience of constant racism can have a "weathering" effect*** Nancy Krieger, "Discrimination and Health Inequalities," in *Social Epidemiology*, eds. Lisa F. Berkman, Ichiro Kawachi, and M. Maria Glymour, 2nd ed. (Oxford, UK: Oxford University Press, 2014), 63–125; David R. Williams and Selina A. Mohammed, "Racism and Health I: Pathways and Scientific Evidence," *American Behavioral Scientist* 57, no. 8 (2013): 1152–73.

72 ***While the general trend since 1990*** Dania Nadeem, "U.S. Life Expectancy Falls to Lowest Level in Almost 20 Years Due to COVID-19 -CDC," Reuters, July 21, 2021, https://www.reuters.com/world/us/us-life-expectancy-fell-year-half-2020-due-covid-19-cdc-2021-07-21/.

72 ***Notably, over the past two decades*** Laura Dwyer-Lindgren et al., "Life Expectancy by County, Race, and Ethnicity in the USA, 2000–19: A Systematic Analysis of Health Disparities," *The Lancet* 400, no. 10345 (July 2022): 25–38, https://doi.org/10.1016/S0140-6736(22)00876-5.

72 ***Growing inequality and the bifurcation in outcomes*** Deirdre Bloome, Daniel Schrage, and Jane Furey, "Rising Class Crystallization? Time Trends and Racial/Ethnic Differences in Multidimensional Social Class Inequality" (Kennedy School of Government, Harvard University, 2021).

72 ***This may lead to the "why try" syndrome*** Catherine DeCarlo Santiago, Martha E. Wadsworth, and Jessica Stump, "Socioeconomic Status, Neighborhood Disadvantage, and Poverty-Related Stress: Prospective Effects on Psychological Syndromes among Diverse Low-Income Families," *Journal of Economic Psychology* 32, no. 2 (2011): 218–30; Adrien Papuchon and Nicolas Duvoux, "Subjective Poverty As Perceived Lasting Social Insecurity: Lessons From a French Survey on Poverty, Inequality and the Welfare State (2015–2018)," SSRN Scholarly Paper (Rochester, NY: Social Science Research Network, September 1, 2019), https://doi.org/10.2139/ssrn.3465214.

Chapter 5: CHANGING HEARTS AND MINDS: How Recognition Chains Amplify the Cultural Agenda

75 ***CBMA's efforts amplified*** "Racial Justice and Movement-Building Visionary Shawn Dove Joins New Profit as a Managing Partner," *New Profit* (blog), February 23, 2022, https://www.newprofit.org/go/racial-justice-and-movement-building-visionary-shawn-dove-joins-new-profit-as-a-managing-partner/.

76 ***CBMA supports many other programs*** "My Brother's Keeper," The White House, accessed September 19, 2021, https://obamawhitehouse.archives.gov/my-brothers-keeper.

77 ***In 2016, she edited a special issue*** "Recognition chains" involve actors, institutions, and classification systems involved in the funding, evaluation, and diffusion of recognition. It is similar to the network of occupations involved in cultural fields. Pierre Bourdieu, *The Field of Cultural Production* (New York: Columbia University Press, 1993). I propose this term to refer specifically to actors who are contributing to the recognition process. For an extension of Bourdieu's argument to global fields, see Larissa Buchholz, "What is a Global Field? Theorizing Fields beyond the Nation-State," *Sociological Review* 64, no. 2 suppl (July 1, 2016): 31–60.

78 ***The space has been*** "About Jack Shainman Gallery," Jack Shainman Gallery, accessed October 11, 2022, https://jackshainman.com/about.

79 ***Under the leadership of Darren Walker*** Darren Walker, "Inclusion Is Patriotism of the Highest Order," *Washington Post*, July 2, 2021, https://www.washingtonpost.com/opinions/2021/07/02/inclusion-is-patriotism-highest-order/.

79 ***focusing on narrative change*** Sujatha Fernandes, *Curated Stories: The Uses and Misuses of Storytelling* (New York: Oxford University Press, 2017).

79 ***With the help of the Ford Foundation*** Brooks Barnes, "Just Who Has Seen 'Roma'? Netflix Offers Clues," *New York Times*, February 6, 2019, https://www.nytimes.com/2019/02/06/business/media/roma-netflix-viewers.html.

80 ***ranging from publishing*** Lila Shapiro, "Publishing's New Power Club: A Wave of Hires Is Set to Pick up Where the Reckoning Left Off," *New York Magazine*, February 23, 2021, https://nymag.com/intelligencer/article/book-publishing-power-club.html; Marcela Valdes, "Inside the Push to Diversify the Book Business," *New York Times*, June 22, 2022, https://www.nytimes.com/2022/06/22/magazine/inside-the-push-to-diversify-the-book-business.html.

80 ***to art museums and art leaders*** The Association of Art Museum Directors, "Latest Art Museum Staff Demographic Survey Shows Number of African American Curators and Women in Leadership Roles Increased," *Press Releases & Statements* (blog), January 28, 2019, https://aamd.org/for-the-media/press-release/latest-art-museum-staff-demographic-survey-shows-number-of-african; Victoria L. Valentine, "On the Rise: 47 Curators and Arts Leaders Who Took on New Appointments in 2019," *Culture Type* (blog), December 27, 2019, https://www.culturetype.com/2019/12/27/on-the-rise-47-curators-and-arts-leaders-who-took-on-new-appointments-in-2019/.

80 ***higher education, and beyond*** Jiannbin Lee Shiao, *Identifying Talent, Institutionalizing Diversity: Race and Philanthropy in Post–Civil Rights America* (Durham, NC: Duke University Press Books, 2004). On changes in the number of racialized leaders in philanthropy see: Floyd Mills, "The State of Change: An Analysis of Women and People of Color in the Philanthropic Sector," Council on Foundations, August 2017, https://cof.org/sites/default/files/documents/files/2017-Gender-Diversity-Report.pdf; Stan Yogi, "The POC Majority: Preparing Your Organization for Demographic Shifts," *Nonprofit Quarterly*, July 1, 2020, https://nonprofitquarterly.org/the-poc-majority-preparing-your-organization-for-demographic-shifts/.

80 ***This leadership change came*** Jennifer Schuessler, "Michelle T. Boone Named President of Poetry Foundation," *New York Times*, April 29, 2021, https://www.nytimes.com/2021/04/29/arts/michelle-t-boone-president-poetry-foundation.html/.

80 ***The Gates Foundation has aimed*** Bill & Melinda Gates Foundation, "Changing the National Conversation About Poverty and Economic Mobility," *Media Center* (blog), June 10, 2020, https://www.gatesfoundation.org/Media-Center/Press-Releases/2020/06/Changing-the-National-Conversation-About-Poverty-and-Economic-Mobility.

80 ***At the same time, progressive foundations*** Rachel Sherman, "The Rich Kid Revolutionaries," *New York Times*, April 27, 2019, https://www.nytimes.com/2019/04/27/opinion/sunday/rich-social-inequality.html; Steve Lohr, "What Can Replace Free Markets? Groups Pledge $41 Million to Find Out," *New York Times*, February 16, 2022, https://www.nytimes.com/2022/02/16/business/neoliberalism-free-market-research.html.

81 ***Some have argued that philanthropic organizations*** They are inspired by the notions of the "prison industrial complex" as well as the original "military

industrial complex" concept, which was popularized by President Dwight Eisenhower in his 1961 farewell presidential speech. Sociologist C. Wright Mills pointed to the phenomenon in the fifties as he described how power is exercised through the coordination of the military hierarchy, the administrative bureaucracy, and corporate wealth. C. Wright Mills, *The Power Elite* (Oxford, UK: Oxford University Press, 1956).

81 ***For some of these critics*** HistPhil, "Movement Capture and the Long Arc of the Black Freedom Struggle," *HistPhil* (blog), July 14, 2020, https://histphil.org/2020/07/14/movement-capture-and-the-long-arc-of-the-black-freedom-struggle; Karen Ferguson, "The Perils of Liberal Philanthropy," *Jacobin*, November 26, 2018, https://jacobinmag.com/2018/11/black-lives-matter-ford-foundation-black-power-mcgeorge-bundy.

81 ***For instance, the Chan-Zuckerberg Foundation*** Aaron Horvath and Walter W. Powell, "Seeing Like a Philanthropist," in *The Nonprofit Sector: A Research Handbook*, 3rd ed. (Stanford, CA: Stanford University Press, 2020); Anand Giridharadas, *Winners Take All: The Elite Charade of Changing the World* (New York: Knopf, 2018); Powell and Bromley, *The Nonprofit Sector: A Research Handbook*, chap. 3.

81 ***Still, it remains to be seen*** Derek Robey, Nicole Letourneau, and Michèle Lamont, "Multicultural Meritocracy in Hollywood and Comedy," Department of Sociology, Harvard University, Unpublished.

81 ***For this to happen, significant changes*** Emma Saunders-Hastings, *Private Virtues, Public Vices: Philanthropy and Democratic Equality* (Chicago: University of Chicago Press, 2022).

82 ***Patreon is one of the platforms*** Benjamin Cannon et al., "Aaron Rodgers Stops by You Made It Weird to Talk about UFO Sightings," The A.V. Club, March 28, 2016, https://www.avclub.com/aaron-rodgers-stops-by-you-made-it-weird-to-talk-about-1798287872.

82 ***Dungey explained to me*** Ben Smith, "How Netflix Beat Hollywood to a Generation of Black Content," *New York Times*, July 6, 2020, https://www.nytimes.com/2020/07/05/business/media/netflix-hollywood-black-culture.html.

83 ***This celebrated show promotes recognition*** Salamishah Tillet, "'Bridgerton' Takes On Race. But Its Core Is Escapism," *New York Times*, January 5, 2021, https://www.nytimes.com/2021/01/05/arts/television/bridgerton-race-netflix.html; Monk, "Inequality without Group."

83 ***Women such as Rhimes and DuVernay*** Yoon, Dasl, and Timothy W. Martin, "Netflix's 'Squid Game' Is the Dystopian Hit No One Wanted—Until Everyone Did," *Wall Street Journal*, October 4, 2021, https://www.wsj.com/articles/netflixs-squid-game-is-the-dystopian-hit-no-one-wanteduntil-everyone-did-11633183200; Darnell Hunt and Ana-Christina

Ramón, "Hollywood Diversity Report 2020: A Tale of Two Hollywoods, Part 1: Film" (Division of Social Sciences at UCLA, 2020); Robey, Letourneau, and Lamont, "Multicultural Meritocracy in Hollywood and Comedy."

84 ***As of 2019, the organization had 171 staff*** "Change.Org Impact Report 2019," Change.org, 2019, https://static.change.org/brand-pages/impact/reports/2020/2020_Impact+Report_Change_EN_final.pdf.

84 ***Ultimately, their story helped*** BBC News, "Medicinal Cannabis: The Family That Changed Australia's Debate," June 30, 2019, https://www.bbc.com/news/world-australia-47796044.

85 ***This and similar networks that work toward recognition*** Bourdieu, *The Field of Cultural Production.*

86 ***Recognition chains work through the media*** Less is known about long-term effects. Bartosz G. Żerebecki et al., "Can TV Shows Promote Acceptance of Sexual and Ethnic Minorities? A Literature Review of Television Effects on Diversity Attitudes," *Sociology Compass*, 2021, 1–16.

86 ***Some focus on the content*** Francesca Polletta, *Inventing the Ties That Bind: Imagined Relationships in Moral and Political Life* (Chicago: University of Chicago Press, 2020).

87 ***Sociologist Heather Haveman*** Benedict Anderson, *Imagined Communities: Reflections on the Origin and Spread of Nationalism* (London: Verso, 1983); Heather A. Haveman, *Magazines and the Making of America: Modernization, Community, and Print Culture, 1741–1860* (Princeton, NJ: Princeton University Press, 2020).

87 ***This has been true across history*** Robert Wuthnow, *Communities of Discourse: Ideology and Social Structure in the Reformation, the Enlightenment, and European Socialism* (Cambridge, MA: Harvard University Press, 1989). A similar resources-based approach was developed by Charles Tilly et al. in their study of the diffusion of social movements across a range of countries from 1768 to 2004. See Charles Tilly et al., *Social Movements, 1768–2018* (New York: Routledge, 2019).

87 ***Understanding these structural changes*** Evan Stewart and Douglas Hartmann, "The New Structural Transformation of the Public Sphere," *Sociological Theory* 38, no. 2 (2020): 170–91; Michèle Lamont and Laurent Thévenot, *Rethinking Comparative Cultural Sociology: Repertoires of Evaluation in France and the United States*, Cambridge Cultural Social Studies (New York: Cambridge University Press, 2000). On how ideas travel globally, see Andreas Wimmer, "Domains of Diffusion: How Culture and Institutions Travel around the World and with What Consequences," *American Journal of Sociology* 126, no. 6 (May 2021): 1389–1438. Also Tim Hallett, Orla Stapleton, and Michael Sauder, "Public Ideas: Their Varieties and Careers," *American Sociological Review* 84, no. 3 (2019): 545–76.

88 ***are now serving more differentiated publics*** Stuart Cunningham and David Craig, *Social Media Entertainment: The New Intersection of Hollywood and Silicon Valley* (New York: NYU Press, 2019); Gabriel Rossman, *Climbing the Charts: What Radio Airplay Tells Us about the Diffusion of Innovation* (Princeton, NJ: Princeton University Press, 2012); Jonas Kaiser et al., "What Happened to the Public Sphere? The Networked Public Sphere and Public Opinion Formation," in *Handbook of Cyber-Development, Cyber-Democracy, and Cyber-Defense*, eds. Elias G. Carayannis, David F. J. Campbell, and Marios Panagiotis Efthymiopoulos (Cham, Switzerland: Springer International Publishing, 2018), 433–59; Yochai Benkler, *The Wealth of Networks: How Social Production Transforms Markets and Freedom* (New Haven, CT: Yale University Press, 2007).

88 ***The online space in particular is democratized*** C. W. Anderson, "Media Ecosystems: Some Notes Toward a Genealogy of the Term and an Application of It to Journalism Research" (ESF Exploratory Workshop on Mapping the Digital News Ecosystem, New York, 2013), https://www.cwanderson.org/wp-content/uploads/2013/04/EcosystemGenealogy.pdf.

88 ***In 2018, for instance, 22 percent*** Stefan Wojcik and Adam Hughes, "Sizing Up Twitter Users," Pew Research Center, April 24, 2019, https://www.pewresearch.org/internet/2019/04/24/sizing-up-twitter-users/.

88 ***television remains the primary medium*** Alexis C. Madrigal, "When Did TV Watching Peak?," *The Atlantic*, May 30, 2018, https://www.theatlantic.com/technology/archive/2018/05/when-did-tv-watching-peak/561464/.

89 ***Nightly local TV news*** Michael Barthel and Kristen Worden, "Newspapers Fact Sheet," *Pew Research Center's Journalism Project* (blog), June 29, 2021, https://www.pewresearch.org/journalism/fact-sheet/newspapers/.

89 ***Print journalism, for instance*** On the causes, see Nicholas Lemann, "Can Journalism Be Saved?," *New York Review*, February 27, 2020, https://www.nybooks.com/articles/2020/02/27/can-journalism-be-saved/; Jill Abramson, *Merchants of Truth: The Business of News and the Fight for Facts* (New York: Simon & Schuster, 2019).

89 ***The* New York Times, *for example*** Sara Fischer, "New York Times Surpasses 10 Million Subscriptions," *Axios*, February 2, 2022, https://www.axios.com/2022/02/02/new-york-times-10-million-subscriptions.

89 ***Compare that to Facebook's*** Mansoor Iqbal, "Facebook Revenue and Usage Statistics (2022)," *Business of Apps*, June 30, 2022, https://www.businessofapps.com/data/facebook-statistics/; S. Dixon, "Twitter - Statistics & Facts," *Statista*, April 27, 2022, https://www.statista.com/topics/737/twitter/.

89 ***their favorite source of information*** Djordjevic Milos, "21 Extraordinary Newspaper Statistics," *Letter.Ly* (blog), February 23, 2021, https://letter.ly/newspaper-statistics/.

89 ***access print publications online often*** Elisa Shearer, "More than Eight-in-Ten Americans Get News from Digital Devices"(Pew Research Center, January 12, 2021), https://www.pewresearch.org/fact-tank/2021/01/12/more-than-eight-in-ten-americans-get-news-from-digital-devices/.

89 ***In February 2022, only 11 percent*** Amy Watson, "Millennials News Consumption Sources in the U.S. 2022," *Statista*, March 24, 2022, https://www.statista.com/statistics/1010456/united-states-millennials-news-consumption/.

90 ***Coverage of state legislatures*** Daniel J. Hopkins, *The Increasingly United States: How and Why American Political Behavior Nationalized* (Chicago: University of Chicago Press, 2018).

90 ***To appeal to more people*** Peck, *Fox Populism*.

90 ***This has had enormous consequences*** Markus Prior, "Media and Political Polarization," *Annual Review of Political Science* 16, no. 1 (2013): 101–27.

90 ***Consequently, politics has increasingly*** Lilliana Mason, *Uncivil Agreement: How Politics Became Our Identity* (Chicago: University of Chicago Press, 2018).

90 ***the United States has seen its share of unionized workers decline*** DeSilver, "American Unions Membership Declines as Public Support Fluctuates"; Shierholz et al., "Latest Data Release on Unionization Is a Wake-up Call to Lawmakers."

91 ***The decline was much less significant among Republicans*** Simon Greer and Richard D. Kahlenberg, "How Progressives Can Recapture Seven Deeply Held American Values," February 26, 2020, https://tcf.org/content/report/progressives-can-recapture-seven-deeply-held-american-values/; Ryan P. Burge, *The Nones: Where They Came From, Who They Are, and Where They Are Going* (Minneapolis: Fortress Press, 2021).

92 ***pitted against creationism*** Amy Binder, *Contentious Curricula: Afrocentrism and Creationism in American Public Schools* (Princeton, NJ: Princeton University Press, 2004).

92 ***However, as of 2021, 24 percent of freshmen*** "College Dropout Rate [2022]: By Year + Demographics," Education Data Initiative, November 22, 2021, https://educationdata.org/college-dropout-rates.

92 ***At the same time, higher education*** Kim Parker, "The Growing Partisan Divide in Views of Higher Education," *Pew Research Center's Social & Demographic Trends Project* (blog), August 19, 2019, https://www.pewresearch.org/social-trends/2019/08/19/the-growing-partisan-divide-in-views-of-higher-education-2/; Neil Gross, *Why Are Professors Liberal and Why Do Conservatives Care?* (Cambridge, MA: Harvard University Press, 2013).

92 ***the American cultural canon around race*** On Gates's contributions, see "2021 PEN/Audible Literary Service Award: Henry Louis Gates Jr.," *PEN America*

(blog), May 10, 2021, https://pen.org/2021-pen-america-audible-literary-service-award-henry-louis-gates/.

93 ***helped institutionalize the field*** Catharine R. Stimpson and Gilbert Herdt, eds., *Critical Terms for the Study of Gender* (Chicago: University of Chicago Press, 2014).

93 ***We are in an era of heightened activism*** For an overview, see James M. Jasper, *Protest: A Cultural Introduction to Social Movements* (Cambridge, UK: Polity, 2014).

93 ***the organization Marshall Plan for Moms*** "Marshall Plan for Moms—About," Marshall Plan for Moms, accessed July 12, 2022, https://marshallplanformoms.com/about/.

93 ***Change agents and recognition chains operate on the right*** For instance, Roger Ebert, "Mephisto Movie Review & Film Summary," January 1, 1982, https://www.rogerebert.com/reviews/mephisto-1982.

93 ***This includes Joe Rogan*** Glenn Greenwald, "As Joe Rogan's Platform Grows, So Does the Media and Liberal Backlash. Why?," *The Intercept*, September 22, 2020, https://theintercept.com/2020/09/22/as-joe-rogans-platform-grows-so-does-the-media-and-liberal-backlash-why/.

93 ***far-right and white nationalist Nick Fuentes*** "Nick Fuentes," in *Wikipedia*, January 27, 2022, https://en.wikipedia.org/w/index.php?title=Nick_Fuentes&oldid=1068290178.

94 ***libertarian youth organization active on campuses*** Binder and Kidder, *The Channels of Student Activism*.

94 ***assembles white nationalist and far-right activists*** "Groyper Army and 'America First,'" Anti-Defamation League, accessed January 31, 2022, https://www.adl.org/resources/backgrounders/groyper-army-and-america-first.

94 ***These movements tend to promote nihilism*** "Red Dead Redemption 2," *Rockstar Games*, accessed January 31, 2022, https://www.rockstargames.com/games/reddeadredemption2.

Chapter 6: STRATEGIES FOR TRANSFORMATION: The Work of Change Agents in Hollywood and Beyond

98 ***to challenge stereotypes about stigmatized groups*** See Naomi McDougall Jones, *The Wrong Kind of Women: Inside Our Revolution to Dismantle the Gods of Hollywood* (Boston: Beacon Press, 2020).

100 ***Over time, these more nuanced depictions*** Destigmatization in cultural industries is often overlooked, as social scientists have been most concerned with shedding light on patterns of stereotyping, discrimination, and exclusion in their field. But see Jack G. Shaheen, "Reel Bad Arabs: How Hollywood

Vilifies a People," *Annals of the American Academy of Political and Social Science* 588 (2003): 171–93; Riva Tukachinsky, Dana Mastro, and Moran Yarchi, "Documenting Portrayals of Race/Ethnicity on Primetime Television over a 20-Year Span and Their Association with National-Level Racial/Ethnic Attitudes," *Communication Faculty Articles and Research*, January 1, 2015, https://doi.org/10.1111/josi.12094.

100 ***the distinct strategies they use for fighting stigmatization*** For a full description of strategies used by these groups, see Robey, Letourneau, and Lamont, "Multicultural Meritocracy in Hollywood and Comedy."

103 ***The situation for comedians is different.*** Ibid.

104 ***In an interview with BET*** BETNetworks, *The Making Of Lizzo's "Truth Hurts" Performance at the BET Awards | Rehearsal 360°*, 2019, https://www.youtube.com/watch?v=1eR25kf4kxQ.

105 ***how to perform "middle classness"*** Lounsbury and Glynn, *Cultural Entrepreneurship*.

105 ***In teaching these women to perform domesticity*** Ibid.

105 ***Oprah Winfrey, too, has worked*** Eva Illouz, *Oprah Winfrey and the Glamour of Misery: An Essay on Popular Culture* (New York: Columbia University Press, 2003).

105 ***who preaches prosperity theology or "gospel capitalism"*** Marla Frederick, *Colored Television: American Religion Gone Global* (Stanford, CA: Stanford University Press, 2015); Susan Friend Harding, *The Book of Jerry Falwell: Fundamentalist Language and Politics* (Princeton, NJ: Princeton University Press, 2001); Micki McGee, *Self Help, Inc.: Makeover Culture in American Life* (Oxford: Oxford University Press, 2007).

105 ***As participants in the rough-and-tumble world*** Paul Lichterman, *How Civic Action Works: Fighting for Housing in Los Angeles* (Princeton, NJ: Princeton University Press, 2020).

107 ***For instance, the Narrative Initiative*** Jacob Swenson-Lengyel, "What We Learned in Minnesota," *Narrative Initiative* (blog), August 2, 2019, https://narrativeinitiative.org/blog/what-we-learned-in-minnesota/.

107 ***In recognition of Goff's important work*** Lesley Goldberg, "Warner Bros. TV Inks Creative Partnership With Center for Policing Equity CEO," *Hollywood Reporter* (blog), March 22, 2021, https://www.hollywoodreporter.com/tv/tv-news/warner-bros-tv-inks-creative-partnership-with-center-for-policing-equity-ceo-4154027/.

108 ***inhospitable to socialism*** Eric Foner, "Why Is There No Socialism in the United States?," *History Workshop* 17 (1984): 57–80; Werner Sombart, *Why Is There No Socialism in the United States?* (London: Palgrave Macmillan UK, 1976).

108 ***Although the DSA*** Todd Chretien, "DSA Convention 2021: Big Accomplishments and the Long Road Ahead," *Pine & Roses*, August 7, 2021, https://pineandroses.org/politics/dsa-convention-2021-big-accomplishments-and-the-long-road-ahead/.

109 ***thirty-three years of age*** Chris Gray and Grace Fors, "Democratic Socialists of America 2021 Convention: What Way for Socialists?," *International Socialist Alternative*, August 1, 2021, https://internationalsocialist.net/en/2021/08/united-states.

109 ***At the same time, capitalism has*** Lydia Saad, "Socialism as Popular as Capitalism Among Young Adults in U.S.," Gallup, November 25, 2019, https://news.gallup.com/poll/268766/socialism-popular-capitalism-among-young-adults.aspx.

110 ***They are somewhat irreverent*** Nellie Bowles, "The Pied Pipers of the Dirtbag Left Want to Lead Everyone to Bernie Sanders," *New York Times*, February 29, 2020, https://www.nytimes.com/2020/02/29/us/politics/bernie-sanders-chapo-trap-house.html.

110 ***In the many speeches West gave*** Judith Hertog, "Prisoner of Hope: Cornel West's Quest for Justice," *The Sun*, September 2018, https://www.thesunmagazine.org/issues/513/prisoner-of-hope.

110 ***In past decades, his moral convictions led him*** Dr. Cornel West, *Never Forget: A Journey of Revelations* (Hidden Beach, 2007).

111 ***the nonprofit lobbyist association Business Roundtable*** "Business Roundtable Redefines the Purpose of a Corporation to Promote 'An Economy That Serves All Americans,'" *Business Roundtable*, August 19, 2019, https://www.businessroundtable.org/business-roundtable-redefines-the-purpose-of-a-corporation-to-promote-an-economy-that-serves-all-americans.

112 ***Recently, several progressive foundations*** Lohr, "What Can Replace Free Markets? Groups Pledge $41 Million to Find Out."

112 ***to fight inequality within the framework of capitalism*** Nancy Fraser, "From Redistribution to Recognition? Dilemmas of Justice in a 'Post-Socialist' Age," *New Left Review*, no. I/212 (August 1, 1995): 68–93.

112 ***Some are working on President Biden's plans*** Ben Zdencanovic, "How Biden Could Save Welfare," *Boston Review*, May 15, 2021, https://bostonreview.net/class-inequality-politics/ben-zdencanovic-how-biden-could-save-welfare.

Chapter 7: THE NEXT GENERATION: How Gen Z Flights for the Future

115 ***Like many children of immigrants*** Tony Tian-Ren Lin, *Prosperity Gospel Latinos and Their American Dream* (Chapel Hill, NC: University of North Carolina Press, 2020).

117 ***my research team interviewed eighty college students*** This analysis draws on a more detailed analysis of these interviews in Shira Zilberstein, Michèle Lamont, and Mari Sanchez, "Recreating a Plausible Future: Combining Cultural Repertoires in Unsettled Times," *Sociological Science*, forthcoming; and Sanchez, Lamont, and Zilberstein, "How American College Students Understand Social Resilience during Covid-19 and the Movement for Racial Justice."

117 ***Only about half of eighteen- to twenty-three-year-olds*** Duffin, "U.S. Higher Education Enrollment Rates, by Age Group 1970-2019."

117 ***The remainder were working class*** For the "less privileged": A quarter are squarely in the working class, with parents who are low-status white-collar workers or blue-collar workers, working as laborers, salespeople, bank clerks, or waitresses. The remaining group have families with lower-middle-class backgrounds, with jobs as assistant teachers, low-level managers, or technical professionals. Students from the Northeast who agreed to be interviewed are generally more privileged than those living in the Midwest.

117 ***Slightly more than half were people of color*** Non-whites make up 57 percent of the group (with 35 percent Black, 23 percent Latino, and 40 percent Asian participants).

117 ***Ideologically, the group leaned toward the liberal*** Alyssa N. Rockenbach et al., "Does College Turn People into Liberals?," *The Conversation*, February 2, 2018, http://theconversation.com/does-college-turn-people-into-liberals-90905.

118 ***a focus on personal balance that dampen the risk of failure*** Barbara Ehrenreich, *Bright-Sided: How Positive Thinking Is Undermining America* (New York: Metropolitan Books, 2009); Greenhalgh and Wessily, "Health for Me"; Illouz, *Saving the Modern Soul.*

119 ***Originally, the term mostly referred to*** Kim Parker and Ruth Igielnik, "On the Cusp of Adulthood and Facing an Uncertain Future: What We Know About Gen Z So Far" (Pew Research Center, May 14, 2020), https://www.pewresearch.org/social-trends/2020/05/14/on-the-cusp-of-adulthood-and-facing-an-uncertain-future-what-we-know-about-gen-z-so-far-2/.

119 ***At the same time, their futures*** Challenges most frequently mentioned in the interviews are polarization (mentioned by fifty-two students), growing inequality (forty-eight), social media and peer pressure (forty-four), interpersonal relationships (thirty-four), financial crisis (thirty-three), disengagement from politics (twenty-eight), climate change (twenty-four), squandered potential (twenty-two), financial crisis and student debt (twenty-two), desire for more cohesion (twenty-two).

119 ***the millennials, who entered*** Jill Filipovic, *OK Boomer, Let's Talk: How My Generation Got Left Behind* (New York: Atria/One Signal Publishers, 2020).

119 ***They have experienced precarity*** Jennifer M. Silva, *Coming Up Short: Working-Class Adulthood in an Age of Uncertainty* (New York: Oxford University Press, 2013); Christopher Ingraham, "Millennials' Share of the U.S. Housing Market: Small and Shrinking," *Washington Post*, January 20, 2020, https://www.washingtonpost.com/business/2020/01/20/millennials-share-us-housing-market-small-shrinking/; Annie Lowrey, "The Next Recession Will Destroy Millennials," *The Atlantic*, August 26, 2019, https://www.theatlantic.com/ideas/archive/2019/08/millennials-are-screwed-recession/596728/.

120 ***they are less likely to experience upward mobility*** Corak, "Income Inequality, Equality of Opportunity, and Intergenerational Mobility."

120 ***in their thirties and forties, fewer marry*** S. Robby Berman, "How Student Loans Stop Americans from Marrying," *Big Think*, October 1, 2018, https://bigthink.com/politics-current-affairs/student-debt-marriage-rate.

120 ***held them back in the labor market*** Robert D. Putnam, *Our Kids: The American Dream in Crisis* (New York: Simon & Schuster, 2016).

120 ***Beyond inclusion, they also emphasize*** Inclusion is mentioned 99 times, authenticity 104 times, and sustainability 88 times. Some students mentioned these challenges more than once.

121 ***This is suggested by a 2018 Pew national survey*** Parker and Igielnik, "On the Cusp of Adulthood and Facing an Uncertain Future."

121 ***would describe themselves as hopeful*** "Spring 2021 Harvard Youth Poll" (Harvard Kennedy School Institute of Politics, April 23, 2021), https://iop.harvard.edu/youth-poll/spring-2021-harvard-youth-poll.

122 ***We already saw how neoliberal ideas*** Hall and Lamont, *Social Resilience in the Neoliberal Era*; Silva, *Coming Up Short*; Allison J. Pugh, ed., *Beyond the Cubicle: Job Insecurity, Intimacy, and the Flexible Self* (New York: Oxford University Press, 2017). This script has roots in the liberal scripts of self predominant in the Anglo world for a few centuries. Cathie Jo Martin, "Imagine All the People: Literature, Society, and Cross-National Variation in Education Systems," *World Politics* 70, no. 3 (July 2018): 398–442.

123 ***opt for vegan or vegetarian diets*** Nina Guilbeault, *The Good Eater: A Vegan's Search for the Future of Food* (New York: Bloomsbury USA, forthcoming).

123 ***A number of young people are suffering*** Natasha Warikoo, "Addressing Emotional Health While Protecting Group Status: Asian American and White Parents in Suburban America," *American Journal of Sociology* 126, no. 3 (2020).

123 ***Shockingly, nearly a third reported*** Harvard Kennedy School Institute of Politics, "Spring 2021 Harvard Youth Poll."

124 ***They support "anything that makes you happy"*** Edgar Cabanas and Eva Illouz, *Manufacturing Happy Citizens: How the Science and Industry of Happiness*

Control Our Lives (Hoboken, NJ: John Wiley & Sons, 2019); Illouz, *Saving the Modern Soul*; Michèle Lamont, Jason Kaufman, and Michael Moody, "The Best of the Brightest: Definitions of the Ideal Self among Prize-Winning Students," *Sociological Forum* 15, no. 2 (2000): 187–224.

124 ***a body that can be optimized.*** Wayne Brekhus, *The Sociology of Identity: Authenticity, Multidimensionality, and Mobility* (Medford, MA: Polity Press, 2020); Ori Schwartz, "'Everything Is Designed to Make an Impression': The Moralisation of Aesthetic Judgement and the Hedonistic Ethic of Authenticity," *European Journal of Cultural Studies* 22, no. 4 (July 26, 2019): 399–415.

125 ***having "a sense of linked fate."*** Michael C. Dawson, *Behind the Mule: Race and Class in African-American Politics* (Princeton, NJ: Princeton University Press, 1995).

125 ***32 percent donate*** Alice Berg, "Gen Z: The Next Generation of Donors," *Classy* (blog), December 8, 2017, https://www.classy.org/blog/gen-z-next-generation-donors/.

125 ***During the COVID-19 crisis, 66 percent*** "Consumer Payment Behaviors," Zelle, 2020, https://www.zellepay.com/sites/default/files/2020-09/Consumer_Payment_Behaviors.pdf. Eric W. Dolan, "Study Finds Millennials Tend to Donate More to Charity—but Do It Less Often," *PsyPost*, July 16, 2019, https://www.psypost.org/2019/07/study-finds-millennials-tend-to-donate-more-to-charity-but-do-it-less-often-54055.

126 ***Spurred by an effective grassroots campaign*** Jonah Engel Bromwich, "How a Minnesota Bail Fund Raised $20 Million," *New York Times*, June 1, 2020, https://www.nytimes.com/2020/06/01/style/minnesota-freedom-fund-bail-george-floyd-protests.html.

126 ***Students from privileged backgrounds*** Sanchez, Lamont, and Zilberstein, "How American College Students Understand Social Resilience during Covid-19 and the Movement for Racial Justice."

126 ***special political and social mission of their generation*** This mission is shared with millennials. See Ruth Milkman, "A New Political Generation: Millennials and the Post-2008 Wave of Protest," *American Sociological Review* 82, no. 1 (2017): 1–31.

126 ***For instance, they blame these generations*** Filipovic, *OK Boomer, Let's Talk*; Kligler-Vilenchik and Literat, "Distributed Creativity as Political Expression: Youth Responses to the 2016 U.S. Presidential Election in Online Affinity Networks."

126 ***They also tend to downplay*** Ibid.

127 ***Attitudes like this may*** Michelle Jackson et al., "Having to Stay Still: Youth and Young Adults in the Covid-19 Crisis," Monitoring the Crisis: American

Voices Project (Stanford, CA: Stanford Center on Poverty and Inequality, Federal Reserve Bank of Boston, and Federal Reserve Bank of Atlanta, February 2021), https://inequality.stanford.edu/covid/youth-young-adults.

127 ***And indeed, the majority of*** Parker and Igielnik, "On the Cusp of Adulthood and Facing an Uncertain Future."

127 ***hold our collective future in their hands*** Lauren Young, "Gen Z Is The Most Progressive—and Least Partisan—Generation," *Teen Vogue*, October 2, 2019, https://www.teenvogue.com/story/how-will-gen-z-vote; Kligler-Vilenchik and Literat, "Distributed Creativity as Political Expression"; Sarah Jackson, Moya Bailey, and Brooke Foucault Welles, *#HashtagActivism: Networks of Race and Gender Justice* (Cambridge, MA: MIT Press, 2020).

127 ***The 2016 survey reported that students*** Courtney Kueppers, "Today's Freshman Class Is the Most Likely to Protest in Half a Century," *Chronicle of Higher Education*, February 11, 2016, http://search.proquest.com.ezp-prod1.hul.harvard.edu/trade-journals/todays-freshman-class-is-most-likely-protest-half/docview/1768189179/se-2?accountid=11311.

128 ***Some are concerned with reparations*** For generational comparison see: Christian Smith and Patricia Snell, *Souls in Transition: The Religious Lives of Emerging Adults in America* (New York: Oxford University Press, 2009); Kenneth Keniston, *The Uncommitted: Alienated Youth in American Society* (New York: Harcourt, Brace & World, 1965); Barbara Epstein, *Political Protest and Cultural Revolution: Nonviolent Direct Action in the 1970s and 1980s* (Berkeley, CA: University of California Press, 1991).

128 ***Signaling this shift*** "Merriam-Webster's Words of the Year 2019," accessed May 12, 2022, https://www.merriam-webster.com/words-at-play/word-of-the-year-2019-they; Abigail C. Saguy and Juliet A. Williams, "A Little Word That Means a Lot: A Reassessment of Singular They in a New Era of Gender Politics," *Gender & Society* 36, no. 1 (February 1, 2022): 5–31.

128 ***A January 2020 Pew Research Center survey*** Parker and Igielnik, "On the Cusp of Adulthood and Facing an Uncertain Future."

128 ***This compares to 18 percent*** Stolzenberg et al., *The American Freshman.*

129 ***In the second round of interviews*** On this topic see Rishika Dugyala, "Anti-Trump, but Not Fully for Biden: Will Gen Z Vote?," *Politico*, October 11, 2020, https://www.politico.com/news/2020/10/11/gen-z-vote-2020-trump-biden-424571; John B. Holbein and D. Sunshine Hillygus, *Making Young Voters: Converting Civic Attitudes into Civic Action* (Cambridge, UK: Cambridge University Press, 2020).

129 ***the intensity of Black Twitter*** Jackson, Bailey, and Welles, *#HashtagActivism.*

130 ***more than to actually help people of color*** Ellen Berrey, *The Enigma of Diversity: The Language of Race and the Limits of Racial Justice* (Chicago: University of Chicago Press, 2015); Dobbin and Kalev, *Getting to Diversity*.

130 ***50 percent of all eligible Americans*** "Half of Youth Voted in 2020, An 11-Point Increase from 2016," Tufts University Center for Information & Research on Civic Learning and Engagement, April 29, 2021, https://circle.tufts.edu/latest-research/half-youth-voted-2020-11-point-increase-2016. Another national survey conducted by the Institute of Politics at the "Spring 2021 Harvard Youth Poll" found that 30 percent of respondents did not vote. This survey included 2,513 young Americans ages eighteen to twenty-nine. Domenico Montanaro, "Poll: Despite Record Turnout, 80 Million Americans Didn't Vote. Here's Why," NPR, December 15, 2020, https://www.npr.org/2020/12/15/945031391/poll-despite-record-turnout-80-million-americans-didnt-vote-heres-why.

130 ***young people was only 39 percent*** "Election Week 2020: Young People Increase Turnout, Lead Biden to Victory," CIRCLE, Tufts University, accessed June 13, 2022, https://circle.tufts.edu/latest-research/election-week-2020.

131 ***Their narratives of change remain*** This analysis is elaborated in Sanchez, Lamont, and Zilberstein, "How American College Students Understand Social Resilience during Covid-19 and the Movement for Racial Justice."

131 ***Working-class (or first gen) students' college experiences*** Anthony Abraham Jack, *The Privileged Poor: How Elite Colleges Are Failing Disadvantaged Students* (Cambridge, MA: Harvard University Press, 2019).

132 ***were particularly hit by the pandemic*** Andreas Kluth, "An Epidemic of Depression and Anxiety Among Young Adults," *Bloomberg*, August 22, 2020.

132 ***These developments are seen as feeding xenophobic*** Gidron and Hall, "The Politics of Social Status."

132 ***Also, like their parents*** Stephanie Ternullo, "'I'm Not Sure What to Believe': Media Distrust and Opinion Formation during the COVID-19 Pandemic," *American Political Science Review* 116, no. 3 (August 2022): 1096–1109, https://doi.org/10.1017/S000305542200003X; Elizabeth A. Bennett et al., "Disavowing Politics: Civic Engagement in an Era of Political Skepticism," *American Journal of Sociology* 119, no. 2 (September 2013): 518–48, https://doi.org/10.1086/674006.

132 ***Surveys show that this group*** Marco Giugni and Maria Grasso, "Youth and Politics in Times of Increasing Inequalities," in *Youth and Politics in Times of Increasing Inequalities* (Cham, Switzerland: Springer International Publishing, 2021), 1–26; Kjell Noordzij, Willem de Koster, and Jeroen van der Waal, "'They Don't Know What it's Like to Be at the Bottom': Exploring the Role of Perceived Cultural Distance in Less-Educated Citizens' Discontent with Politicians," *British Journal of Sociology* 72, no. 3 (2021): 566–79.

132 ***Whether these young people feel "seen"*** Arjun Appadurai, "The Capacity to Aspire: Culture and the Terms of Recognition," in *Culture and Public Action*, eds. Vijayendra Rao and Michael Walton (Stanford, CA: Stanford University Press, 2004), 59–84; Amartya Sen, "Capability and Well-Being," in *The Quality of Life* (Oxford: Clarendon Press, 1993). Scholars are aware of the importance of making cultural scripts and institutional resources available for this capacity to aspire to develop. On this topic, see Barbara Hobson, ed., *Recognition Struggles and Social Movements: Contested Identities, Agency and Power* (Cambridge, UK; New York: Cambridge University Press, 2003).

133 ***who appreciate sexist and vulgar humor*** Mark Makela, "Transcript: Donald Trump's Taped Comments About Women," *New York Times*, October 8, 2016, https://www.nytimes.com/2016/10/08/us/donald-trump-tape-transcript.html. On how humor contributes to attracting workers in politics, see Peck, *Fox Populism*, and Giselinde Kuipers, "Humor and Polarization: How Humor Can Drive People Apart, in Politics and Beyond," live presentation presented at the Hot Politics Lab, University of Amsterdam, November 5, 2021.

134 ***Students value higher education*** Education was mentioned forty-eight times as a source of hope in our interviews. On the role of institutions such as education in diffusing cultural messages, see Frank and Meyer, *The University and the Global Knowledge Society*.

135 ***acts as a buffer against uncertainty*** Gowoon Jung and Hyunjoon Park, "Bridging Sociology of Religion to Transition to Adulthood: The Emerging Role of Religion in Young Adults' Lives," *Social Compass* 67, no. 3 (September 1, 2020): 428–43.

135 ***In contrast to change agents*** For a recent analysis on the impact of networks on political attitudes, with a focus on polarization, see Craig M. Rawlings, "Becoming an Ideologue: Social Sorting and the Microfoundations of Polarization," *Sociological Science* 9 (August 1, 2022): 313–45, https://doi.org/10.15195/v9.a13. For a more elaborate model of diffusion, taking into consideration communication sources, messages, and channels and how they affect political polarization, see John T. Jost et al., "Cognitive–Motivational Mechanisms of Political Polarization in Social-Communicative Contexts," *Nature Reviews Psychology* 1, no. 10 (October 2022): 560–76, https://doi.org/10.1038/s44159-022-00093-5.

136 ***We saw that young people in 2016*** Kueppers, "Today's Freshman Class Is the Most Likely to Protest in Half a Century."

136 ***turn increasingly into a "social movement society"*** David S. Meyer and Sidney Tarrow, *The Social Movement Society: Contentious Politics for a New Century* (Rowman & Littlefield Publishers, 1997).

136 ***Some have argued that the postmaterialist values*** Ronald Inglehart, *The Silent Revolution: Changing Values and Political Styles Among Western Publics* (Princeton University Press, 1977); Paul R. Abramson, "Critiques and Counter-Critiques of the Postmaterialism Thesis: Thirty-Four Years of Debate," Center for the Study of Democracy, April 20, 2011, https://escholarship.org/uc/item/3f72v9q4.

137 ***are now much more salient*** Matthew Yglesias and Milan Singh, "Democrats Have Changed a Lot since 2012," *Slow Boring* (blog), May 11, 2022, https://www.slowboring.com/p/shifting-left.

137 ***the broad moral features of this cultural context*** Of relevance is the work of social scientists studying the moral aspects of social movements, such as Jeffrey Alexander, Nina Eliasoph, James Jasper, Doug McAdams, and others.

137 ***progressive "old boomers" maintained progressive*** Gary Alan Fine, *Fair Share: Senior Activism, Tiny Publics, and the Culture of Resistance* (Chicago: University of Chicago Press, 2023); Jack Whalen, *Beyond the Barricades: The Sixties Generation Grows Up*, 1st edition (Philadelphia: Temple University Press, 1989); Susan Krauss Whitbourne and Sherry L. Willis, eds., *The Baby Boomers Grow Up: Contemporary Perspectives on Midlife* (Mahwah, NJ: Psychology Press, 2006); Doug McAdam, "The Biographical Consequences of Activism," *American Sociological Review* 54, no. 5 (1989): 744–60.

137 ***political variations within this group considered at large*** Longitudinal panel data for an extended duration needed for a long-term assessment of generational trends is insufficient (personal correspondence with Pippa Norris, Harvard University). However, these two articles provide useful information on the US and UK cases: Patrick Fisher, "Generational Cycles in American Politics, 1952–2016," *Society* 57, no. 1 (2020): 22–29; Maria Teresa Grasso et al., "Socialization and Generational Political Trajectories: An Age, Period and Cohort Analysis of Political Participation in Britain," *Journal of Elections, Public Opinion and Parties* 29, no. 2 (2019): 199–221.

Chapter 8: DIFFERENT YET THE SAME: Solutions for Building an Inclusive Society

139 ***the gap between the "winners" and the "losers"*** Bloome, Schrage, and Furey, "Rising Class Crystallization?" (Kennedy School of Government, Harvard University, 2021).

139 ***For this group, life expectancy has declined*** Nadeem, "U.S. Life Expectancy Falls to Lowest Level in Almost 20 Years Due to COVID-19 -CDC."

140 ***Occupations such as software developer*** Steve Lohr, "Millions Have Lost a Step Into the Middle Class, Researchers Say," *New York Times*, January 14, 2022, https://www.nytimes.com/2022/01/14/business/middle-class-jobs-study.html.

140 ***But equally important is devising new narratives*** Shiller, *Narrative Economics.*

140 ***This practice needs to*** This approach to cultural change, which connects individual agency with meso-level resources, is made explicit in Michèle Lamont and Paul Pierson, "Inequality Generation & Persistence as Multidimensional Processes: An Interdisciplinary Agenda," *Daedalus: Journal of the American Academy of Arts and Sciences* 148, no. 3 (2019): 5–18.

140 ***Other researchers have given*** A rapidly growing body of knowledge on the political polarization, populism, and illiberalism from across the social sciences offers a wide array of solutions concerning how to effect change by transforming the digital environment (reducing fake news, transforming algorithms), the political environment, and others causal paths. For examples, see Fletcher, et al., "How Polarized Are Online and Offline News Audiences?"; Jacob S. Hacker and Paul Pierson, "Confronting Asymmetric Polarization," in *Solutions to Political Polarization in America*, ed. Nathaniel Persily (Cambridge, UK: Cambridge University Press, 2015), 59–70; Gordon Pennycook and David G. Rand, "Who Falls for Fake News? The Roles of Bullshit Receptivity, Overclaiming, Familiarity, and Analytic Thinking," *Journal of Personality* 88, no. 2 (2020): 185–200; Daniel DellaPosta, "Pluralistic Collapse: The 'Oil Spill' Model of Mass Opinion Polarization," *American Sociological Review* 85, no. 3 (June 1, 2020): 507–36. Conversely, on the production of national cohesion and nationalism, see Feinstein, *Rally 'round the Flag*; Bart Bonikowski, Yuval Feinstein, and Sean Bock, "The Partisan Sorting of 'America': How Nationalist Cleavages Shaped the 2016 U.S. Presidential Election," *American Journal of Sociology* 127, no. 2 (September 2021): 492–561; Yascha Mounk, *The Great Experiment: Why Diverse Democracies Fall Apart and How They Can Endure* (New York: Penguin Press, 2022).

140 ***In* The Sum of Us** Heather McGhee, *The Sum of Us: What Racism Costs Everyone and How We Can Prosper Together* (New York: One World, 2022).

140 ***Duke sociologist Chris Bail*** Christopher Bail, *Breaking the Social Media Prism: How to Make Our Platforms Less Polarizing* (Princeton, NJ: Princeton University Press, 2021).

140 ***She concludes that to overcome*** Polletta, *Inventing the Ties That Bind*; Bloemraad et al., "Membership without Social Citizenship?"

140 ***His solution is to celebrate work*** Sandel, *The Tyranny of Merit.*

141 ***how we have reduced stigmatization*** Clair et al., "Destigmatization and Health"; Michèle Lamont, "Addressing Recognition Gaps: Destigmatization and the Reduction of Inequality," *American Sociological Review* 83, no. 3 (June 2018): 419–44.

141 ***resulted in less absenteeism*** Erin Kelly et al., "7 Strategies to Improve Your Employees' Health and Well-Being," *Harvard Business Review*, October 12, 2021, https://hbr.org/2021/10/7-strategies-to-improve-your-employees

-health-and-well-being; Phyllis Moen et al., "Changing Work, Changing Health: Can Real Work-Time Flexibility Promote Health Behaviors and Well-Being?," *Journal of Health and Social Behavior* 52, no. 4 (2011): 404–29.

141 ***working conditions for the majority of US mothers*** Caitlyn Collins, *Making Motherhood Work: How Women Manage Careers and Caregiving* (Princeton, NJ: Princeton University Press, 2019).

142 ***Broad exposure to a wide range of people*** Jonathan JB Mijs, "Institutions as Inferential Spaces: How People Learn About Inequality" (Dissertation, Department of Sociology, Harvard University, 2017).

142 ***Moreover, frequent interactions with people*** Diana C. Mutz, *Hearing the Other Side: Deliberative Versus Participatory Democracy* (New York: Cambridge University Press, 2006); Mijs, "Why Don't We Care about Growing Inequality?"

142 ***direct them away from the "excellent sheep" pathway*** William Deresiewicz, *Excellent Sheep: The Miseducation of the American Elite and the Way to a Meaningful Life* (New York: Free Press, 2015).

142 ***in countries like Denmark and Sweden*** Christian Albrekt Larsen and Thomas Engel Dejgaard, "The Institutional Logic of Images of the Poor and Welfare Recipients: A Comparative Study of British, Swedish and Danish Newspapers," *Journal of European Social Policy* 23, no. 3 (July 1, 2013): 287–99.

143 ***Whereas more privileged Americans*** See, for instance, McCall, *The Undeserving Rich*. On changing perceptions of the deservingness of the poor over the last decades, see Bloemraad et al., "Membership without Social Citizenship?"; Silja Häusermann and Hanna Schwander, "Varieties of Dualization? Labor Market Segmentation and Insider-Outsider Divides across Regimes" (Green Templeton College, University of Oxford, 2010), https://mwpweb.eu/1/22/resources/publication_418_1.pdf.

143 ***Anthropologist Bhrigupati Singh*** He studies the life of laborers living in extreme poverty in Rajasthan, India. Bhrigupati Singh, *Poverty and the Quest for Life: Spiritual and Material Striving in Rural India* (Chicago: University of Chicago Press, 2015).

143 ***This strengthened social resilience*** Ioana Sendroiu, "Among Crises: Making Sense of COVID-19" (Unpublished, Weatherhead Center for International Affairs, Harvard University, Cambridge, MA, 2021).

143 ***These alternative standards help bolster*** Hojman and Miranda, "Agency, Human Dignity, and Subjective Well-Being"; Andersson and Hitlin, "Subjective Dignity and Self-Reported Health." On how agency and dignity are connected to hope, see Sanchez, Lamont, and Zilberstein, "How American College Students Understand Social Resilience during Covid-19 and the Movement for Racial Justice."

143 ***The impact of income on happiness plateaus*** Cory Stieg, "From the 'perfect' Salary to Keeping up with the Joneses, Here's How Money Really Affects Your Happiness," CNBC, May 26, 2020, https://www.cnbc.com/2020/05/26/how-your-salary-and-the-way-you-spend-money-affect-your-happiness.html.

143 ***Developmental economist and Nobel laureate*** Amartya Sen, *Development as Freedom* (New York: Oxford University Press, 1999); Joseph E. Stiglitz, Amartya Sen, and Jean-Paul Fitoussi, *Mismeasuring Our Lives: Why GDP Doesn't Add Up* (New York: New Press Distributed by Perseus, 2010); Appadurai, "The Capacity to Aspire."

143 ***the United Nations' annual Human Development Report*** Human Development Report 2021/2022. *Uncertain Times, Uncertain Lies: Shaping our Future in a Transforming World* (New York: United Nations Development Program). I cochaired the advisory committee to this report, which incorporates notions of social resilience, uncertainty, and solidarity.

144 ***we urgently need to lift up "ordinary universalism"*** Lamont and Aksartova emphasize the particular universalisms that are grounded in "the cultural repertoires of universalism that are differentially available to individuals across race and national context." Michèle Lamont and Sada Aksartova, "Ordinary Cosmopolitanisms: Strategies for Bridging Racial Boundaries among Working- lass Men," *Theory, Culture & Society* 19, no. 4 (2002): 1–25.

144 ***how people bridge boundaries*** See also Ann Morning and Marcello Maneri, *An Ugly Word: Rethinking "Race" in Italy* (New York: Russell Sage Foundation, 2022). Michèle Lamont, Ann Morning, and Margarita Mooney, "Particular Universalisms: North African Immigrants Respond to French Racism," *Ethnic and Racial Studies* 25, no. 3 (2002): 390–414. Also Maureen A. Craig and Jennifer A. Richerson, "Stigma-Based Solidarity: Understanding the Psychological Foundations of Conflict and Coalition Among Members of Different Stigmatized Groups," *Current Directions in Psychological Science* 25, no. 1 (2016): 21–27.

144 ***When asked about how they are similar*** Lamont, Morning, and Mooney, Ibid. Also Craig and Richeson, Ibid.

144 ***polarization and political sectarianism*** Alan I. Abramowitz, *The Great Alignment: Race, Party Transformation, and the Rise of Donald Trump* (New Haven, CT: Yale University Press, 2018); Finkel et al., "Political Sectarianism in America."

145 ***A recent study of female janitors*** Ramaswami Mahalingam and Patturaj Selvaraj, "Ambedkar, Radical Interdependence and Dignity: A Study of Women Mall Janitors in India," *Journal of Business Ethics* 177, no. 4 (2022): 813–28.

145 ***Social psychologists Matthew Feinberg*** Matthew Feinberg and Robb Willer, "From Gulf to Bridge: When Do Moral Arguments Facilitate Political Influence?," *Personality and Social Psychology Bulletin* 41, no. 12 (2015): 1665–81.

146 ***This includes a form of "aesthetic cosmopolitanism"*** Vincenzo Cicchelli et al., "A Tale of Three Cities: Aesthetico-Cultural Cosmopolitanism as a New Capital among Youth in Paris, São Paulo, and Seoul," *Journal of Consumer Culture* 21, no. 3 (2018): 576–97; Motti Regev, *Pop-Rock Music: Aesthetic Cosmopolitanism in Late Modernity* (Cambridge, UK: Polity, 2013).

146 ***middle-class Turkish immigrants in Berlin*** Gökçe Yurdakul and Tunay Altay, "Getting Respect in Berlin: Turkish Immigrant Parents' Quest for Privilege in Berlin's Private Schools." Workshop on Practicing Intersectionality in Racism Research: Methods and Analysis, 2021; Gökçe Yurdakul and Tunay Altay, "Overcoming Stigma: The Boundary Work of Privileged Mothers of Turkish Background in Berlin's Private Schools," *Ethnic and Racial Studies*, DOI: 10.1080/01419870.2022.2152720; Jürgen Gerhards, Silke Hans, and Sören Carlson, *Social Class and Transnational Human Capital: How Middle and Upper Class Parents Prepare Their Children for Globalization* (Abingdon, UK: Routledge, 2017); Çetin Çelik and Tuğçe Özdemir, "When Downward Mobility Haunts: Reproduction Crisis and Educational Strategies of Turkish Middle Class under the AK Party Rule," *British Journal of Sociology of Education* 43, no. 2 (February 17, 2022): 260–77.

146 ***Nationalist populism, Islamophobia, and xenophobia*** Erik Bleich and A. Maurits van der Veen, *Covering Muslims: American Newspapers in Comparative Perspective* (Oxford, UK: Oxford University Press, 2021).

146 ***It weakens the boundaries between groups*** Lamont and Molnár, "The Study of Boundaries in the Social Sciences"; Wimmer, *Ethnic Boundary Making*; Richard Alba and Victor Nee, *Remaking the American Mainstream: Assimilation and Contemporary Immigration* (Cambridge, MA: Harvard University Press, 2005); Rogers Brubaker, *Grounds for Difference* (Harvard University Press, 2015).

146 ***The turn toward "superdiversity"*** Steven Vertovec, "Super-Diversity and Its Implications," *Ethnic and Racial Studies* 30, no. 6 (2007): 1024–54; Elijah Anderson, *The Cosmopolitan Canopy: Race and Civility in Everyday Life* (New York: W. W. Norton, 2012).

146 ***So does the use of the category*** Cristina Mora, *Making Hispanics: How Activists, Bureaucrats, and Media Constructed a New American* (Chicago: University of Chicago Press, 2014); Mari Sanchez. "The Expansion & Diffusion of the POC Category 1975–1995: A Focus on Sociocultural Processes" (Unpublished manuscript, Department of Sociology, Harvard University, 2022).

146 ***These changes in terminology*** John Skrentny, *The Minority Rights Revolution* (Cambridge, MA: Harvard University Press, 2002); Frank Dobbin, *Inventing Equal Opportunity* (Princeton, NJ: Princeton University Press, 2011).

146 ***affirmative action in universities and nonprofits*** Berrey, *The Enigma of Diversity*; Natasha K. Warikoo, *The Diversity Bargain: And Other Dilemmas of Race, Admissions, and Meritocracy at Elite Universities* (Chicago: University of Chicago Press, 2016).

146 ***affinity groups in the corporate sector*** Lumumba Babushe Seegars, "Organizing in the Shadows of White Hegemony: Comparing How Black versus Asian Employees Collectively Contest Racial Marginalization in the Workplace" (Working Paper, Harvard Business School, 2021).

146 ***One way that some corporations*** Dobbin and Kalev, *Getting to Diversity*.

146 ***"happy talk" or empty, symbolic gestures*** Joyce M. Bell and Douglas Hartmann, "Diversity in Everyday Discourse: The Cultural Ambiguities and Consequences of 'Happy Talk,'" *American Sociological Review* 72, no. 6 (2007): 895–914.

147 ***the marginalization of certain groups*** Jennifer Lee and Min Zhou, *The Asian American Achievement Paradox* (Russell Sage Foundation, 2015).

147 ***They are also criticized*** Adia Wingfield, *Flatlining: Race, Work, and Health Care in the New Economy* (Berkeley, CA: University of California Press, 2019).

147 ***This dynamic has worsened*** Gidron, Adams, and Horne, *American Affective Polarization in Comparative Perspective*.

147 ***When groups feel they are competing*** John T. Jost et al., "Political Conservatism as Motivated Social Cognition," *Psychological Bulletin* 129, no. 3 (2003): 339–75.

147 ***Few acknowledge that there is a common quest*** Rory McVeigh and Kevin Estep, *The Politics of Losing: Trump, the Klan and the Mainstreaming of Resentment* (New York: Columbia University Press, 2019).

147 ***suffering is commensurate with the other's*** See for instance Eduardo Bonilla-Silva, "On the Racial Fantasies of White Liberals in Trump's America and Beyond," *American Studies* 66, no. 1 (2021): 53–58.

147 ***Progressive finger-wagging can only stoke working-class resentment*** There are any other factors that should influence the likelihood that the Democratic Party will be able to attract more working-class voters moving forward. For a cogent discussion of these conditions and the broader situation, see Jared Abbott, "A Populism of the Left Can Realign American Politics," *Jacobin*, December 5, 2022, https://jacobin.com/2022/12/a-populism-of-the-left-can-realign-american-politics.

148 ***become less stigmatized in recent decades*** Clair, Daniel, and Lamont, "Destigmatization and Health."

148 ***people labeled as obese*** Abigail C. Saguy, *What's Wrong with Fat?* (Oxford, UK: Oxford University Press, 2012).

148 ***For example, they used language*** Gerald Rosenberg, *The Hollow Hope: Can Courts Bring about Social Change?* (Chicago: University of Chicago Press, 1991); Charles R. Epp, *The Rights Revolution: Lawyers, Activists, and Supreme Courts in Comparative Perspective* (Chicago: University of Chicago Press, 1998).

148 ***They also used the law*** Ibid.

149 ***in 1987, Lady Diana was photographed*** Skrentny, *The Minority Rights Revolution*, p. 141.

149 ***and eventually, beyond national boundaries*** Kristopher Velasco, "Queering the World Society: Global Norms, Rival Transnational Networks, and the Contested Case of LGBT Rights," *SocArXiv*, July 25, 2020, https://doi.org/doi:10.31235/osf.io/3rtje; Ferguson, "'There Is an Eye on Us.'"

150 ***we need to devise and diffuse new narratives*** On the emotional dimension of engaging in different strategies for marginalized groups, see James M. Jasper, "Strategic Marginalizations, Emotional Marginalities: The Dilemma of Stigmatized Identities," in *Surviving Against Odds: The Marginalized in a Globalizing World*, ed. Debal K. SinghaRoy (Delhi, India: Manohar Publishers, 2010), 27–35.

150 ***support from "outsiders" is validating*** Lamont et al., *Getting Respect*.

150 ***By broadening who appears in ads*** Jordan Foster and David Pettinicchio, "A Model Who Looks like Me: Communicating and Consuming Representations of Disability," *Journal of Consumer Culture* (2021): 1–19.

150 ***Weiner also assisted Mattel in launching Barbie*** Anna Livsey, "Barbie Comes out in Support of Same-Sex Marriage," *The Guardian*, November 29, 2017, https://www.theguardian.com/lifeandstyle/2017/nov/29/barbie-comes-out-in-support-of-same-sex-marriage.

151 ***effective means for diffusing at scale*** Michèle Lamont and Viràg Molnár, "How Blacks Use Consumption to Shape Their Collective Identity: Evidence from African-American Marketing Specialists," *Journal of Consumer Culture* 1, no. 1 (2001): 31–45; Mora, *Making Hispanics*.

151 ***In the past, marketers worked to convince*** Lamont and Molnár, Ibid.

151 ***American society for most of the twentieth century*** Alba, *The Great Demographic Illusion*; Tomás R. Jimenez, *The Other Side of Assimilation: How Immigrants Are Changing American Life* (Oakland, CA: University of California Press, 2017); Adrian Favell, *The Integration Nation: Immigration and Colonial Power in Liberal Democracies* (London: Polity Press, 2022).

151 ***Governments play an important role*** Arturo Rodriguez Morató and Matías Zarlenga, "Analysis of the Influence of Gender and Rising Diversity in the Configuration of the Values of Culture," UNCHARTED: Understanding, Capturing and Fostering the Societal Value of Culture (University of Barcelona, October 2020).

151 ***Sociologist Jeffrey Reitz*** Jeffrey G. Reitz, "Multiculturalism Policies and Popular Multiculturalism in the Development of Canadian Immigration," in *The Multiculturalism Question: Debating Identity in 21st Century Canada* (Kingston and Montreal: McGill-Queen's University Press, 2014), 107–26.

151 ***In Canada, for instance, such efforts*** Jeffrey G. Reitz, Emily Laxer, and Patrick Simon, "National Cultural Frames and Muslims' Economic Incorporation: A Comparison of France and Canada," *International Migration Review*, January 10, 2022, https://doi.org/10.1177/01979183211035725.

152 ***In 1971, in response to a movement for independence*** Elke Winter, "Rethinking Multiculturalism After Its 'Retreat': Lessons From Canada," *American Behavioral Scientist* 59, no. 6 (May 1, 2015): 637–57.

152 ***and favored "interculturalism" over multiculturalism*** Gérard Bouchard, *Interculturalism: A View from Quebec*, trans. Howard Scott (University of Toronto Press, 2015). See also Nasar Meer, Tariq Modood, and Ricard Zapata-Barrero, eds., *Multiculturalism and Interculturalism: Debating the Dividing Lines* (Edinburgh University Press, 2016).

152 ***This has led Canadian immigrants to be more involved*** Matthew Wright and Irene Bloemraad, "Is There a Trade-off between Multiculturalism and Socio-Political Integration? Policy Regimes and Immigrant Incorporation in Comparative Perspective," *Perspectives on Politics* 10, no. 1 (2012): 77–95.

152 ***The latter "work bonus" program*** Jennifer Sykes et al., "Dignity and Dreams: What the Earned Income Tax Credit (EITC) Means to Low-Income Families," *American Sociological Review* 80, no. 2 (April 1, 2015): 243–67.

153 ***Or laws can enact segregation*** Lamont et al., *Getting Respect.*

153 ***The ongoing battle over abortion rights*** Jocelyn Viterna et al., "Governance and the Reversal of Women's Rights," in *Towards Gender Equity in Development* (Oxford University Press, 2018).

153 ***self-presentation as acceptable*** Prudence L. Carter, *Stubborn Roots: Race, Culture, and Inequality in U.S. and South African Schools* (New York: Oxford University Press, 2012).

154 ***We all have to be carriers*** Again, these changes cannot be reduced to that of a self-serving liberal new middle class. There exists an excellent and detailed literature on the politics of this group, such as: Steven Brint, *In an Age of Experts: The Changing Role of Professionals in Politics and Public Life* (Princeton, NJ: Princeton University Press, 1994).

154 ***many efforts of civic action and imagination*** Lichterman, *How Civic Action Works*; Hahrie Han, *How Organizations Develop Activists: Civic Associations and Leadership in the 21st Century* (Oxford University Press, 2014); Gianpaolo Baiocchi et al., *Civic Imagination: Making a Difference in American Political Life* (New York: Routledge, 2014); Julien Talpin, *Community Organizing* (Raisons D'Agir, 2016).

CONCLUSION: Strengthening Our Capacity to Live Better Together

156 ***a condition for our social resilience*** Hall and Lamont, *Social Resilience in the Neoliberal Era.*

157 ***The decision to migrate*** Noel B. Salazar, "The Power of Imagination in Transnational Mobilities," *Identities* 18, no. 6 (2011): 576–98; Filiz Garip, *On the Move: Changing Mechanisms of Mexico-U.S. Migration* (Princeton, NJ: Princeton University Press, 2016).

157 ***One's basic notions about agency*** Robert H. Frank, *Success and Luck: Good Fortune and the Myth of Meritocracy* (Princeton, NJ: Princeton University Press, 2016); Helga Nowotny, *The Cunning of Uncertainty* (London: Polity Press, 2016); Michael Sauder, "A Sociology of Luck," *Sociological Theory* 38, no. 3 (2020): 193–216.

157 ***renewed threats to LGBTQ+ rights*** Lucas Acosta, "A List of Trump's 'Unprecedented Steps' for the LGBTQ Community," Human Rights Campaign, June 11, 2020, https://www.hrc.org/news/the-list-of-trumps-unprecedented-steps-for-the-lgbtq-community.

157 ***decision in* Roe v. Wade** "An Overview of U.S. Refugee Law and Policy" (1331 G Street NW, Suite 200, Washington, DC, 20005: American Immigration Council, September 20, 2021), https://www.americanimmigrationcouncil.org/research/overview-us-refugee-law-and-policy.

157 ***Befriending someone from*** Ben Baumberg Geiger, "Does Diversity Help Students Learn about Inequality?," *Inequalities Blog* (blog), July 2, 2018, https://inequalitiesblog.wordpress.com/2018/07/02/does-diversity-help-students-learn-about-inequality/; Mijs, "Why Don't We Care about Growing Inequality?"

158 ***More generally, increasing contact between groups*** Gordon W. Allport, *The Nature of Prejudice* (Basic Books, 1954). Many study the impact of contact on the decline of prejudices and discrimination: Elizabeth Levy Paluck, Seth A. Green and Donald P. Green, "The Contact Hypothesis Re-Evaluated," *Behavioral Public Policy* 3, no. 2 (2018): 129–58. For example, Salma Mousa, "Building Social Cohesion between Christians and Muslims Through Soccer in Post-ISIS Iraq," *Science* 369 (6505) (2020): 866–70. Also, Chagai M. Weiss, "Diversity in Health Care Institutions Reduces Israeli Patients' Prejudice

toward Arabs," *Proceedings of the National Academy of Sciences* 118, no. 14 (April 6, 2021).

158 ***This remains one of the most effective approaches*** Alba, *The Great Demographic Illusion*. On the large literature on the conditions that lead to the production of porous boundaries, see Lamont and Molnár, "The Study of Boundaries in the Social Sciences"; Wimmer, *Ethnic Boundary Making*; and Steven Vertovec, "The Social Organization of Difference," *Ethnic and Racial Studies* 44, no. 8 (2021): 1273–95.

158 ***only if integration occurs at a social level*** Warikoo, *The Diversity Bargain*; Mitchell L. Stevens, *Creating a Class: College Admissions and the Education of Elites* (Cambridge, MA: Harvard University Press, 2007).

159 ***by regaining working-class voters*** A detailed discussion of the electoral dynamics of the Democratic Party and other liberal or progressive parties in relation to the working class is beyond the purpose of this study. But see Abbott, "A Populism of the Left Can Realign American Politics." For a recent analysis in a comparative perspective, see Amory Gethin, Clara Martínez-Toledano, and Thomas Piketty, eds., *Political Cleavages and Social Inequalities: A Study of Fifty Democracies, 1948–2020* (Cambridge, MA: Harvard University Press, 2021).

159 ***Middle-class white people need to recognize*** Geismer, *Don't Blame Us*.

159 ***Many avoid conversations*** Robin DiAngelo, *White Fragility: Why It's So Hard for White People to Talk About Racism* (Boston, MA: Beacon Press, 2018).

159 ***This avoidance, euphemistically called "color-blindness"*** Eduardo Bonilla-Silva, *Racism Without Racists: Color-blind Racism and the Persistence of Racial Inequality in the United States* (Lanham, MD: Rowman & Littlefield Publishers, 2006).

160 ***a world where everyone has dignity and respect*** For a related perspective focused on political messaging, see Jan G. Voelkel and Robb Willer, "Resolving the Progressive Paradox with Professor Robert Willer," https://www.thirdway.org/interview/resolving-the-progressive-paradox-with-professor-robb-willer. Also Luiza A. Santos, Jan G. Voelkel, Robert Willer, and Jaml Zaki, "Belief in the Utility of Cross-Partisan Empathy Reduces Partisan Animosity and Facilitates Political Persuasion," *Psychological Science* 33, no. 9 (2022): 1557–73.

160 ***Some countries, such as Germany*** Cynthia Miller-Idriss, *The Extreme Gone Mainstream: Commercialization and Far Right Youth Culture in Germany* (Princeton, NJ: Princeton University Press, 2018).

160 ***In Massachusetts, where I live*** "Civics Project Guidebook: Guidance to Support Implementation of Chapter 296 of the Acts of 2018, An Act to Promote and Enhance Civic Engagement" (Massachusetts Department of Elementary and Secondary Education, December 2021), https://

www.doe.mass.edu/instruction/hss/civics-project-guidebook/index.html#/; Danielle Allen and Paul Carrese, "Our Democracy Is Ailing. Civics Education Has to Be Part of the Cure," *Washington Post*, March 2, 2021, https://www.washingtonpost.com/opinions/2021/03/02/our-democracy-is-ailing-civics-education-has-be-part-cure/.

160 ***All our cultural institutions*** American Academy of Arts & Sciences, *Investing in Civic Education & Our Democracy*, 2021, https://www.youtube.com/watch?v=w92zVnL7fas.

161 ***Research on what helps increase diversity*** Alexandra Kalev, Frank Dobbin, and Erin Kelly, "Best Practices or Best Guesses? Assessing the Efficacy of Corporate Affirmative Action and Diversity Policies," *American Sociological Review* 71, no. 4 (2006): 589–617.

161 ***into our own psyche, to find "grit"*** Duckworth, *Grit.*

162 ***trends of mindfulness, positive psychology, and other "quick fixes"*** Singal, *The Quick Fix.*

162 ***trendy ideas about "tribalism"*** For an example, see Nigel Nicholson, "How Hardwired Is Human Behavior?," *Harvard Business Review*, 1998, https://hbr.org/1998/07/how-hardwired-is-human-behavior; Joseph Henrich, *The Secret of Our Success* (Princeton, NJ: Princeton University Press, 2017).

162 ***in favor of our ingroup members*** Greene, *Moral Tribes*; Ryan D. Enos, *The Space between Us: Social Geography and Politics* (New York: Cambridge University Press, 2017). Evolutionary psychologists discuss learning as historical, but largely conditioned by evolution. While space limitation precludes a full engagement with this topic, I thank Yossi Harpaz for helping me familiarize myself with this literature.

162 ***It is influenced by outside factors*** Gidron, Adams, and Horne, *American Affective Polarization in Comparative Perspective.*

162 ***our sense of community waxes and wanes*** Paul Gilbert and Jaskaran Basran, "The Evolution of Prosocial and Antisocial Competitive Behavior and the Emergence of Prosocial and Antisocial Leadership Styles," *Frontiers in Psychology* 10 (2019).

162 ***We may feel differently*** Lamont et al., *Getting Respect.*

162 ***how much "groupness" a group experiences*** Michael A. Hogg et al., "Uncertainty, Entitativity, and Group Identification," *Journal of Experimental Social Psychology* 43, no. 1 (January 1, 2007): 135–42.

162 ***In response, some redouble their efforts*** Charles Tilly, *Durable Inequality* (Berkeley, CA: University of California Press, 1998).

162 ***as if awareness*** Frank Dobbin and Alexandra Kalev, "Why Diversity Programs Fail," *Harvard Business Review*, August 2016; Calvin K. Lai et al.,

"Reducing Implicit Racial Preferences: II. Intervention Effectiveness across Time," *Journal of Experimental Psychology: General* 145, no. 8 (2016): 1001–16.

162 ***In order to feed solidarity*** Claude S. Fischer, *Made in America: A Social History of American Culture and Character* (Chicago: University of Chicago Press, 2010); Mario Luis Small, *Someone to Talk To* (New York: Oxford University Press, 2017).

162 ***by making narratives of inclusion widely available*** Jan G. Voelkel and Robb Willer, "Resolving the Progressive Paradox: Conservative Value Framing of Progressive Economic Policies Increases Candidate Support" (Department of Sociology, Stanford University, Stanford, CA, April 22, 2019).

163 ***Cuing can help*** Ibid.

163 ***promoted a distinctive and popular "China dream,"*** Jeffrey Wasserstrom, "Here's Why Xi Jinping's 'Chinese Dream' Differs Radically from the American Dream," *Time*, October 19, 2015.

163 ***Some of the US's problems are also present*** Phillip Inman, "Social Mobility in Richest Countries 'Has Stalled since 1990s,'" *The Guardian*, June 15, 2018, https://www.theguardian.com/society/2018/jun/15/social-mobility-in-richest-countries-has-stalled-since-1990s; Bloemraad et al., "Membership without Social Citizenship?"

163 ***skyrocketing income inequality*** Milanovic, *Global Inequality*; Savage, *The Return of Inequality*.

163 ***Everywhere, young people have faced setbacks and are mobilizing*** Paul Mason, "How the Covid Shock Has Radicalised Generation Z," *The Guardian*, June 2, 2021, https://www.theguardian.com/world/2021/jun/02/how-the-covid-shock-has-radicalised-generation-z; Cecile Van de Velde, "What Have You Done to Our World? From the Indignados to the pro-Climate Movement, the Rise of a Global Generational Voice" (ISA World Forum of Sociology, February 27, 2021).

163 ***the suicide rate in several strongly neoliberal countries*** Prianka Padmanathan et al., "Social Media Use, Economic Recession and Income Inequality in Relation to Trends in Youth Suicide in High-Income Countries: A Time Trends Analysis," *Journal of Affective Disorders* 275 (October 1, 2020): 58–65; "Young Americans Increasingly End Their Own Lives," *The Economist*, December 9, 2022, sec. United States, https://www.economist.com/united-states/2022/12/03/young-americans-increasingly-end-their-own-lives.

163 ***America's reckoning for racial justice inspired progressive movements elsewhere*** Milman and Ajayi, "Black Lives Matter in Europe"; Jada Nagumo and Nana Shibata, "#BlackLivesMatter Shines Light on Racism in Japan and across Asia," *Nikkei Asia*, August 11, 2020, https://asia.nikkei.com/Spotlight/Asia-Insight/BlackLivesMatter-shines-light-on-racism-in-Japan-and-across-Asia.

163 ***Countries such as France*** Benjamin Dodman, "As George Floyd Outrage Spreads, France Confronts Its Own Demons," France 24, June 3, 2020, https://www.france24.com/en/20200603-it-happens-here-too-as-george-floyd-outrage-spreads-france-confronts-its-own-demons.

163 ***others around the world feel more empowered.*** See the findings of the "world society" school on these issues. For instance: David John Frank and Elizabeth H. Mceneaney, "The Individualization of Society and the Liberalization of State Policies on Same-Sex Sexual Relations, 1984–1995," *Social Forces* 77, no. 3 (1999): 911–43. On recognition struggles and women's movements, see Hobson, *Recognition Struggles and Social Movements.*

163 ***Asians in France launched an anti-Asian hate hashtag*** Fontana, *Recognition Politics*; Howard Ramos, "Opportunity for Whom?: Political Opportunity and Critical Events in Canadian Aboriginal Mobilization, 1951–2000," *Social Forces* 87, no. 2 (2008): 795–823.

164 ***different in every country and region*** "The American-Western European Values Gap" (Pew Research Center, November 17, 2011), https://www.pewresearch.org/global/2011/11/17/the-american-western-european-values-gap/.

164 ***countries face persistent challenges with xenophobia and racism*** Adrian Favell, "Immigration, Integration and Citizenship: Elements of a New Political Demography," *Journal of Ethnic and Migration Studies* 48, no. 1 (January 2, 2022): 3–32.

164 ***We can all feed or fight social and spatial segregation*** On the role of residential segregation based on class and race in the social reproduction of inequality, see Douglas S. Massey and Jonathan Tannen, "Suburbanization and Segregation in the United States: 1970-2010," *Ethnic and Racial Studies* 41, no. 9 (2018): 1594–1611 and Annette Lareau and Kimberly Goyette, eds., *Choosing Homes, Choosing Schools* (New York, NY: Russell Sage Foundation, 2014).

165 ***Explicitly acknowledging how workers are penalized by the cultural dominance*** This point is also made by Bonilla-Silva, "On the Racial Fantasies of White Liberals in Trump's America and Beyond."

Appendix B: College Students

185 ***Chapter 6 draws on original analyses*** Sanchez, Lamont, and Zilberstein, "How American College Students Understand Social Resilience during Covid-19 and the Movement for Racial Justice"; Zilberstein, Lamont, and Sanchez, "Recreating a Plausible Future."

185 ***the use of theoretical sampling focused on class is justified*** Mario Luis Small, "'How Many Cases Do I Need?': On Science and the Logic of Case Selection in Field-Based Research," *Ethnography* 10, no. 1 (March 2009): 5–38.

186 ***Indeed, a January 2020 Pew Research Center survey*** Parker and Igielnik, "On the Cusp of Adulthood and Facing an Uncertain Future."

INDEX

INDEX

INDEX

ABOUT THE AUTHOR

MICHÈLE LAMONT is professor of sociology and of African and African American Studies and the Robert I. Goldman Professor of European Studies at Harvard University.

A cultural and comparative sociologist, she is the author or coauthor of a dozen books and edited volumes and more than one hundred articles on a range of topics including culture, inequality, racism, stigma, social change, and qualitative methods.

After directing the Weatherhead Center for International Affairs, Harvard University (2014–2021), she now leads its research cluster on Comparative Inequality and Inclusion. Recent honors include a Carnegie Fellowship (2019–2021), a Russell Sage Foundation fellowship (2019–2020), the 2017 Erasmus Prize, and honorary doctorates from six countries. She served as the 108th president of the American Sociological Association in 2016–2017.